TEACH YOURSELF BOOKS

Beginner's
RUSSIAN

Beginner's RUSSIAN

AN EASY INTRODUCTION

Rachel Farmer

TEACH YOURSELF BOOKS

To Peter, Lucy and Catherine.

———— Acknowledgements ————

My very warm thanks to Liza Lacy for her extensive help during the writing of this book.

Long-renowned as the authoritative source for self-guided learning – with more than 30 million copies sold worldwide – the *Teach Yourself* series includes over 200 titles in the fields of languages, crafts, hobbies, sports, and other leisure activities.

British Library Cataloguing in Publication Data

A catalogue for this title is available from The British Library

Library of Congress Catalog Card Number: 95-73147

First published in UK 1996 by Hodder Headline Plc, 338 Euston Road, London NW1 3BH

First published in US 1996 by NTC Publishing Group, 4255 West Touhy Avenue, Lincolnwood (Chicago) Illinois 60646 – 1975 U.S.A.

Typeset by Transet Ltd, Coventry, Warwickshire.
Printed in Great Britain by Cox & Wyman Ltd, Reading, Berkshire.

Impression number   10 9 8 7 6 5 4 3 2 1
Year   1999 1998 1997 1996

CONTENTS

Introduction to the course

Teach Yourself Beginner's Russian is the course to use if you are a complete beginner or have just a smattering of Russian. It is a self-study course, and will help you to speak, understand and read the language sufficiently for you to visit Russia or receive Russian visitors at home.

The course works best with the accompanying 90 minute cassette, but it is not essential. The recorded dialogues and exercises will give you practice in understanding the language and in pronouncing it correctly, and will give you confidence to speak out loud. Each unit contains at least one activity which requires the cassette, but the material will always be covered by other activities as well. If you don't have the cassette, use the **Pronunciation guide** to help you pronounce the words correctly. Always read the words and dialogues out loud in a strong, clear voice.

How the units work

In units 1–2 you will learn to read the Russian alphabet, and in units 3–10 you will learn the basic structures of the language which you will need in different situations. In unit 11 you will learn to read the hand-written Russian script and to write it if you choose, and in units 12–20 you will learn how to cope with practical situations in more detail.

Within each unit you will find:

● a list of things you can expect to learn

● **Информа́ция** *Information*

These notes provide some basic background information on the Russian customs and way of life relevant to the unit. You should bear in mind that in recent times there have been many changes in Russian life and even in the language as it absorbs many new international words. You may therefore find if you visit Russia that details of everyday life have changed. This is particularly likely to be true with matters relating to the economic state of the country.

● **Ключевы́е слова́** *Key words*

These are key words and phrases which will be used in the unit. Try to learn them by heart as they will help you with the rest of the unit and will often appear again later in the book. In units 3–10, while you are getting used to the Russian alphabet, each word will have its pronunciation in English letters next to it. Try not to become dependent on this, but just use it to check any sounds you are not sure of.

● **Диало́ги** *Dialogues*

If you have the cassette, listen to the dialogue once or twice to try and get the gist of it. Then use the pause button to break it up into phrases and repeat each phrase out loud to develop your accent. If you only have the book, read the dialogue through several times before you look up the words and say the phrases out loud. As you become more confident, you could cover up part of the dialogue and try to remember what to say.

● **Механи́зм языка́** *Mechanics of the language*

All languages work by following certain patterns, and this section shows you examples of the mechanics of constructing Russian. Once you have become used to the patterns you can make up sentences yourself by changing words or their endings.

● **Упражне́ния** *Exercises*

The exercises allow you to practise the language which you have just learned in the *Mechanics of the language* section. For some of the exercises you need the cassette. It is important to do the exercises and to check your answers in the back of the book so that you are sure you understand the language in one unit before moving on.

● **Анекдо́т** *Anecdote*

In the later units you may find a short Russian anecdote or joke.

● **Прове́рьте себя́** *Test yourself*

At the end of units 3–10 you will find a short revision section.

How to succeed in learning Russian

1 Spend a little bit of time on Russian each day, rather than a marathon session once a week. It is most effective to spend no more than 20–30 minutes at a time.

2 Go back and revise words and language patterns regularly until things which seemed difficult become easier.

3 Say the words and phrases out loud and listen to the cassette whenever you can.

4 Take every opportunity to use the language. Try to meet a Russian speaker or join a class to practise with other people.

5 Don't worry if you make mistakes. The most important thing is to communicate, and by jumping in at the deep end and trying things out, you may surprise yourself with how well you can make yourself understood!

Symbols and abbreviations

This indicates that the cassette is needed for the following section.

This indicates dialogue.

This indicates exercises – places where you can practise using the language.

This indicates key words or phrases.

This indicates grammar or explanations – the nuts and bolts of the language.

This draws your attention to points to be noted and key tips to help you learn.

(*m*) masculine	(*sing*) singular
(*f*) feminine	(*pl*) plural

At the back of the book

At the back of the book is a reference section which contains:

Отве́ты   *Answers.* (page 226)
Ци́фры   *Numbers.* (page 235)
A brief summary of Russian language patterns. (page 237)
An English–Russian vocabulary list. (page 242)
A Russian–English vocabulary list containing all the words in the course. (page 245)

Pronunciation guide

First, here are a few tips to help you acquire an authentic accent:

1   Listen carefully to the cassette or Russian speaker, and whenever possible, repeat words and phrases loudly and clearly.
2   Make a recording of yourself and compare it with the cassette.
3   Ask a Russian speaker to listen to your pronunciation and tell you how to improve it.
4   Practise specific sounds which you find difficult.
5   Make a list of words which give you trouble and practise them.

Russian sounds

Most English speakers can pronounce most of the Russian sounds without difficulty. What is more, reading Russian is often easier than reading English with its complicated spelling, e.g. *enough, plough, cough.* In Russian, what you see is more or less what you get, and if you join together the sound of the individual letters you will usually end up with the sound of the whole word. The first two units will take you through the sounds in detail, but here is a reference guide to help you.

Consonants

Б	б	**b**	as in *bag*
В	в	**v**	as in *visitor*
Г	г	**g**	as in *good*
Д	д	**d**	as in *duck*
Ж	ж	**zh**	as in *pleasure*

З	з	z	as in *zoo*
К	к	k	as in *kiss*
Л	л	l	as in *lane*
М	м	m	as in *moon*
Н	н	n	as in *note*
П	п	p	as in *pin*
Р	р	r	as in *rabbit*
С	с	s	as in *sit*
Т	т	t	as in *tennis*
Ф	ф	f	as in *funny*
Х	х	ch	as in *loch*
Ц	ц	ts	as in *cats*
Ч	ч	ch	as in *chicken*
Ш	ш	sh	as in *ship*
Щ	щ	shsh	as in *Spanish sherry*

When you listen to spoken Russian, you may notice that the first five consonants will change their sound if they occur at the end of a word. Don't worry about this, but try to get into the habit of imitating the way that Russians speak.

Б	б	b	at the end of a word sounds like **p**
В	в	v	at the end of a word sounds like **f**
Г	г	g	at the end of a word sounds like **k**
Д	д	d	at the end of a word sounds like **t**
Ж	ж	zh	at the end of a word sounds like **sh**
З	з	z	at the end of a word sounds like **s**

Vowels

If a word has more than one syllable there will be one vowel which is pronounced more strongly than the others. This is called a stressed vowel. When vowels are stressed they are pronounced clearly and strongly. When they are in an unstressed position they are pronounced more weakly. Listen to the cassette whenever possible and notice what happens to vowels in different positions as you repeat the words.

А	а	a	as in *father*
Е	е	ye	as in *yesterday*
Ё	ё	yo	as in *yonder*
И	и	ee	as in *street*
Й	й	y	as in *toy*
О	о	o	as in *born*

У	у	oo	as in *boot*
	ы		sounds rather like **i** in *ill* (say it by keeping your mouth very slightly open and drawing your tongue back as far as it will go).
Э	э	e	as in *leg*
Ю	ю	yoo	as in *universe*
Я	я	ya	as in y*ard*

The soft and hard signs

ь The soft sign has the effect of softening the preceding consonant, as if adding a soft **y** sound to it.

ъ The hard sign is rare, is not pronounced, and makes a tiny pause between syllables.

1

In this unit you will learn

- how to read twenty letters of the Russian alphabet
- how to ask where something is
- how to show where something is
- how to thank someone

Before you start

You may think that Russian will be difficult to learn because of its different alphabet, but you will probably be surprised how quickly you can learn to recognise the letters. The Russian alphabet is called the Cyrillic alphabet after the monk, St. Cyril, who invented it. In order to follow this course, you will need to know how to read Russian in its printed form, so that is what you will concentrate on for the first two units. Later, in unit 11, you will have the chance to see how Russian is written by hand. One of the good things about Russian is that words are pronounced more or less as they are written, so in that way it is easier than English with its complicated spellings.

f you have the cassette, make sure you have it handy as you'll be using it o practise the pronunciation of the words. Russian has some sounds which vill be new to you, but if you listen carefully and repeat the words clearly, ou should soon make progress. It might be helpful to record yourself and ompare what you sound like with the cassette. If you don't have the assette, use the **Pronunciation guide** on page 4.

emember that it is more effective to study little and often than to try and o a long session every now and then. Your concentration will probably be est in 20-minute bursts.

──── The Russian alphabet ────

The Russian alphabet can be divided into four groups of letters: those which look and sound like English letters; 'false friends' which look like English letters but sound different; a group of unfamiliar letters with familiar sounds; and those which are quite unlike English letters.

English look- and sound-alikes

The first group (those which look and sound like their English counterparts) contains five letters

A a   sounds like   **a**   in   *father*

T т   sounds like   **t**   in   *tennis*

O o   sounds like   **o**   in   *born*

M м   sounds like   **m**   in   *moon*

К к   sounds like   **k**   in   *kiss*

With these letters you can already read the following Russian words:

áтом   atom
мáма   mum
кот   cat

✳ You will notice that **áтом** and **мáма** have an accent over the letter **á**. This is called a 'stress mark' and is used to show you which syllable to emphasise in words of more than one syllable. In English, if we underlined every stress syllable, it would look like this: *the piano player wants to record a record.* When you are speaking Russian, put lots of energy into the stressed syllable and pronounce it clearly. The vowels in unstressed syllables are underplayed and do not need to be pronounced so clearly. For example, in the syllable before the stress, **o** will sound like **a** in *father*, and in any other position it will sound like **a** in *again*. You will soon get used to where the stress falls on words which you use often, but to help you, the stress marks will be shown throughout the book.

False friends

The next group of letters contains seven letters:

C c   sounds like   **s**   in   *sit*

Р р	sounds like	**r**	in	*rabbit*
Е е	sounds like	**ye**	in	*yesterday.* When unstressed, like **yi** or **i**.
В в	sounds like	**v**	in	*visitor*
Н н	sounds like	**n**	in	*note*
У у	sounds like	**oo**	in	*boot*
Х х	sounds like	**ch**	in	*loch* (Scots)

Reading practice

To practise the twelve letters which you have now met, see if you can read the words in the following exercises. They are mostly international words, so you should recognise them without too much difficulty. When you have done this, listen to them on the cassette if you have it, and repeat them. Then try reading them again without looking at the English meaning until you can say them easily.

1 Firstly we have five cities. See if you can match them up with their English names.

If you decide that (*a*) is Tomsk, write (*a*) (*ii*). You can check the answers in the back of your book. Don't forget to say the words out loud.

(*a*) **Томск**   (*b*) **Торóнто** (*c*) **Вéна**   (*d*) **Омск**   (*e*) **Мýрманск**
(*i*) Vienna   (*ii*) Tomsk   (*iii*) Murmansk (*iv*) Toronto (*v*) Omsk

2 Now try to identify these five Russian names.

(*a*) **Свéта** (*b*) **Антóн** (*c*) **Вéра**   (*d*) **Ромáн** (*e*) **Áнна**
(*i*) Anna   (*ii*) Vera   (*iii*) Sveta   (*iv*) Anton (*v*) Roman

3 Imagine you are walking around Moscow and you see the following places signposted. What are they?

(*a*)   (*b*)   (*c*)

МЕТРÓ   ТЕÁТР   РЕСТОРÁН

(*i*) theatre   (*ii*) restaurant   (*iii*) metro

4 A Russian friend gives you a shopping list. What do you need to buy?

(*a*) **сóус**	(*i*) cocoa
(*b*) **какáо**	(*ii*) sauce
(*c*) **сáхар**	(*iii*) rum
(*d*) **ром**	(*iv*) sugar

If you have managed to read these words out loud and have practised them until you are fairly confident, you are ready to move on to another group of letters.

Unfamiliar letters with familiar sounds

The next group of letters contains thirteen new letters. To make it easier, you are going to meet only five of them to begin with.

П п   sounds like   **p**   in   *pin*

Л л   sounds like   **l**   in   *lane*

И и   sounds like   **ee**   in   *street*

З з   sounds like   **z**   in   *zoo*

Д д   sounds like   **d**   in   *duck*

Now see if you can read words containing the seventeen letters you have met so far. Remember to say them all out loud, and check your pronunciation with the cassette if you have it.

Reading practice

5 These words are to do with sport. Read them and match them up with the pictures below. The English words will appear in the correct order in the answers at the back of the book.

теннис   снукер   стадион   крикет

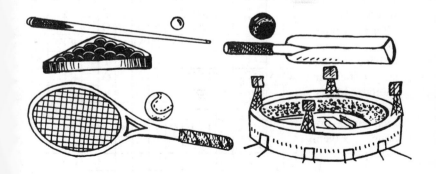

Now match up the remaining words about sport with the English words below.

старт	нокáут	трéнер	рекóрд	атлéтика	спорт	спортсмéн
record	knockout	sport	trainer	start	sportsman	athletics

6 Next you can identify the names of the nine cities around the world. Draw lines linking the Russian and English names.

(*a*) **Минск**	(*i*)	Moscow
(*b*) **Москвá**	(*ii*)	Samarkand
(*c*) **Амстердáм**	(*iii*)	Tokyo
(*d*) **Кúев**	(*iv*)	London
(*e*) **Тóкио**	(*v*)	Madrid
(*f*) **Лóндон**	(*vi*)	Minsk
(*g*) **Одéсса**	(*vii*)	Kiev
(*h*) **Мадрúд**	(*viii*)	Amsterdam
(*i*) **Самаркáнд**	(*ix*)	Odessa

7 Match up these four words connected with travel and transport with their English equivalents below

вúза	трáктор	пáспорт	таксú
taxi	passport	tractor	visa

8 In this grid you will find nine words which refer to occupations or leisure activities. They are written in capital letters. Read them out loud and pronounce them clearly.

Д	И	П	Л	О	М	А	Т						
					У			Д					
					Р			О		Т			
				Х	И	М	И	К		Р			
					С			Т		А			
К	О	С	М	О	Н	А	В	Т		О		К	
	Т							Р		Т			
	У									О			
А	Д	М	И	Н	И	С	Т	Р	А	Т	О	Р	
	Е									И			
	Н									С			
	Т						К	А	П	И	Т	А	Н

Here they are again in lower case letters. You will notice that in their printed form, most Russian capital letters are just bigger versions of lower case letters. Check their meanings against the list in English, which again is in the wrong order.

дипломáт   турúст   космонáвт   хúмик   студéнт
администрáтор   дóктор   тракторúст   капитáн
administrator   captain   diplomat   doctor   student (male)
tractor driver   tourist   cosmonaut   chemist

9 Below is a list of ten Russian names, five for men and five for women. The women's names are the ones ending in -**a**. See if you can read them all out loud, and underline the feminine ones.

Ивáн   Нúна   Алексáндр   Владúмир   Екатерúна   Лúза
Лев   Ирúна   Валентúн   Ларúса

10 You overhear a conversation between **Вéра** (Vyera) and **Алексáндр** (Alexander). **Вéра** cannot find her friend, and asks **Алексáндр** if he knows where she is. Using your cassette if you have one, listen to the conversation and repeat it. Otherwise, read it out loud. You will hear three unfamiliar words.

где?   pronounced   gdye   *where is?*
вот   pronounced   vot   *there is*
спасúбо   pronounced   spaseeba   *thank you*

Вéра   **Алексáндр, где Ирúна?**
Алексáндр   **Вот Ирúна.**
Вéра   **Спасúбо, Алексáндр.**

11 Your next set of words are all to do with science. See if you can read them. Don't look at their meanings in English until you have finished.

áтом   комéта   метеóр   клúмат   механúзм   микроскóп
спýтник   килó   литр   планéта   лунá   киломéтр
kilo microscope sputnik comet litre atom kilometre planet
mechanism moon meteor climate

12 Now see if you can recognise these pieces of technical equipment. There is one word in this list which doesn't belong. Underline it, and don't forget to pronounce all the words clearly. Cover up the English version until you have tried to read the Russian.

телеви́зор	radio
кассе́та	printer
монито́р	television
кинока́мера	cassette
лимона́д	cine-camera
ра́дио	monitor
при́нтер	lemonade

Unfamiliar letters with familiar sounds – three more!

Once you are confident reading the seventeen letters you have met so far, you are ready to learn three more from the group of unfamiliar letters with familiar sounds.

Ф ф sounds like **f** in *funny*
Ю ю sounds like **yoo** in *universe*
Г г sounds like **g** in *good*

Reading practice

13 Here are some signs which might help you as you walk around a Russian town if you do not have a **план** (plan) *a town plan*. Match them up with their English meanings. Remember that they would not normally have accents to show where the stress is.

stadium park telephone kiosk zoo café institute grocer's (gastronom) *university*

ТЕЛЕФО́Н   ИНСТИТУ́Т

университе́т

14 Nina is always getting lost. She supports the football team **Дина́мо** (Deen<u>a</u>mo) and she is looking for the stadium. If you have the cassette, listen to the conversation and repeat it. If not, try to read it out loud.

Ни́на	**Ива́н, где стадио́н?**
Ива́н	**Стадио́н? Вот стадио́н.**
Ни́на	**А, вот стадио́н. Спаси́бо Ива́н.**

When Nina says «**А**» it is like saying *Aah* in English.

15 You are visiting friends in their flat (**кварти́ра** kvart<u>ee</u>ra) in a block of flats (**дом** dom). You hear them mention the following domestic objects as they show you around. Try to read them out loud before looking at the English equivalents to check the meaning.

ла́мпа   стул   коридо́р   дива́н   ми́ксер   ва́за   то́стер
газ   лифт
gas   corridor   lamp   mixer   vase   toaster   lift   sofa (divan)
chair

16 As you listen carefully to their conversation, you hear the following words and realise they are interested in music.

саксофо́н   компози́тор   гита́ра   пиани́но   орке́стр
соли́ст   о́пера   пиани́ст   компа́кт-ди́ск   хе́ви металл-ро́к

piano   opera   composer   pianist   saxophone   compact disc
orchestra   guitar   soloist   heavy metal rock

17 You are in a concert hall when you hear a pianist asking his colleague, the composer, for help in finding something. Repeat the conversation. What has the pianist lost?

Пиани́ст	**Влади́мир, где пиани́но?**
Компози́тор	**Пиани́но? Где, где пиани́но? А, вот пиани́но, Валенти́н!**
Пиани́ст	**А, вот пиани́но! Спаси́бо.**

18 Now you are in a restaurant looking at a menu. Work out what is on it and underline the drinks. Read out the whole list as if you were giving your order to the waiter. The menu is on the next page.

Меню́

омле́т	сала́т
ви́ски	фрукт
ко́фе	мю́сли
котле́та	вино́
пепси-ко́ла	суп министро́не

---

*pepsi-cola   muesli   salad   coffee   wine   minestrone soup
whisky   omelette   cutlet (flat meat ball)   fruit*

Congratulations! You can now read twenty letters of the Cyrillic alphabet, and you have only thirteen more to learn. To test yourself, read back over all the Russian words you have met and say them out loud without looking at the English. Check your pronunciation with the cassette if you have it. Then read the English words and see if you can remember them in Russian. Don't worry if you don't get them all exactly right. Then you are ready to move on to unit 2.

2

In this unit you will learn

- how to read the remaining thirteen letters of the Russian alphabet
- how to say you don't know
- how to ask who someone is
- how to say no

Before you start

Make sure that you can read and say all the Russian words in unit 1. Remember to use the cassette if you have it, and say each new word aloud to practise your pronunciation.

More letters and sounds

You already know these twenty letters of the Russian alphabet:

- those which look and sound like English letters: **а т о м к**
- the 'false friends' which look like English letters but sound different: **с р е в н у х**
- and the unfamiliar letters with familiar sounds: **п л и з д ф ю г**

Unfamiliar letters with familiar sounds – the last five

There are still five letters to learn in the group of unfamiliar letters with familiar sounds, and we will begin with these.

Б б	sounds like	**b**	in	*bag*
Э э	sounds like	**e**	in	*leg*
Й й	sounds like	**y**	in	*toy*
Ё ё	sounds like	**yo**	in	*yonder*
Я я	sounds like	**ya**	in	*yak* except in the syllable before the stress, when it sounds like *yi*.

The letter **я** on its own means *I*, so that is another word to add to your repertoire! To practise these new letters along with those you already know, see if you can read the words in the following exercises. Try to work out what they mean before you look at the English meanings. If you have the cassette, listen to the words and repeat them carefully. Remember to emphasise each syllable which has a stress mark. Wherever **ё** appears in a word, that syllable will be stressed. So **ёлка** (y<u>o</u>lka) *a Christmas tree*, will be emphasised on the first syllable.

Reading practice

1 First try matching up these cities with their English names.

(*a*) **Берли́н** (*b*) **Я́лта** (*c*) **Санкт-Петербу́рг** (*d*) **Софи́я**
(*e*) **Бухаре́ст** (*f*) **Багда́д**
(*i*) Sofia (*ii*) Baghdad (*iii*) Berlin (*iv*) Saint Petersburg (*v*) Bucharest (*vi*) Yalta

You can check the answers in the back of your book.

2 All these words are to do with travel and transport. Write the correct letter next to each English word to show that you have understood.

(*a*)	**стюарде́сса**	trolleybus
(*b*)	**платфо́рма**	airport
(*c*)	**экску́рсия**	signal
(*d*)	**авто́бус**	express
(*e*)	**трамва́й**	stewardess
(*f*)	**аэропо́рт**	Aeroflot
(*g*)	**экспре́сс**	platform
(*h*)	**си́гнал**	tram
(*i*)	**Аэрофло́т**	excursion
(*j*)	**тролле́йбус**	bus

3 If you want to read the sports pages of a Russian newspaper, here are some words which will be useful. Match them up with the English words below.

ФУТБО́Л	ВОЛЕЙБО́Л	БАДМИНТО́Н
МАРАФО́Н	*БОКС*	ПИНГ-ПО́НГ
СЕ́РФИНГ	**ФИНА́Л**	РЕ́ГБИ
ХОККЕ́Й		БАСКЕТБО́Л

rugby   marathon   boxing   volleyball   football   hockey   basket-ball   final   surfing   badminton   ping-pong

4 You are visiting your music-loving Russian friends again. This time their conversation is about music, theatre and books, and you hear them mention the following words. Try to read them out loud before looking at the English words to check their meaning.

симфо́ния   балери́на   поэ́т   актри́са   бестсе́ллер   актёр балет   три́ллер
best-seller   actress   ballet   symphony   ballerina   thriller   poet   actor

5 You pick up a magazine about science, and work out the following words.

эне́ргия   килова́тт   атмосфе́ра   килогра́мм   электро́ника эксперимéнт
kilogram   experiment   atmosphere   energy   kilowatt   electronics

6 Your friends have an atlas, and you browse through it recognising these countries.

Аме́рика   Ме́ксика   А́фрика   Пакиста́н   Аргенти́на А́нглия   Росси́я   Украи́на   Кана́да   И́ндия   Австра́лия Норве́гия
Argentina   Mexico   Russia   Australia   America   Norway   England Ukraine   Canada   Pakistan   India   Africa

7 You play a game with their little girl, **Ле́на** (Lyena). You ask her where certain countries are on a world map and she shows you. Occasionally she doesn't know and then she says: **Я не зна́ю**   (Ya nye znayoo)   *I don't know.*

Listen to the conversation on the cassette or read it out loud.

You	**Лéна, где Канáда?**
Лéна	**Канáда? Вот Канáда.**
You	**Где Росси́я?**
Лéна	**Вот Росси́я, и вот Москвá.**
You	**Где А́нглия?**
Лéна	**А́нглия? Я не знáю. Где А́нглия?**
You	**Вот А́нглия, и вот Лóндон.**

Did you work out what **и** means?

и   (ee)   *and*

The last eight letters and sounds

Once you are happy with those new letters you are ready to move on to learn the remaining eight letters of the Russian alphabet, which are quite unlike English letters. The first five letters of this group make sounds which will be familiar to you, but in English you would need more than one letter to show the whole sound.

Ж ж sounds like **zh**   as in   *pleasure*

Ц ц sounds like **ts**   as in   *cats*

Ч ч sounds like **ch**   as in   *chicken*

Ш ш sounds like **sh**   as in   *ship*

Щ щ sounds like **shsh**   as in   *spanish sherry*

The last three letters of the group never occur at the beginning of a word. They are:

ы   sounds rather like **i** in *ill*, but with the tongue further back in the mouth

ь   is a 'soft sign' which adds a soft 'y' sound to the letter before it. Think of how you would pronounce the **p** in *pew*. When you see a Russian word written using English letters in this book, a soft sign will be indicated by an apostrophe '. So for example, the word for computer **компьюóтер** will be written **komp'yooter**.

ъ   is a 'hard sign'. This is very rare, and makes a tiny pause between syllables.

Now you have met all the letters of the Russian alphabet. The Russian alphabet is shown in its correct order in your alphabet guide on page 74.

Remember that Russian spelling and pronunciation are simpler than English, and if you just join together every letter in a word you will come fairly close to pronouncing it correctly. Now have a go at reading some more words in which any letter of the alphabet may appear! Good luck!

✅ *Reading practice*

8 Imagine you are walking around the centre of Moscow. You see these signs outside some of the buildings. What are they?

(*a*) **бар** (*b*) **Мело́дия** (*c*) **Пи́цца Хат** (*d*) **музе́й** (*e*) **цирк** (*f*) **банк** (*g*) **библиоте́ка** (*h*) **Кремль** (*i*) **по́чта** (*j*) **Большо́й теа́тр**

9 Signs outside some other buildings tell you what you can find inside. Match the signs and the English words.

| сувени́р | | милиция | | информа́ция |

| пи́цца | | проду́кты |

information   souvenirs   pizza   provisions   militia (police)

10 Traditional Russian cookery is delicious, and includes such dishes as **борщ** (borshsh) which is beetroot soup, and **щи** (shshee) which is cabbage soup. They are often served with bread **хлеб** (khlyep) and sour cream **смета́на** (smet<u>a</u>na). **Во́дка** (v<u>o</u>tka) vodka is a traditional Russian drink, and **чай** (chai) tea is also frequently drunk, usually without milk. However, many Russians now enjoy Western-style food as well. See if you can match the words with the pictures.

(*a*) **чи́збургер** (*b*) **бана́н** (*c*) **ко́фе каппучи́но** (*d*) **пи́цца су́пер суприм**

11 As well as Western-style food, many Western words concerning the world of work have also come to Russia. What are these?

(*a*) **ме́неджер**   (*b*) **факс**   (*c*) **бри́финг**   (*d*) **ма́ркетинг**
(*e*) **фло́ппи диск**   (*f*) **бизнесме́н**   (*g*) **но́у-хау**   (*h*) **бро́кер**
(*i*) **уи́к-энд**   (*j*) **компью́тер**

12 Here is a family portrait. It has been labelled for you. Can you read who everyone is?

бабушка   кот   де́душка   ма́ма   па́па   сын   дочь

Pointing to the picture and speaking out loud, answer the following questions. (In answer to the first one you would say: «**Вот ма́ма**».)

Где ма́ма?	**Где дочь?**
Где сын?	**Где де́душка?**
Где ба́бушка?	**Где кот?**
Где па́па?	

The children are described in Russian as **сын** (syn) *son* and **дочь** (doch') *daughter*. You could also describe them as **брат** (brat) *brother* and **сестра́** (sistra) *sister*.

13 Just as many English words are familiar to Russians, names of many famous Russians are familiar to us. Can you work out who these people are?

Writers	Composers	Political leaders
(*a*) Чёхов	(*d*) Чайко́вский	(*g*) Ле́нин
(*b*) Толсто́й	(*e*) Рахма́нинов	(*h*) Горбачёв
(*c*) Пу́шкин	(*f*) Шостако́вич	(*i*) Е́льцин

Writers: (i) Pushkin (ii) Tolstoy (iii) Chekhov. **Composers:** (i) Rachmaninov (ii) Tchaikovsky (iii) Shostakovich. **Political leaders:** (i) Lenin (ii) Yeltsin (iii) Gorbachev

14 For your last alphabet reading exercise, imagine you have to visit the doctor in Russia. Let's hope it never happens, but if it does here are some words which might prove useful:

(*a*) температу́ра　(*b*) бакте́рия　(*c*) антибио́тик　(*d*) масса́ж
(*e*) табле́тка　(*f*) диа́гноз　(*g*) пеницилли́н　(*h*) инфе́кция

Well done! You have managed to read words containing any letter of the Russian alphabet except for the hard sign ъ. That is because it is so rare, but just for good luck, here is a word which contains a hard sign: объе́кт (ob-y<u>e</u>kt) *object*. So now there is nothing which can surprise you! With every new word, just say each sound in order, emphasising the stressed syllable, and you should be pronouncing it well enough for a Russian to understand you.

Механи́зм языка́
Mechanics of the language

Now that you can pronounce Russian and feel confident with the sounds, you'll be glad to know that it is a logical language and that all you need to make up your own sentences is an understanding of the patterns of the language. Before learning any more words and phrases, here are some key points on starting to use those patterns. Russian is very logical, and while some things may seem to be more complicated than English, some things are definitely easier.

1　The and *a*

The good news is that there are no words in Russian for *the* or *a*. So студе́нт means either *the student* or *a student*.

2   *To be*

More good news! In Russian the verb *to be* is not used when you are talking about things happening now. So you do not need to learn to say *I am*, *you are*, *he is* and so on. In English you would say *I am a businessman*, but in Russian this is simply **Я – бизнесмéн**, literally *I businessman*. This may sound like Tarzan speaking, but don't worry, it is real Russian. So if you hear **Антóн – студéнт**, it means *Anton is a student*. Note that Russian may use a dash to replace the verb *to be*.

3   *Gender of nouns*

A noun is a word that names someone or something: **мéнеджер** *manager*, **Ларúса** *Larisa*, **Россúя** *Russia*, **автóбус** *bus*, **кот** *cat*, **электрóника** *electronics*. Russian nouns are divided randomly into three groups called 'gender groups': masculine, feminine and neuter. Later it will be helpful to know which group a noun belongs to. As you might expect, **бизнесмéн** *businessman* is masculine and **балерúна** *ballerina* is feminine, but even non-living things in Russian have a gender. The good thing is that you do not have to memorise which gender each noun has. You can tell simply by looking at the ending. Here are the most common endings:

Masculine
Most masculine nouns end in a consonant or **-й**. (Look at your pronunciation guide if you are not sure what a consonant is.) So **стадиóн** *stadium*, **чúзбургер** *cheeseburger*, **Лóндон** *London*, and **дом** *house* or *block of flats* are all masculine. So are **музéй** *museum*, and **трамвáй** *tram*.

Feminine
Most feminine nouns end in **-a** or **-я**. So **кассéта** *cassette*, **Одéсса** *Odessa*, **Áнглия** *England*, and **энéргия** *energy* are all feminine. If you meet a word like **студéнтка** which ends in **-a**, you know that this must be a female student. A male student, as you know, is **студéнт**. (There are exceptions to this rule, e.g. **пáпа** *Dad* which ends in **-a** but which is masculine because of its meaning.)

Neuter
Most neuter nouns end in **-o** or **-e**. So **метрó** *metro*, **винó** *wine* and **кафé** *café* are all neuter.

Soft sign ь

There is also a small group of nouns ending in a soft sign **ь**. These may be either masculine or feminine, and you have to learn which gender they are. **Кремль** (Kryeml') *Kremlin* is masculine and **медаль** (medal') *medal* is feminine. **Дочь** *daughter* is, of course, feminine. Every time you meet a new noun ending in **ь** it will have (*m*) or (*f*) next to it to show you whether it is masculine or feminine.

To summarise:

Masculine nouns end in	**a consonant**	парк
	й	музей
	ь	Кремль
Feminine nouns end in	**а**	кассета
	я	энергия
	ь	дочь
Neuter nouns end in	**о**	метро
	е	кафе

Упражнения: *exercises*

15 Listen to the cassette to find out what jobs people do. Match up the numbers and the letters. So if you think Nina is an actress write (a) iv.

(*a*)	**Нина**	(*i*)	**бизнесмен**
(*b*)	**Александр**	(*ii*)	**поэт**
(*c*)	**Анна**	(*iii*)	**администратор**
(*d*)	**Владимир**	(*iv*)	**актриса**
(*e*)	**Борис**	(*v*)	**стюардесса**

16 Look at the pictures below and make up a sentence about each person, using the words in brackets. For example, **Лариса – студентка** (*Larisa is a student*).

Йгорь   Лари́са   Анто́н   Ната́ша   Бори́с

(теннисйст, студе́нтка, футболйст, балери́на, турйст)

17 Ната́ша is at a party. She is rather short-sighted so she asks Лари́са for help in spotting her friends. But Лари́са doesn't know them all. In this conversation, which is on your cassette if you have one, you will meet two new words:

Кто? (Kto?) *Who?*
Нет (Nyet) *No*

Ната́ша **Лари́са, где Анто́н?**
Лари́са **Анто́н? Кто Анто́н?**
Ната́ша **Анто́н – студе́нт.**
Лари́са **А, вот Анто́н.**
Ната́ша **Спаси́бо, Лари́са. Где А́нна?**
Лари́са **А́нна? Кто А́нна? Актри́са?**
Ната́ша **Нет. А́нна – балери́на.**
Лари́са **Балери́на? А, вот А́нна.**

18 Read this list of words and decide which are masculine, feminine and neuter. Write (m), (f) or (n) in the brackets at the side to show their gender.

(*a*) а́том ( )	(*e*) Аме́рика ( )	(*i*) кино́ ( )
(*b*) кассе́та ( )	(*f*) теа́тр ( )	(*j*) дочь ( )
(*c*) сала́т ( )	(*g*) трамва́й ( )	(*k*) волейбо́л ( )
(*d*) пиани́но ( )	(*h*) информа́ция ( )	(*l*) вино́ ( )

19 These words are grouped according to gender, but there is one word in each group which has the wrong gender. Find the odd-one-out in each group and underline it.

Masculine	Feminine	Neuter
суп	гита́ра	метро́
Кремль	А́нглия	кафе́
план	меда́ль	ра́дио
па́спорт	во́дка	саксофо́н
сестра́	стадио́н	кака́о
трамва́й	кассе́та	пиани́но

20 You are in a restaurant ordering three items. Can you find them hidden in the string of letters below?

абресуптономлетхалисалаткуд

Which gender are all three things which you ordered?

21 See if you can decipher these jumbled words using the clues. The first letter of each word is in bold print. They are all feminine.

(*a*) та**с**ре**с**   (a relative)
(*b*) **ф**ими**с**оян   (orchestral music)
(*c*) г**А**нетиран   (a country)
(*d*) аке**б**итбило   (a place for bookworms)
(*e*) урме**т**ерпата   (this is high if you are feverish)

Did you know that you can already say and read more than 350 words in Russian! When you are confident that you understand everything in these first two units, you are ready to move on to unit 3.

3

ДО́БРЫЙ ДЕНЬ!
Good day!

In this unit you will learn

- how to say hello and goodbye
- how to greet and address someone
- how to say you don't understand
- how to ask if anyone speaks English

Before you start

✳ It is very important for you to read the introduction to the course on page 1. This gives some useful advice on studying alone and how to make the most of the course. If you are working with the cassette, keep it handy as you will need it for the **Key words** and **Dialogue** sections. If you don't have the cassette, use the Pronunciation guide on page 4.

—— Информа́ция: *information* ——

Russian names

If you have ever seen a Russian play or read a Russian book in English you will have noticed that one Russian person may appear to have many names. Actually, Russians have three names each.

Their first name **и́мя** (<u>ee</u>mya) is their given name, for example, **Ива́н** (Eev<u>a</u>n) or **Ни́на** (N<u>ee</u>na). Then they have a 'patronymic' name, **о́тчество** (<u>o</u>tchestvo). This is formed from their father's first name plus a special ending: **-о́вич** (<u>o</u>veech) or **-е́вич** (y<u>e</u>veech) for boys and **-о́вна** (<u>o</u>vna) or **-е́вна** (y<u>e</u>vna) for girls. Finally they have a family name, **фами́лия** (fam<u>ee</u>liya), which has the same function as our surname. So you would be able to work out that **Влади́мир Ива́нович Козло́в** (Vlad<u>ee</u>mir Eev<u>a</u>novich Kazl<u>o</u>v) had a father called **Ива́н** (Eev<u>a</u>n), and **Еле́на Алекса́ндровна Попо́ва** (Ily<u>e</u>na Aliks<u>a</u>ndrovna Pap<u>o</u>va) had a father called **Алекса́ндр** (Aliks<u>a</u>ndr). Notice that the man's name has masculine endings (consonants) and the woman's name has feminine endings (**-a**).

и́мя	<u>ee</u>mya	*given name*
о́тчество	<u>o</u>tchestvo	*patronymic*
фами́лия	fam<u>ee</u>liya	*family name*

How to address Russians

Adult Russians who are on formal terms will call each other by their first name and patronymic. This is a mark of respect, and young people will address older people in this way, for example, a schoolchild will address a teacher as **Гали́на Миха́йловна** (Gal<u>ee</u>na Mikh<u>a</u>ilovna). In Soviet times, another official form of address was **това́рищ** (tav<u>a</u>rishsh) *comrade*, used either with the surname or on its own to address someone whose name was not known. Nowadays, **това́рищ** is losing popularity and the pre-Revolutionary **господи́н** (gaspad<u>ee</u>n) *sir* and **госпожа́** (gaspazh<u>a</u>) *madam* have reappeared.

Adult Russians who are close friends will call each other by their first name, and children will usually be addressed by their first name. People on first name terms will often use 'diminutive' forms. This is like using Mike for Michael or Annie for Annabel but each Russian name has lots of possible diminutives. For example, **Еле́на** (Ily<u>e</u>na) might be called **Ле́на** (Ly<u>e</u>na) for short, **Ле́ночка** (Ly<u>e</u>nochka) or **Лену́ся** (Lyin<u>oo</u>sya) affectionately, **Лено́к** (Lyin<u>o</u>k) jokingly, **Ле́нка** (Ly<u>e</u>nka) perhaps by an angry parent, and more rarely but affectionately, **Алёна** (Aly<u>o</u>nya) and **Алёнушка** (Aly<u>o</u>nooshka).

Ключевы́е слова́:
key words and phrases

Диало́г 1 *Dialogue 1*

До́брое у́тро	D<u>o</u>broye <u>oo</u>tra	*Good morning*
До́брый день	D<u>o</u>bry dyen'	*Good day*
До́брый ве́чер	D<u>o</u>bry vy<u>e</u>cher	*Good evening*
Здра́вствуйте	Zdr<u>a</u>stvooeetye	*Hello*
До свида́ния	Da sveed<u>a</u>nya	*Goodbye*

Диало́г 2 *Dialogue 2*

Меня́ зову́т	Miny<u>a</u> zav<u>oo</u>t	*I am called*
О́чень прия́тно	<u>O</u>chen preey<u>a</u>tna	*Pleased to meet you* (lit. *very pleasant*)
Как вас зову́т?	Kak vas zav<u>oo</u>t?	*What are you called?*
Как дела́?	Kak dyel<u>a</u>?	*How are things?*
хорошо́	kharash<u>o</u>	*good, well*

Диало́г 3 *Dialogue 3*

извини́те	eezveen<u>ee</u>tye	*excuse me/I'm sorry*
молодо́й челове́к	malad<u>o</u>y	
chilovy<u>e</u>k		*young man*
вы vy		*you*
нет nyet		*no*
я ya		*I*
не nye		*not*
де́вушка dy<u>e</u>vushka		*young woman/miss*
да da		*yes*

Диало́г 4 *Dialogue 4*

Я не понима́ю	Ya nye paneem<u>a</u>yoo	*I don't understand*
Ме́дленнее, пожа́луйста		
My<u>e</u>ddlyn-ye-ye, pazh<u>a</u>l-sta		*slower please*
Вы говори́те по-англи́йски?		
Vy gavar<u>ee</u>tye pa-angl<u>ee</u>sky?		*Do you speak English?*
Я говорю́ по-ру́сски	Ya gavary<u>oo</u>	
pa-r<u>oo</u>sky		*I speak Russian*
пло́хо pl<u>o</u>kha		*badly*

Диало́ги: *dialogues*

Listen to the dialogues on the tape, or read them through several times until you feel comfortable with them. Pretend to be one of the people in each dialogue and try to memorise what they say. Pause the tape and say your part out loud. Then check your pronunciation with the tape or with the pronunciation given in the **Key words** box. If you are not working with a tape, remember to emphasise the stressed syllables and to under-play the unstressed ones.

📼 Диало́г 1

In this dialogue people are greeting each other and saying goodbye in Russian at different times of day.

Ви́ктор	**До́брое у́тро, Ната́ша.**	Бори́с	**До́брый день, А́нна.**
Ната́ша	**До́брое у́тро, Ви́ктор.**	А́нна	**До́брый день, Бори́с.**
Све́та	**До́брый ве́чер, Ле́на.**	Ири́на	**Здра́вствуйте!**
Ле́на	**До́брый ве́чер, Све́та.**	Анто́н	**Здра́вствуйте!**
Та́ня	**До свида́ния, Ива́н.**		
Ива́н	**До свида́ния, Та́ня.**		

Now cover up the text and see if you can remember how to say: (*a*) good morning (*b*) good evening (*c*) hello (*d*) good day (*e*) goodbye.

📼 Диало́г 2

In this dialogue Igor and Alison meet and introduce themselves.

Igor   *Alison*
До́брый ве́чер. Меня́ зову́т Йгорь.

                                          О́чень прия́тно.

Как вас зову́т?

                                          Меня́ зову́т А́лисон.

О́чень прия́тно. Как дела́, А́лисон?

                                          Хорошо́, спаси́бо.

Practise the dialogue, then imagine that you are Alison. Cover up the right hand side of the dialogue. Say you are pleased to meet Igor and answer his questions. Now cover up the left hand side and practise Igor's part of the conversation.

Диало́г 3

In connection with an advert about a flat, Volodya has arranged to meet a young man called Sasha and his girlfriend Nastya outside a metro station. (Incidentally, **Воло́дя** is a diminutive of **Влади́мир**, **Са́ша** is a diminutive of **Алекса́ндр** and **На́стя** is a diminutive of **Анаста́сия**.) Read their conversation carefully.

Воло́дя	**Извини́те, молодо́й челове́к, вы Са́ша?**
Ми́ша	**Нет, я не Са́ша.**
Воло́дя	**Извини́те. . . . Де́вушка, вы не На́стя?**
Ве́ра	**На́стя? Нет, я не На́стя.**
Воло́дя	**Извини́те, вы Са́ша и На́стя?**
Са́ша и На́стя	**Да. Вы Воло́дя?**
Воло́дя	**Да, я Воло́дя. О́чень прия́тно, Са́ша. О́чень прия́тно, На́стя.**

Repeat the dialogue, and check that you know how to say *excuse me* or *sorry*, and how to address an unknown young man or woman.

▦ Диало́г 4

In the second dialogue in this unit, Alison managed to understand what Igor said to her. Andrew is not quite so lucky and has a few problems understanding a new acquaintance at a party.

Никола́й	**Здра́вствуйте.**
Andrew	**Здра́вствуйте.**
Никола́й	**Как вас зову́т?**
Andrew	**Ме́дленнее, пожа́луйста.**
Никола́й	**Как вас зову́т?**
Andrew	**Извини́те, я не понима́ю.**
Никола́й	**Как вас зову́т? Меня́ зову́т Никола́й Петро́вич. Как вас зову́т?**
Andrew	**А, меня́ зову́т А́ндрю. Вы говори́те по-англи́йски?**
Никола́й	**Да, я говорю́ по-англи́йски.**
Andrew	**Oh good! Хорошо́! Я пло́хо понима́ю по-ру́сски.**

Practise the dialogue several times until you are happy with the new words.

Механи́зм языка́
Mechanics of the language

1 Two ways of saying you

In Russian, as in many languages, there are two different words for *you*. English used to have two words – *you* and *thou* – but now we nearly always use *you*. The two Russian words are **вы** (vy) and **ты** (ty). **Вы** is used whenever you are speaking to more than one person, or to an adult with whom you are on formal or polite terms. **Ты** is used whenever you are speaking informally to one person only. So you would nearly always use **ты** to address a child or a close friend or relation. (Let your Russian friends decide whether to use **вы** or **ты** with you. The younger generation often prefer the less formal **ты** while older people may feel more comfortable using **вы** even when they have known you for years.)

There are also two ways of saying *hello*, depending on whether you call someone **вы** or **ты**. If you are talking to more than one person or formally to one adult, you say **здра́вствуйте** as you have already learned, but if you are talking to a child, close friend or relative, you say **здра́вствуй**, missing off the last two letters. So, if you picked up the phone and heard your Russian boss calling, you might say: **Здра́вствуйте, Влади́мир Ива́нович. Где вы?** Hello, Vladeemir Eevanovich. Where are you?

If, on the other hand, it was your long-lost friend, you would say: **Здра́вствуй, Ле́на. Где ты?** Hello, Lyena. Where are you?

2 Asking questions

A statement can easily be turned into a question in Russian simply by varying the rise and fall of your voice. If you make a statement in Russian, your voice should fall:

Ива́н – студе́нт. Ivan is a student.

If you want to make the statement into a question, your voice should rise:

Ива́н – студе́нт? Is Ivan a student?

If the question contains a question word, like *who? what? where? why? when? how?* then your voice should rise on the question word itself:

Как дела́? How are things?

3 To do or not to do

You have already met people saying that they can and can't do things, and you have probably noticed the little word **не** (nye) which means *not*. In unit 2, little Ле́на said **Я не зна́ю** *I don't know*. In the last dialogue, Andrew said **Я не понима́ю** *I don't understand*. Никола́й told him: **Я говорю́ по-англи́йски** *I speak English*. So you can work out that:

Я зна́ю Ya znayoo	means	*I know*
Я понима́ю Ya paneemayoo	means	*I understand*
Я говорю́ Ya gavaryoo	means	*I speak*

If you want to say that you can't do any of these things, simply slip **не** *not* between **я** and the word which says what you are doing.

Я не зна́ю	*I don't know*
Я не понима́ю	*I don't understand*
Я не говорю́	*I don't speak*

The action words *to know*, *to understand*, *to speak* may be described as verbs. If you want to say that you do any of these things well or badly, slip **хорошо́** *well* or **пло́хо** *badly* between **я** and the verb.

Я хорошо́ зна́ю А́лисон	*I know Alison well*
Я хорошо́ понима́ю А́ндрю	*I understand Andrew well*
Я пло́хо говорю́ по-ру́сски	*I speak Russian badly*

By the end of the course you should be able to say truthfully *I speak Russian well*. Why not try it out now! **Я хорошо́ говорю́ по-ру́сски**.

4 Who's who?

You already know how to say *I* (**я**) and *you* (**ты** or **вы**) in Russian. Now you should be ready to learn *he*, *she*, *we* and *they*.

In Russian, *he* is **он** (on). So you could say: **Он – поэ́т.** *He is a poet.*

She is similar to *he* but has a feminine ending: **она́** (an<u>a</u>). So you could say: **Она́ – балери́на.** *She is a ballerina.*

We is **мы** (my), rhyming with **ты** and **вы**. So you might hear: **Мы – ма́ма и па́па.** *We are Mum and Dad.*

They is **они́** (an<u>ee</u>). So you might say: **Они́ –Са́ша и На́стя.** *They are Sasha and Nastya.*

Now you can refer to anyone in a conversation, even if you don't know what they are called.

я	*I*	**мы**	*we*
ты	*you* (one person, familiar)	**вы**	*you* (more than one person,
он	*he*		or formal acquaintance)
она́	*she*	**они́**	*they*

———— Упражне́ния: *exercises* ————

1 Imagine you have to fill in a form for a male Russian friend. Match the names provided with the blanks on the form.

(*a*) **и́мя** _____   (*i*) **Влади́мирович**
(*b*) **о́тчество** _____   (*ii*) **Смирно́в**
(*c*) **фами́лия** _____   (*iii*) **Бори́с**

Now do the same for a female Russian friend.

(*a*) **и́мя** _____   (*i*) **Ни́на**
(*b*) **о́тчество** _____   (*ii*) **Горбачёва**
(*c*) **фами́лия** _____   (*iii*) **Бори́совна**

What is the first name of your male friend's father? And your female friend's father?

2 How would you say hello at these times of day?

(*a*) 9.15
(*b*) 14.45
(*c*) 20.30

3 You meet a Russian who asks you what your name is: **Как вас зову́т?** How do you answer: *My name is . . .*?

М_____ з_____ Stuart.
He says he is pleased to meet you. How does he say that in Russian?
О_____ п_____.

4 Imagine that you are working in Russia and an old friend and colleague Áнна Миха́йловна calls to see you. What should you say?

(a) Как вас зову́т? (b) Я не понима́ю (c) Де́вушка
(d) До свида́ния (e) Здра́вствуйте (f) Извини́те

5 (a) You want to attract the attention of the young man serving behind the counter of a crowded shop in St. Petersburg. How do you address him?

(b) You step on someone's foot. What do you say?

(c) You want to ask the girl at the cash-desk a question. How do you address her?

(d) You think you recognise a girl called Nina whom you met on the tram yesterday. What do you say to her?

Choose your answers from the suggestions below:
(i) Де́вушка! (ii) Извини́те, вы Ни́на? (iii) Молодо́й челове́к!
(iv) Извини́те!

6 How do you pronounce these words and phrases?

(a) Здра́вствуйте	(e) Где Бори́с?
(b) Спаси́бо	(f) Я не зна́ю
(c) Я говорю́ по-англи́йски	(g) Ме́дленнее, пожа́луйста
(d) Хорошо́	(h) Извини́те

What do they all mean?

7 Draw lines to link the matching phrases in Russian and English.

(a)	**Я говорю́ по-англи́йски.**	(i)	*I don't know.*
(b)	**Я не понима́ю.**	(ii)	*I understand Russian well.*
(c)	**Я хорошо́ понима́ю по-ру́сски.**	(iii)	*I speak English.*
(d)	**Я не зна́ю.**	(iv)	*I understand.*
(e)	**Я понима́ю.**	(v)	*I don't understand.*

8 Which word is missing? Refer to the words in brackets below if you need to.

(a) Меня́ _____ Ива́н.
(b) _____ ве́чер.
(c) Я ____ понима́ю.

(*d*) Вы _____ по-англи́йски?

(*e*) Молодо́й _____.

(До́брый, челове́к, зову́т, не, говори́те)

9 Using your cassette, check that you understand which is the right answer.

(*a*) The speaker says (*i*) good morning (*ii*) good day (*iii*) good evening.

(*b*) She is called (*i*) Nina Petrovna (*ii*) Nina Borisovna (*iii*) Anna Petrovna.

(*c*) She (*i*) speaks English (*ii*) doesn't speak English (*iii*) speaks English well.

10 Match up the questions and answers so that they make sense.

(*a*) Кто он?

(*b*) Кто ты?

(*c*) Кто она́?

(*d*) Кто вы?

(*e*) Кто они́?

(*i*) Они́ – ба́бушка и де́душка.

(*ii*) Она́ – стюарде́сса.

(*iii*) Мы – брат и сестра́.

(*iv*) Он – студе́нт.

(*v*) Я – космона́вт.

Прове́рьте себя́ *Test yourself: end of unit revision*

You have arrived at the end of unit 3. Now you know how to say hello and goodbye, find out who people are and exchange greetings. You also know how to cope if you don't understand. How would you:

1 say hello?

2 say goodbye?

3 say excuse me?

4 ask for someone's name?

5 find out if someone speaks English?

6 say you don't understand?

You'll find the answers to this little test at the end of the book. If most of them are correct you are ready to move on to the next unit. If you still need practice, spend some more time revising this unit until you feel confident enough to move on. You should expect to take quite a while over each unit because you are still getting used to the new alphabet, so do not be discouraged if your progress seems slow. Look back to the start of unit 1 to remind yourself how much you have learned since then! Well done!

4

ГДЕ БАНК?
Where's the bank?

In this unit you will learn

- how to name some important places in a town
- how to ask and say where things are
- how to describe things which you see
- how to understand a Russian address
- how to count to ten

Before you start

Look back at page 24 to make sure that you can recognise whether a noun is masculine, feminine or neuter. Just to check, write *m, f,* or *n* in the brackets after these words: автóбус (   ) óпера (   ) пианúно (   ) метрó (   ) мáма (   ) банк (   ).

✳ —— Информáция: *information* ——

Пассажúрский трáнспорт: *passenger transport*

Passenger transport in Russian cities includes the **автóбус** (av<u>to</u>boos) *bus*, **трамвáй** (tramv<u>a</u>y) *tram* and **троллéйбус** (trolly<u>ei</u>boos) *trolleybus* and, in some cities, an underground system **метрó** (mitr<u>o</u>). Tickets for the bus, tram and trolleybus services may be bought from the driver and each ticket **талóн** (tal<u>o</u>n) must have holes punched in it when it is used. A token **жетóн** (zhet<u>o</u>n) has to be inserted into an entry barrier to gain access to the metro.

автóбус, троллейбус, трамвáй и метрó

талóны

Russian addresses

Russian addresses are written in a different order from most of Europe, starting with the city **гóрод** (g<u>o</u>rat), then the street **ýлица** (<u>oo</u>leetsa), the number of the block of flats **дом** (dom), the building section number **кóрпус** (k<u>o</u>rpoos) and finally the flat number **квартúра** (kvart<u>ee</u>ra). If a name is included, this will be written after the rest of the address with the surname first. So a typical address **áдрес** (<u>a</u>dryes) might look like this:

Москвá,
Ботанúческая ýлица,   (*Botanical street*)
дом 8, кóрпус 4, квартúра 10.

Ключевы́е слова́:
Key words and phrases

Диало́г 1

москви́ч/москви́чка	maskv<u>ee</u>ch/ maskv<u>ee</u>chka	*Muscovite (m, f)*
э́то	<u>e</u>to (*rhymes with letter*)	*it is/is it?*
вон там	von tam	*over there*

Диало́г 2

кинотеа́тр	keenoti<u>a</u>tr	*cinema*
спра́вочное бюро́	spr<u>a</u>vuchnoye byur<u>o</u>	*information office*
Не́ за что!	Ny<u>e</u> za shto!	*Don't mention it!*

Диало́г 3

здесь	zdyes'	*here, around here*
он/она́/оно́	on/on<u>a</u>/an<u>o</u>	*it (m/f/n)*
скажи́те	skazh<u>ee</u>tye	*tell me*
гости́ница	gast<u>ee</u>neetsa	*hotel*

Диало́г 4

како́й э́то го́род?	kak<u>o</u>y <u>e</u>to g<u>o</u>rat?	*What sort of city is it?*
како́й/кака́я/како́е	kak-<u>o</u>y/-<u>a</u>ya/-<u>o</u>ye	*what sort of (m/f/n)?*
го́род	g<u>o</u>rat	*city/town*
большо́й/больша́я/большо́е	bol'sh-<u>o</u>y/-<u>a</u>ya/-<u>o</u>ye	*big (m/f/n)*
краси́вый/краси́вая/краси́вое	kras<u>ee</u>v-y/-aya/-oye	*beautiful (m/f/n)*

Диало́г 5

хоро́ший/хоро́шая/хоро́шее	khor<u>o</u>sh-y/-aya/-eye	*good (m/f/n)*
там	tam	*there*

Диало́г 6

ма́ленький/ма́ленькая/ма́ленькое	m<u>a</u>lyen'-ky/-aya/-oye	*little (m/f/n)*

Диало́ги: *dialogues*

 **Диало́г 1**

Andrew's Russian is getting better every day, and he has gone out to find his way around Moscow. First he needs to change some money.

Andrew	Извини́те, пожа́луйста, э́то банк?
Москви́чка	Нет, э́то по́чта.
Andrew	Где банк?
Москви́чка	Банк вон там.

Диало́г 2

He has read in the paper that there is a good film on at the «Ко́смос» cinema.

Andrew	Молодо́й челове́к, э́то кинотеа́тр «Ко́смос»?
Москви́ч	Нет, э́то кинотеа́тр «Плане́та».
Andrew	Где кинотеа́тр «Ко́смос»?
Москви́ч	Извини́те, я не зна́ю.
Andrew	Где спра́вочное бюро́?
Москви́ч	Вон там.
Andrew	Спаси́бо.
Москви́ч	Не́ за что! До свида́ния.

Диало́г 3

Andrew is feeling hungry, but can't make up his mind whether to eat at a restaurant, hotel or café.

Andrew	Извини́те, где здесь рестора́н?
Москви́ч	Вот он.
Andrew	Скажи́те, пожа́луйста, где здесь гости́ница?
Москви́ч	Вот она́.
Andrew	Спаси́бо. Где здесь кафе́?
Москви́ч	Вот оно́.

Диало́г 4

While he is having lunch, he asks a Muscovite what sort of city Moscow is.

Andrew	Скажи́те, како́й э́то го́род?
Москви́ч	Э́то большо́й, краси́вый го́род.

Диало́г 5

Meanwhile, Volodya asks Sasha and Nastya about the flat in the advert.

Володя	Скажи́те, кака́я э́то кварти́ра?
Са́ша	Э́то больша́я, хоро́шая кварти́ра. Там лифт, телефо́н и краси́вый балко́н.

Диало́г 6

The pianist from unit 1 has found his piano, but he is disappointed with it, and complains to the composer.

Пиани́ст	Э́то о́чень ма́ленькое пиани́но!
Компози́тор	Нет, э́то не ма́ленькое пиани́но. Пиани́но – большо́е, краси́вое.

Numerals 0-10

0	ноль	nol'		
1	оди́н	ad<u>ee</u>n	6 шесть	shest'
2	два	dva	7 семь	syem'
3	три	tree	8 во́семь	v<u>o</u>syem'
4	четы́ре	chyet<u>i</u>rye	9 де́вять	dy<u>e</u>vyat'
5	пять	pyat'	10 де́сять	dy<u>e</u>syat'

Number practice

Read all the numbers aloud or listen to the tape and repeat the numbers after you hear them spoken. Try to say the first three numbers without looking, then add another three until you can say them all without looking. If you have a pack of playing cards shuffle the pack and then turn over a card at a time calling out the number, or throw some dice, calling out the score each time. Do this until you can say the numbers up to 10 in random order as soon as you see them. Then read these numbers out loud in the right order.

пять де́вять четы́ре два шесть ноль во́семь оди́н де́сять три семь

Now try reciting the numbers from 10 down to 0.

Механизм языка
Mechanics of the language

1 Это *This is*

You already know that you do not need a verb *to be* in Russian if you are talking about things happening now. For example, **Антон студент** *Anton is a student*. But there is a very useful word in Russian meaning *this is* or *these are*: **это**. So, **Это телефон** means *This is a telephone*. You can also use **это** as a question word: **Это телефон?** *Is this a telephone?*

Это ресторан?   Нет, это не ресторан. Это кафе.

2 Он, она, оно *it*

In English we use *it* to refer to anything we have already mentioned which is not a person, for example, *it (the bus) is late*. In Russian, every time you want to use *it* you must think whether the noun you are referring to is masculine, feminine or neuter. Look back at page 24 to remind yourself how to tell whether a word is masculine, feminine or neuter. You already know that **он** means *he* and **она** means *she*. **Он** and **она** also mean *it* when referring to a masculine and feminine noun respectively. **Оно** is what you use to refer to a neuter noun. Notice that the endings of these words do what you would expect: the masculine **он** ends in a consonant, the feminine **она** ends in -**a** and the neuter **оно** ends in -**o**.

Где автобус? *Where is the bus?*   Вот он. *(m) There it is.*
Где ваза?   *Where is the vase?*   Вот она. *(f) There it is.*
Где радио? *Where is the radio?* Вот оно. *(n) There it is.*

3 Какой это . . .? *What sort of . . .?*

Just as there are three similar words for *it* in Russian, so there are also three forms of the word meaning *What sort of . . .?* when you are asking about a singular noun. Again you choose which to use by remembering whether the noun you are referring to is masculine, feminine or neuter.

Какой? means *what sort of?* when it refers to a masculine noun.
Какая? means *what sort of?* when it refers to a feminine noun.
Какое? means *what sort of?* when it refers to a neuter noun.

Notice that **какóй** has a typical masculine ending in **-й**, **какáя** has a typical feminine ending in **-я**, and **какóе** has a typical neuter ending in **-е**.

Какóй э́то суп? What sort of soup is it? (*m*)
Какáя э́то гитáра? What sort of guitar is it? (*f*)
Какóе э́то винó? What sort of wine is it? (*n*)

4 *Adjectives*

When you want to describe a singular noun, possibly in answer to a question like **Какóй э́то суп?** you will need to choose a masculine, feminine or neuter ending for the adjective (or describing word) you want to use. Again this will depend on the gender of the noun to which you are referring. This is called making the adjective 'agree' with the noun. If you want to describe something as beautiful, work out which gender the noun is, and use the correct ending to make the adjective agree.

Masculine	*Feminine*	*Neuter*
Э́то краси́вый парк.	Э́то краси́вая вáза.	Э́то краси́вое рáдио.
It's a beautiful park.	*It's a beautiful vase.*	*It's a beautiful radio.*

Look at the other adjectives in your **Key words** list. You will notice that the most common endings are **-ый** (*m*), **-ая** (*f*) and **-ое** (*n*). Sometimes, as in **мáленький**, the masculine ending will be spelt **-ий** because of a spelling rule which need not concern us here, (see p. 237). Similarly, the neuter form may sometimes be spelt **-ее** as in **хорóшее**. Finally, any masculine adjective with the last syllable stressed will have the ending **-óй** as in **большóй**. In your word lists from now on, adjectives will appear in singular masculine form only, unless there is anything unusual about them. Don't worry – even if you get the endings wrong you will still be understood!

☑———— **Упражнéния:** *exercises* ————

1 Look at the map of part of Moscow and imagine that you are a tourist asking someone where certain places are. So you might ask out loud: **Где здесь парк?** Now imagine what the reply will be and say it aloud: **Вот он**. Carry on until you can say where everything on the map is.

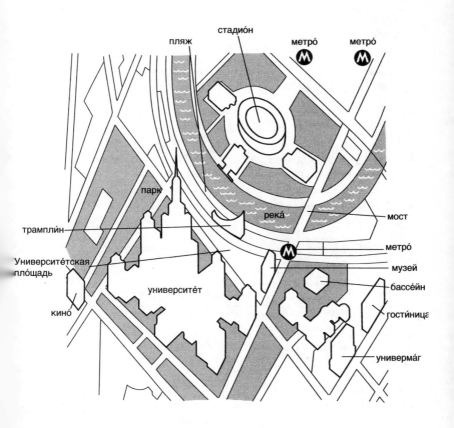

Здесь (zdyes') means *here*, and if you include it in the question, it implies that you do not have a particular park in mind, or you do not know if you are looking in the right area, but you just want to know where there might be a park around here.

Ключ *Key*		
река́ ryik<u>a</u>	*river*	
мост most	*bridge*	
стадио́н stadee<u>o</u>n	*stadium*	
музе́й moozy<u>ey</u>	*museum*	
парк park	*park*	
метро́ mitr<u>o</u>	*metro*	
бассе́йн bassy<u>ei</u>n	*swimming pool*	
универма́г ooniverm<u>a</u>k t<u>ee</u>nitsa	*department store* **гости́ница** *gas-hotel*	
кино́ keen<u>o</u>	*cinema*	
университе́т ooniversity<u>e</u>t	*university*	
трампли́н trampl<u>ee</u>n	*ski jump*	
пляж plyash	*beach*	
Университе́тская пло́щадь (f) ooniversity<u>e</u>tskaya pl<u>o</u>shshad'	*University square*	

2 Here are some more signs that you might see. Try to work out what they mean.

(*a*) **бульва́р**   (*b*) проспе́кт   (*c*) **ке́мпинг**

(*d*) **стоя́нка такси́**   (*e*) **кафе́-бар**   (*f*) **тури́стская гости́ница**

(*g*) *ботани́ческий сад*   (*h*) **медпу́нкт**   (*i*) яхт-клу́б

(*j*) **кулб тури́стов**   (*k*) **кана́л**

(*l*) **Кра́сная Пло́щадь**

3 Underline the correct answer to each of these questions:

(*a*) Где вокза́л? Вот он/она́/оно́.
(*b*) Где ста́нция? Вот он/она́/оно́.
(*c*) Где трамва́й? Вот он/она́/оно́.
(*d*) Где метро́? Вот он/она́/оно́.
(*e*) Где шко́ла? Вот он/она́/оно́.
(*f*) Где университе́т? Вот он/она́/оно́.
(*g*) Где гости́ница? Вот он/она́/оно́.
(*h*) Где спра́вочное бюро́? Вот он/она́/оно́.

4 What are these numbers? Say them out loud.

4 5 *10* 2 8

0 6 1 7 **3** 9

5 Listen to your cassette and write down the scores of these entirely fictional, amazingly high-scoring international football matches as you hear them. The countries involved are Russia, Italy, Spain, France and England.

Металли́ст (Росси́я) [ ]   Юве́нтус (Ита́лия) [ ]
Реа́л (Испа́ния) [ ]   Дина́мо (Росси́я) [ ]
Нант (Фра́нция) [ ]   Спарта́к (Росси́я) [ ]
А́стон Ви́лла (А́нглия) [ ]   Ла́цио (Ита́лия) [ ]
Ньюка́сл юна́йтед   Атле́тик (Испа́ния) [ ]
   (А́нглия) [ ]
На́поли (Ита́лия) [ ]   Торпе́до (Росси́я) [ ]

6 Listen to your cassette and fill in the columns to say which number bus, tram or trolleybus people are looking for.

автобус   трамва́й   тролле́йбус

(*a*)
(*b*)
(*c*)
(*d*)

7 A Russian tourist asks you:

(*a*) Где спра́вочное бюро́?   *Tell him it's over there.*
(*b*) Где тролле́йбус?   *Tell him you are sorry, you don't know.*
(*c*) Э́то библиоте́ка?   *Tell him no, it's the post office.*
(*d*) Спаси́бо.   *Tell him not to mention it.*

8 Rearrange the following information into an address, and read it out loud including the numbers.

(*a*) кварти́ра 3
(*b*) Краснода́р
(*c*) ко́рпус 7
(*d*) Восто́чная у́лица (*East Street*)
(*e*) дом 5

9 Try out a few new adjectives. They are all colours.

кра́сный	krasny	*red*	**зелёный**	zilyony	*green*
бе́лый	byely	*white*	**чёрный**	chorny	*black*
жёлтый	zholty	*yellow*			

In the box above, each adjective is in its masculine form. Below you have the same adjectives in different forms: masculine, feminine and neuter. They have become separated from their nouns. See if you can match them up.

бе́лая
зелёный
кра́сное
чёрный
жёлтый

вино́
бана́н
табле́тка
кот
сала́т

Прове́рьте себя́   *Test yourself: end of unit revision*

By now you know about the public transport system in Russian cities, you can read a Russian address, and you can request and give information about where places are. You can also give a description of something, and you can count to ten. To test yourself, see if you can unjumble the Russian sentences below to put this conversation into Russian.

Tourist   *Excuse me. Where is the park?*
Tour guide   *There it is. Over there.*
Tourist   *What sort of park is it?*

Tour guide   *It is a beautiful big park!*
Tourist   *Thank you. Goodbye.*

(*a*) Какой это парк? (*b*) Спасибо. До свидания. (*c*) Вот он. Вон там. (*d*) Извините. Где парк? (*e*) Это красивый, большой парк!

If you managed that and the exercises in this unit, you are now ready to move on. If you need to spend more time on this unit don't worry – there's a lot to absorb. It is best to work slowly and be sure of things before you move on to new information.

5

ИДИ́ТЕ ПРЯ́МО
Go straight ahead

In this unit you will learn

- how to ask for and give directions
- how to ask whether things are available
- how to make plural forms
- how to say whether somewhere is open or closed
- how to count from ten to thirty

Before you start

If you are at all unsure about how to tell whether a noun is masculine, feminine or neuter, go back to page 24 again.

Look back at page 44 and re-read the section on how to choose adjective endings, as you will have the chance to practise this later in this unit.

Revise your numbers 0 – 10 on page 42, as this will help you to learn the numbers up to 30.

✳ In this unit you will be asking for directions. Remember that in real life, the Russians whom you ask for directions probably won't have read this book, and they may give you rather complicated answers! Don't panic, but just try to pick out the essential words. Remember that you can always ask them to speak more slowly, and in this unit you will also learn how to ask someone to repeat something.

—— Информа́ция ——

Телефо́н-автома́т (Telef<u>o</u>n-avtom<u>a</u>t) *Pay phone*

To use a public telephone, you will need to buy a **жето́н** (zhet<u>o</u>n) similar to the one you need for the **метро́**. In some cities the same **жето́н** works for both the telephone and underground systems. When you get through to a home number, if the person you want does not pick up the phone, ask **Са́ша до́ма?** (S<u>a</u>sha d<u>o</u>ma?) *Is Sasha at home?*

Кио́ск (Ki<u>o</u>sk) *Kiosk*

Kiosks can be found on many city streets in Russia. They sell all manner of goods, including theatre tickets, newspapers, maps, flowers, confectionery and tobacco. Look out for the following signs: **театра́льный** (tiyatr<u>a</u>l'ny) for theatre tickets, **газе́тный** (gaz<u>ye</u>tny) for newspapers and magazines, and **цветы́** (tsvyet<u>y</u>) for flowers. Russians love to give and receive flowers, but you should remember to give an odd number of blooms on happy occasions as an even number is associated with sad events. In winter you may see glass cases of flowers for sale on the streets, with candles burning inside to stop the flowers from freezing. **Таба́к** (Tab<u>a</u>k) means that cigarettes are for sale, and you may see people smoking a version of a cigarette called **папиро́са** (papir<u>o</u>sa) which has a cardboard mouthpiece.

Ключевы́е слова́

Диало́г 1

как попа́сть в...?	kak pop<u>a</u>st' v ...?	*How do I/you get to?*
центр	tsentr	*the centre*
иди́те	eed<u>ee</u>tye	*go*
пря́мо	pry<u>a</u>ma	*straight ahead*
пото́м	pat<u>o</u>m	*then*
нале́во	naly<u>e</u>va	*to the left*
кра́сный	kr<u>a</u>sny	*red*
пло́щадь (f)	pl<u>o</u>shshad'	*square*
повтори́те	pavtar<u>ee</u>tye	*repeat*

Диало́г 2

Куда́ вы идёте?	Kood<u>a</u> vy eedy<u>o</u>tye?	*Where are you going?*
Я иду́ в ...	Ya eed<u>oo</u> v ...	*I am going to ...*
далеко́	dalyik<u>o</u>	*far, a long way*
недалеко́	nidalyik<u>o</u>	*not far*
напра́во	napr<u>a</u>va	*to the right*
интере́сный	intiry<u>e</u>sny	*interesting*

Диало́г 3

закры́т/а/о	zakr<u>y</u>t/zakr<u>y</u>ta/zakr<u>y</u>to	*closed*
на ремо́нт	na rim<u>o</u>nt	*for repairs*
Ой, как жаль!	Oy, kak zhal'!	*Oh, what a pity!*
галере́я	galiry<u>e</u>ya	*gallery*
откры́т/а/о	otkr<u>y</u>t/otrk<u>y</u>ta/otkr<u>y</u>to	*open*

Диало́г 4

У вас есть ...?	Oo vas yest' ...)	*Do you have ...?*
сувени́р/сувени́ры soovin<u>ee</u>r/soovin<u>ee</u>ry		*souvenir/s*
матрёшка/матрёшки matry<u>o</u>shka/matry<u>o</u>shky		*set/s of stacking wooden dolls*
конфе́та/конфе́ты	konf<u>ye</u>ta/konf<u>ye</u>ty	*sweet/s*
ру́сский	r<u>oo</u>sky	*Russian*
америка́нский	amirik<u>a</u>nsky	*American*
кни́га/кни́ги	kn<u>ee</u>ga/kn<u>ee</u>gy	*book/s*
Дом Кни́ги	dom kn<u>ee</u>gy	*House of the Book (book shop)*

Диало́ги

Диало́г 1

Andrew is still exploring Moscow. Now he is heading for Red Square and the Kremlin.

Андрю	Де́вушка, извини́те, как попа́сть в центр?
Де́вушка	В центр? Иди́те пря́мо, пото́м нале́во, и там Кра́сная Пло́щадь и Кремль.
Андрю	Повтори́те, пожа́луйста.
Де́вушка	Иди́те пря́мо, пото́м нале́во.
Андрю	Спаси́бо.

Диало́г 2

Alison is looking for the museum when Igor sees her.

И́горь	Здра́вствуйте, А́лисон. Куда́ вы идёте?
А́лисон	Я иду́ в музе́й. Э́то далеко́?
И́горь	Нет, э́то недалеко́. Иди́те пря́мо, и музе́й напра́во. Музе́й о́чень интере́сный.
А́лисон	Спаси́бо. До свида́ния.

Диало́г 3

As Alison sets off, Igor suddenly remembers something.

И́горь	А́лисон, музе́й закры́т. Закры́т на ремо́нт.
А́лисон	Ой, как жаль!
И́горь	Но галере́я откры́та. И галере́я о́чень интере́сная.
А́лисон	Как попа́сть в галере́ю?
И́горь	Иди́те нале́во, пото́м напра́во, и галере́я пря́мо. Э́то недалеко́.

Диало́г 4

A tourist called Colin is asking a **киоскёр** (kiosky<u>or</u>) *stall-holder* about the souvenirs she is selling.

Ко́лин	У вас есть сувени́ры?
Киоскёр	Да. Вот матрёшки и конфе́ты. Здесь кассе́ты и там ру́сская во́дка и ру́сское вино́.
Ко́лин	Э́то ру́сский шокола́д?
Киоскёр	Нет, америка́нский. О́чень хоро́ший шокола́д.
Ко́лин	А у вас есть кни́ги?
Киоскёр	Нет, иди́те в Дом Кни́ги. Э́то недалеко́.
Ко́лин	Где Дом Кни́ги?
Киоскёр	Иди́те нале́во, пото́м пря́мо, и Дом Кни́ги напра́во.

Numerals 11–30

11	одиннадцать	adeenatsat'	18	восемнадцать	vasyemnatsat'
12	двенадцать	dvyenatsat'	19	девятнадцать	dyevitnatsat'
13	тринадцать	treenatsat'	20	двадцать	dvatsat'
14	четырнадцать	chyetirnatsat'	21	двадцать один	dvatsat' adeen
15	пятнадцать	pitnatsat'	22	двадцать два	dvatsat' dva
16	шестнадцать	shesnatsat'	23	двадцать три	dvatsat' tree
17	семнадцать	syemnatsat'	30	тридцать	treetsat'

Number practice

Read all the numbers aloud or listen to the tape and repeat them. You
will notice that 11 – 19 are made up more or less of the numbers 1 – 9
plus the ending **-надцать** which is a contracted form of **на десять** *on
ten*. To practise numerals this time, you could add 10 or 20 to the
numbers on your playing cards or dice. Or make up sums:

13 + 8 = 21   тринадцать плюс восемь – двадцать один
30 – 11 = 19   тридцать минус одиннадцать – девятнадцать

Механизм языка
Mechanics of the language

1 Как попасть в ...?   *How do I get to ...?*

To ask how to get somewhere in Russian, simply say **как попасть в ...**
How to get to? and add the place to which you want to go. This simple
rule works for masculine and neuter nouns, like **театр** and **кафе** but for
feminine words you should try to remember to change the ending of the
noun from **-а** to **-у** and **-я** to **-ю**. (For those people with an interest in
grammar, these endings are called *accusative* endings, and you use them
after **в** and **на** when movement to a place is indicated.)

Masculine	*Feminine*	*Neuter*
Как попасть в театр?	Как попасть в библиотеку? Как попасть в галерею?	Как попасть в кафе?

When talking about going to a certain place, occasionally you need to use **на** instead of **в** to mean *to*: for example, **Как попáсть на стадиóн?** *How do I get to the stadium?* **Как попáсть на пóчту?** *How do I get to the post office?*

If you meet a new word in your vocabulary list which needs **на** instead of **в** you will see (**на**) next to it.

2 Кудá?/Где? *Where to?/Where?*

You already know the word **Где?** *Where?* In Диалóг 2 you met a different word which you use to ask *Where to?* **Кудá?**

Где музéй? *Where is the museum?*
Кудá вы идёте? *Where are you going to?*

In the same dialogue, you also met part of the verb *to go*. This refers to going somewhere on foot, not by transport.

я идý *I am going*　　　　　　вы идёте *you are going*

3 Откры́т/закры́т *Open/closed*

Note that these words have different endings depending on the gender of the noun they refer to.

Masculine	*Feminine*	*Neuter*
Медпýнкт откры́т.	Пóчта откры́та.	Спрáвочное бюрó откры́то.
Бассéйн закры́т.	Гостíница закры́та.	Кафé закры́то.

4 Plural forms of nouns

To make a plural form in English we usually add -*s*: *rabbit/rabbits*. In Russian, to make the plural forms of masculine nouns you usually add **-ы** unless the spelling rule (see page 237) makes you use **-и** instead. For feminine plural forms, you remove the last letter (usually **-а** or **-я**) and then add **-ы** or **-и**. You will remember that nouns ending in a soft sign **-ь** may be either masculine or feminine, and these also lose the last letter before adding **-и**.

Masculine	**Feminine**
рестора́н/рестора́ны *restaurants*	гости́ница/гости́ницы *hotels*
кио́ск/кио́ски *kiosk/s*	библиоте́ка/библиоте́ки *library/libraries*
рубль/рубли́ *rouble/s*	пло́щадь/пло́щади *square/s*

Neuter nouns also lose their last letter before adding **-а** or **-я** to make the plural form, so **у́тро** *morning* becomes **у́тра**. But most of the neuter nouns which you have met so far (бюро́, кака́о, кафе́, кило́, кино́, метро́, пиани́но, ра́дио) do not change their form at all when they become plural. This is because neuter nouns which have been borrowed directly from other languages are exempt from all the usual rules. So you have to try to tell from the context whether there is one piano or many!

Упражне́ния

1   Look at the town plan and its key. Only new words are shown in English. Make sure you know how to say all the places in Russian. Then sit yourself down with a Russian friend in the window of a café in the left hand corner and ask whether the places shown on the plan are far away or not, for example:

Гости́ница далеко́?   Да, э́то далеко́.
Институ́т далеко́?   Нет, э́то недалеко́.

2   Now you can try asking your friend for directions. **Как попа́сть в библиоте́ку?** *How do I get to the library?* To begin with, all the places that you ask about are feminine, so you will need to change **-а** to **-у** and **-я** to **-ю**. Underline the correct form of the question.

(*a*) (*i*) Как попа́сть на по́чту?   (*ii*) Как попа́сть на по́чта?
(*b*) (*i*) Как попа́сть в гости́ница? (*ii*) Как попа́сть в гости́ницу?
(*c*) (*i*) Как попа́сть в поликли́нику? (*ii*) Как попа́сть в поликли́ника?
(*d*) (*i*) Как попа́сть на фа́брику?   (*ii*) Как попа́сть на фа́брика?

Now ask for directions to all the places on the town plan, including the masculine and neuter places, remembering that their endings do not change: **Как попа́сть в рестора́н?** *How do I get to the restaurant?* Ask your questions in the order given in the key so that you can check them in the back of the book.

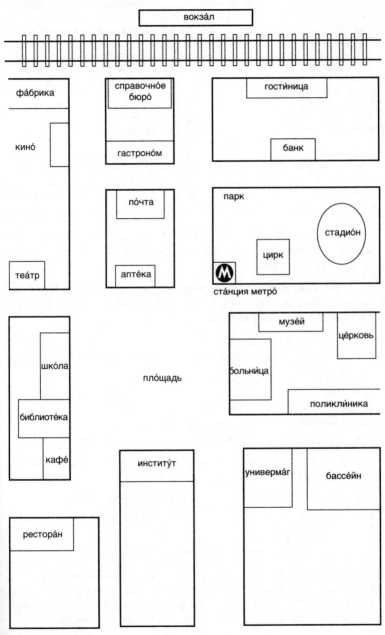

план

Ключ *Key*

1	ресторáн	14	аптéка (aptyeka) *pharmacy*
2	институ́т	15	цирк
3	универмáг	16	стáнция метрó (на)
4	бассéйн		(stantseeya metro) *metro station*
5	кафé	17	пóчта (на)
6	библиотéка	18	парк
7	шкóла (shkola) *school*	19	стадиóн (на)
8	плóщадь (на)	20	кинó
9	поликли́ника	21	гастронóм
	(polykleenika) *health centre*	22	банк
10	цéрковь (f) (tserkov') *church*	23	фáбрика (на) (fabreeka) *factory*
11	больни́ца (bal'neetsa) *hospital*	24	спрáвочное бюрó
12	музéй	25	гости́ница
13	теáтр	26	вокзáл (на) (vakzal) *train station*

What will your friend say in reply? Make up suitable answers using **иди́те напрáво** *go to the right*, **иди́те налéво** *go to the left*, and **иди́те прямо** *go straight ahead*.

3 Now ask your Russian friend where he or she is going: **Кудá вы иди́те?** *Where are you going?* and supply suitable answers. **Я иду́ в гости́ницу** *I am going to the hotel*.

4 Match up these nouns and adjectives to make sentences. Use one word from each column, for example: *a* **Úгорь хорóший футболи́ст**.

(*a*)	Úгорь	ру́сская	гóрод
(*b*)	Лéна	большóй	кафé
(*c*)	Хард-Рок	краси́вая	газéта (*newspaper*)
(*d*)	Лóндон	америкáнское	футболи́ст
(*e*)	Прáвда	хорóший	балери́на

 5 Listen to the conversations on your cassette, and tick the statements which are true.

(*a*) Музéй откры́т.   (*d*) Ресторáн закры́т.
(*b*) Библиотéка закры́та. (*e*) Пóчта откры́та.
(*c*) Кафé откры́то.

6 Match up these questions with suitable answers.

(*a*) У вас есть кни́ги?   (*i*) Нет, иди́те в аптéку.
(*b*) У вас есть кóфе?   (*ii*) Нет, иди́те в киóск.
(*c*) У вас есть таблéтки?   (*iii*) Нет, иди́те в гастронóм.
(*d*) У вас есть проду́кты?   (*iv*) Нет, иди́те в кафé.

(*e*) У вас есть сувениры?   (*v*) Нет, идите в ресторан.
(*f*) У вас есть котлета и салат? (*vi*) Нет, идите
в библиотеку.

7 Read Ivan's shopping list, and wherever he wants more than one of something (e.g. bananas), put a tick. The first one has been done for you.

Гастроном	**Аптека**	**Табак**	**Киоск**	**Театр**
бананы ✓	таблетки	сигареты	цветы	билет
кофе		и папиросы	конфеты	
сахар				
фрукты				

8 When you are reasonably confident with your numbers, listen to your cassette and jot down the missing numbers from each six digit phone number **номер телефона** as it is read out. The numbers will be read in pairs: *17-25-10* **семнадцать – двадцать пять – десять**.

(*a*) 12 – ____ – 1__   (*d*) 1__ – ____ – 24
(*b*) 25 – ____ – __7   (*e*) ____ – ____ – 12
(*c*) 14 – 3__ – ____

If you do not have the cassette or if you want more practice, you could make up and jot down some more phone numbers, and read them out clearly.

9 Look at these road signs and see if you can match them up with their captions. You do not need to understand every word to do this.

(*i*)   (*v*)   (*ix*)

(*ii*)   (*vi*)   (*x*)

(*iii*)   (*vii*)   (*xi*)

(*iv*)   (*viii*)

(*a*) инвалиды   (*g*) автобусы
(*b*) движение прямо   (*h*) движение направо
(*c*) телефон   (*i*) разводной мост
(*d*) кемпинг   (*j*) тракторы

(*e*) гости́ница/моте́ль   (*k*) движе́ние нале́во
(*f*) больни́ца

10 You are visiting another town. Read the instructions below to identify the buildings on your new plan. Match up the letters with the numbers.

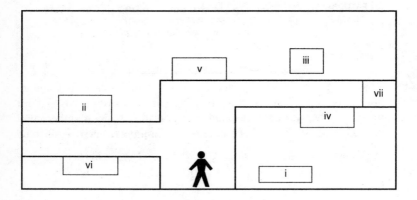

(*a*) Теа́тр пря́мо.
(*b*) Иди́те пря́мо, пото́м напра́во и библиоте́ка напра́во.
(*c*) Иди́те нале́во, и гастроно́м напра́во.
(*d*) Иди́те пря́мо, пото́м напра́во, и вокза́л нале́во.
(*e*) Иди́те нале́во, и рестора́н нале́во. Э́то недалеко́.
(*f*) Иди́те пря́мо, пото́м напра́во, и гости́ница пря́мо.
(*g*) Вот кафе́, напра́во.

☑ *Прове́рьте себя́*

Now you should be able to find your way around a Russian town happily understanding numbers up to 30, never rattling a shop door which says **закры́т**, and finding out what is available in shops which are open! Well done! To test yourself, see if you can put the following phrases into Russian. If your memory needs jogging, the answers are written below, but in the wrong order. Good luck!

1 Excuse me, how do I get to the restaurant?
2 Go straight ahead, then to the left and the restaurant is on the right.

3 Is it far? No, it's not far.
4 Is the museum open?
5 Do you have any chocolate?

(*i*) Музей открыт?

(*ii*) Извините, как попасть
в ресторан?

(*iii*) Это далеко? Нет, это недалеко.

(*iv*) У вас есть шоколад?

(*v*) Идите прямо, потом налево,
и ресторан направо.

How did you manage? If you think you could make yourself understood then you are ready to move on to unit 6. However, now that you have completed five units, you may decide it would be helpful to look back over everything you have done so far. If nothing else, you may find that things which seemed difficult at the time now seem easier!

6

ЧТО ВЫ ХОТИТЕ?
What do you want?

In this unit you will learn

- how to say what you want
- how to pay for something in a shop
- how to say that something belongs to you
- how to make plural forms of adjectives
- how to count from 30 to 100

Before you start

You have already spent two units finding your way around a Russian city. In this unit you will learn more things to say when you finally find the shop or café you were looking for. Since you already know lots of words and phrases you could try rehearsing them in your own environment. Be as active in your language learning as possible.

✳ Every time you talk to a friend, colleague, salesperson or waiter in your own language, try to repeat the transaction to yourself in Russian. Wherever you are, try to name what you see around you in Russian. When you are going somewhere, even if it is just down the corridor, pretend to give directions to a visiting Russian. Say telephone numbers, bus numbers and number plates to yourself in Russian.

If there was anything you didn't understand in an earlier unit, look back at it before you go on. It may be clearer now that you understand more.

Revise your numbers 0-30 on page 235, as this will make learning the higher numbers much easier.

—— Информа́ция ——

Универма́г (Oonivermak) *Department store*

The most famous Russian department store is **ГУМ (Госуда́рстве-нный универса́льный магази́н)** *State department store* in Red Square in Moscow. This used to be centrally run, but since *perestroika* it has been divided up into individual shops which are leased out to leading Russian and Western retailers.

Ры́нок (Rynok) *Market*

If you want to buy fresh vegetables and fruit **о́вощи и фру́кты** (ovashshee ee frookty), milk and dairy produce **молоко́** (malako) meat and fish **мя́со и ры́ба** (myasa ee ryba) the local markets can be a good source of supply, although in the winter months there is inevitably less choice.

Кафе́ *Café*

The waiter **официа́нт** (afitsiant) and waitress **официа́нтка** (afitisiantka) in a café or restaurant may be addressed as **молодо́й челове́к** and **де́вушка**, forms of address which apply to anyone up to about fifty years of age!

Ка́сса (Kassa) *Cash desk*

In some shops you may need to pay for your purchases at a cash desk **ка́сса** (kassa), and then take your receipt **чек** (chek) back to the counter to collect your goods.

—— Ключевы́е слова́ ——

Диало́г 1			
что shto		*what?*	
Что вы хоти́те купи́ть?	Shto vy	*What do you want to buy?*	
khateetye koopeet'?			

подарок/подарки padarak/ padarky	present/presents
я хочу́ ya khachoo	I want
балала́йка balalaika	balalaika (stringed instrument)
пойдём paeedyom	Let's go

Диало́г 2

покажи́те pakazheetye	show (me)
ско́лько сто́ит? skol'ka stoeet?	How much is it?
ты́сяча рубле́й tysacha rooblyei	1,000 roubles
где плати́ть? gdye plateet'?	Where do I pay?
ка́сса kassa	cash desk

Диало́г 3

фрукто́вый сок frooktovy sok	fruit juice
и́ли eely	or
официа́нтка afitsiantka	waitress
иди́те сюда́ eedeetye syooda	come here
Что у вас есть? Shto oo vas yest'?	What have you got?
минера́льная вода́ miniral'naya vada	mineral water
с s	with
с лимо́ном s leemonum	with lemon
с са́харом s sakharum	with sugar
с молоко́м s mulakom	with milk
сейча́с seychas	now, right away

Диало́г 4

ваш/ва́ша/ва́ше/ва́ши vash/vasha/ vashe/vashy	your (m/f/n/p)
мой/моя́/моё/мои́ moy/maya/mayo mayee	my (m/f/n/p)
джаз dzhaz	jazz

 ——————— **Диало́ги** ———————

Диало́г 1

Peter is visiting Russia on business, but before returning home he goes shopping for presents with a colleague, Anton Pavlovich. Anton Pavlovich speaks some English, but they have agreed to speak only Russian in the morning and English in the afternoon.

Анто́н Па́влович **Что вы хоти́те купи́ть, Пи́тер?**
Пи́тер   **Сувени́ры и пода́рки.**
Анто́н Па́влович **Каки́е сувени́ры и пода́рки?**

Пи́тер	Я хочу́ купи́ть кни́ги, матрёшки, шокола́д, во́дку и балала́йку.
Анто́н Па́влович	Хорошо́. Пойдём в Дом Кни́ги.

🖳 Диало́г 2

In Дом Кни́ги Peter soon gets into his stride.

Пи́тер	Молодо́й челове́к, у вас есть кни́га «А́нна Каре́нина»?
Молодо́й челове́к	Да.
Пи́тер	Покажи́те, пожа́луйста.
Молодо́й челове́к	Вот она́.
Пи́тер	Ско́лько сто́ит?
Молодо́й челове́к	Ты́сяча рубле́й.
Пи́тер	Где плати́ть?
Молодо́й челове́к	Иди́те в ка́ссу.
Пи́тер	Спаси́бо.

Диало́г 3

Later in the morning, Peter and Anton Pavlovich pop into a café.

Анто́н Па́влович	Что вы хоти́те, Пи́тер?
Пи́тер	Я хочу́ фрукто́вый сок и́ли чай, пожа́луйста.
Анто́н Па́влович	Де́вушка, иди́те сюда́, пожа́луйста. У вас есть фрукто́вый сок?
Официа́нтка	Извини́те, нет.
Анто́н Па́влович	Что у вас есть?
Официа́нтка	Чай, ко́фе, минера́льная вода́, пепси-ко́ла.
Пи́тер	Да́йте, пожа́луйста, чай с лимо́ном и с са́харом.
Анто́н Па́влович	И ко́фе с молоко́м.
Официа́нтка	Чай с лимо́ном и с са́харом, и ко́фе с молоко́м. Сейча́с.

🖳 Диало́г 4

While they wait for their drinks, Peter and Anton Pavlovich look at their purchases.

Анто́н Па́влович	Что у вас есть?

Пи́тер	**Вот кни́га «А́нна Каре́нина» и матрёшки.**
Анто́н Па́влович	**Как хорошо́. Э́то о́чень краси́вые матрёшки. Пи́тер, э́то ва́ша кассе́та?**
Пи́тер	**Да, э́то моя́ кассе́та, «Ру́сский джаз».**
Анто́н Па́влович	**И вот мой компа́кт-ди́ск. О́пера «Бори́с Годуно́в».**
Официа́нтка	**Вот чай и ко́фе.**
Пи́тер	**Спаси́бо.**
Анто́н Па́влович	*Oh look, it's twelve o'clock. We can speak English now!*

Numerals 10–100

10	**де́сять** dyesyat'	60	**шестьдеся́т** shesdisyat
20	**два́дцать** dvatsat'	70	**се́мьдесят** syemdyesyat
30	**три́дцать** treetsat'	80	**во́семьдесят** vosyemdyesyat
40	**со́рок** sorak	90	**девяно́сто** dyevinosta
50	**пятьдеся́т** pidisyat	100	**сто** sto
146	**сто со́рок шесть** sto sorak shest' etc.		

If you are hoping to visit Russia, you will need to learn relatively high numbers to cope with the high prices in roubles.

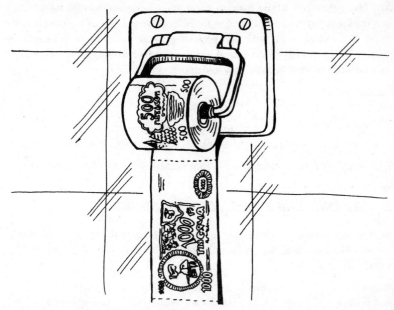

The only thing to your advantage is that prices are often rounded up to the nearest hundred or thousand roubles. A rouble is **рубль** in Russian, and you may hear it in different forms: **рубль, рубля, рублей**. As long as you recognise the number which goes with it this should be no problem, and if you do get confused, you could carry a notepad and ask salespeople to write down the price for you: **Напишите, пожалуйста** (napeesheetye, pazhalsta), *write please*. Practise the numbers in this unit until you can say them almost without thinking. Every time you see a number in your daily life, say it in Russian, as long as doing so doesn't distract you from driving or working!

Language patterns

1 Plural adjectives

In English, the adjective form is the same whether you are describing one or several items: *big blue balloon, big blue balloons*. In Russian, you will remember that there are three forms of singular adjectives to match the singular nouns: masculine, feminine and neuter. (See page

44.) Now that you know how to form plural nouns, (**конфе́ты** *sweets*) you may want to use adjectives with them. This is easy as it doesn't matter if the plural noun you are referring to is masculine, feminine or neuter. There is only one type of plural adjective ending: **-ые**. This may also be written **-ие** if the spelling rule applies (page 237).

краси́вые кни́ги	*beautiful books*
хоро́шие конфе́ты	*good sweets*
больши́е пи́ццы	*big pizzas*

The same ending is used with the plural form **каки́е...?** *what sort of...?*

Каки́е сувени́ры и пода́рки? What sort of souvenirs and presents?

2 My balalaika and your balalaika

In the same way as there are masculine, feminine, neuter and plural forms of adjectives and nouns, there are also different forms of the words *my* and *your*.

Masculine	*Feminine*	*Neuter*	*Plural*
мой па́спорт	**моя́** балала́йка	**моё** пиани́но	**мои́** кассе́ты
my passport	*my balalaika*	*my piano*	*my cassettes*
ваш па́спорт	**ва́ша** балала́йка	**ва́ше** пиани́но	**ва́ши** кассе́ты
your passport	*your balalaika*	*your piano*	*your cassettes*

As you would expect, these words use the typical endings: **-й** and the consonant **-ш** for masculine forms, **-я** and **-а** for feminine forms, **-ё** and **-е** for neuter forms, and **-и** for plurals.

3 I want to buy a balalaika

Did you notice what happens to the endings of the feminine nouns in Диало́г 1? Peter says: Я хочу́ купи́ть кни́ги, матрёшки, шокола́д, во́дку и балала́йку. Во́дка and балала́йка have changed to во́дку and балала́йку. Once again, this is the accusative form. It will always occur when a feminine noun is the person or thing which has something done to it, or in grammatical terms, is the direct object of a verb. By direct object, we mean that a noun answers the question *what?* asked after the verb. Here are some examples of direct objects in English:

She baked **bread**.	She baked **what**? **Bread**.
He likes **opera, books, wine**.	He likes **what**? **Opera, books and wine**.

He plays the **balalaika.**   He plays **what?**   **Balalaika.**

And some in Russian:
Я хочу́ купи́ть   You want to buy   **Balalaika.**
балала́йку.   **what?**
Я хочу **пепси-ко́лу.** You want **what?**   **Pepsi-cola.**

4 Imperatives. Do this, do that!

Did you realise that you can already give people eight different orders or requests in Russian? **Здра́вствуйте** *hello* was the first one you learned, and it means literally *Be healthy!*

Others which you know are
извини́те *excuse (me)*   покажи́те *show (me)*
повтори́те *repeat*   иди́те *go*
напиши́те *write*   да́йте *give (me)*
скажи́те *tell (me)*
Add пожа́луйста to be polite, and you should be able to get things done!

Упражне́ния

1 Choose a question word from the list below to complete these dialogues.

(*a*) _____ теа́тр?   Вот он.
(*b*) _____ вас зову́т?   Меня́ зову́т Ни́на.
(*c*) _____ вы идёте?   Я иду́ на по́чту.
(*d*) _____ вы хоти́те?   Я хочу́ суп, хлеб и во́дку.
(*e*) _____ э́то?   Э́то Са́ша. Он - мой сын.

Как? Что? Где? Кто? Куда́?

2 You work in a Russian kiosk. You cannot keep everything on display, but you have a list so that you know what is tucked away in boxes. A tourist comes up and asks if you have various items. Carry out an imaginary conversation with the tourist. If you have the items he asks for, tell him all about them. If not, say Извини́те, нет. Here is your list.

хоро́шие бана́ны   лимона́д
биле́ты в теа́тр   матрёшки
ру́сская во́дка   папиро́сы и сигаре́ты
кассе́ты   план
америка́нские конфе́ты   сувени́ры
ко́фе   цветы́

The first example has been done for you.

(*a*) Tourist   **У вас есть сувени́ры?**
      You   **Да, есть. Вот краси́вые ру́сские матрёшки.**
(*b*) Tourist   **У вас есть балала́йка?**
(*c*) Tourist   **У вас есть сигаре́ты? Каки́е? Ру́сские и́ли**
                америка́нские?
(*d*) Tourist   **У вас есть бана́ны?**

Now carry on the conversation. You could ask him if he wants any sweets, or he could ask you how much something costs.

3   Say the following phone numbers, and check them off below.

(*a*) 65 – 43 – 74   (b) 14 – 58 – 92   (c) 123 – 89 – 12
(*d*) 135 – 91 – 36   (e) 117 – 54 – 22

(*i*)   сто семна́дцать – пятьдеся́т четы́ре – два́дцать два
(*ii*)   сто два́дцать три – во́семьдесят де́вять – двена́дцать
(*iii*)   сто три́дцать пять – девяно́сто оди́н – три́дцать шесть
(*iv*)   шестьдеся́т пять – со́рок три – се́мьдесят четы́ре
(*v*)   четы́рнадцать – пятьдеся́т во́семь – девяно́сто два

4   Which orders or requests would you use in the following circumstances? You want someone to:

(*a*)   repeat something   (*e*)   tell you something
(*b*)   show you something   (*f*)   write something
(*c*)   give you something   (*g*)   excuse you
(*d*)   go somewhere

(*i*) иди́те, пожа́луйста (*ii*) повтори́те, пожа́луйста (*iii*) скажи́те, пожа́луйста (*iv*) покажи́те, пожа́луйста (*v*) напиши́те, пожа́луйста (*vi*) извини́те, пожа́луйста (*vii*) да́йте, пожа́луйста

5 You are in a possessive mood. Every time Boris claims that an item belongs to him, you contradict him and say it is yours.

Бори́с Э́то мой микроско́п.
Вы   Нет, э́то не ваш микроско́п. Э́то мой микроско́п.

Choose from **мой/моя́/моё/мои́** and **ваш/ва́ша/ва́ше/ва́ши** to fill in the blanks.

(a) **Бори́с** Э́то моё ра́дио.   **Вы** Нет, э́то не в ____ ра́дио.
                                            Э́то м ____ ра́дио.

(b) **Бори́с** Э́то моя́ кни́га.   **Вы** Нет, э́то не в ____ кни́га.
                                            Э́то м ____ кни́га.

(c) **Бори́с** Э́то мои́ гита́ры.   **Вы** Нет, э́то не в ____
                                            гита́ры. Э́то м ____
                                            гита́ры.

(d) **Бори́с** Э́то мой биле́т.   **Вы** Нет, э́то не в ____ биле́т.
                                            Э́то м ____ биле́т.

For more practice, you could try the same thing in a more generous mood, adding your own ideas.

Бори́с Э́то ва́ши сигаре́ты? **Вы** Нет, э́то не мои́ сигаре́ты.
Э́то ва́ши сигаре́ты.

6 Listen to your cassette to find out what people want. Tick off the items on the list below as you hear them mentioned. Then listen again and underline each feminine item asked for. These will have changed their endings from **-а** to **-у** and **-я** to **-ю**. If you don't have the cassette, make up sentences on this model: **Я хочу́ котле́ту, сала́т и ко́фе с молоко́м.**

вино́	конфе́ты	чай с лимо́ном
во́дка	пи́цца	ко́фе с са́харом
суп	смета́на	омле́т
борщ	фру́кты	пепси-ко́ла

7 Link each adjective to a suitable noun by joining them with a line.

Большо́й	сад
ма́ленькое	конфе́ты
краси́вые	челове́к
ру́сские	вино́
интере́сная	папиро́сы
молодо́й	теа́тр
ботани́ческий	кни́га
хоро́шие	ра́дио
бе́лое	цветы́

8 Use this grid to work on your numbers. Cover up all but one line of numbers, and read out the ones you see. Try it again in a day or two, and see if you are any quicker.

1	14	36	97	12
8	122	3	88	45
64	199	20	17	150
7	13	65	10	63
144	21	19	5	111

☑ Проверьте себя

There are many situations which you could now handle if you were visiting Russia. Answer these questions to test yourself.

1 Что вы хотите?

2 Куда вы идёте?

3 Что это?

4 Метро закрыто?

5 Это ваш билет? (*Yes*).

7

В ГОСТИ́НИЦЕ
At the hotel

In this unit you will learn

- how to give your particulars when booking into a hotel
- how to say the letters of the alphabet and fill in a form
- how to say what nationality you are and what you do
- how to say where you work
- how to specify *this* or *that*
- how to count from 100 to 1,000

Before you start

If you are thinking of visiting Russia at any time you will need somewhere to stay. You may be fortunate enough to have friends there, or you may need to book into a **гости́ница** (gasteenitsa) *hotel*. The language in this unit will enable you to do this, and it will also be useful whenever you need to give or ask for personal details. You may find it particularly helpful to be able to use the alphabet in case anyone asks **Как э́то пи́шется?** (Kak eta peeshetsa?) *How is that written?* In this unit, you will also learn to count up to 1,000 so make sure you know your numbers up to 100 first.

Информа́ция

Hotel accommodation

If you are travelling to Russia on a tourist visa you will have to arrange your accommodation before you arrive. At present this means getting a private invitation to stay in a home or booking a hotel. Getting a business visa means that you do not need to prebook accommodation. When you arrive at your hotel you will meet the **администра́тор** *administrator* at the reception desk. Each floor of a big hotel will also usually have a **дежу́рная** (dyizh<u>oo</u>rnaya), a woman on duty who sits at a table on the landing, often dispensing tea and mineral water.

▣ *Saying the alphabet in Russian*

In Russian, as in English, the name of a letter sometimes sounds different from the sound that the letter makes. If you had not thought of this before, say *h*, *w*, or *y* out loud in English and think how confusing the letter names might be to a foreign visitor. You may need to know the names of Russian letters to spell something, for example your name or the name of your home town, so here they are, in the correct order. Familiarise yourself with them before you move on to the dialogues. Read down each column in turn. You will see the letter first, for example С с. Then you see the name of the letter in Russian **эс** and finally the English transliteration of the letter name (es). You can listen to them on your tape.

Alphabet Guide

Аа	**а**	(a)	Кк	**ка**	(ka)	Хх	**ха**	(kha)
Бб	**бэ**	(beh *as in bed*)	Лл	**эль**	(el')	Цц	**цэ**	(tse)
Вв	**вэ**	(veh)	Мм	**эм**	(em)	Чч	**че**	(che)
Гг	**гэ**	(geh)	Нн	**эн**	(en)	Шш	**ша**	(sha)
Дд	**дэ**	(deh)	Оо	**о**	(o)	Щщ	**ща**	(shsha)
Ее	**е**	(yeh)	Пп	**пэ**	(peh)	ъ	**твёрдый знак**	(tvy<u>o</u>rdy znak *hard sign*)
Ёё	**ё**	(yoh)	Рр	**эр**	(air)	ы	**ы**	(iy)
Жж	**жэ**	(zheh)	Сс	**эс**	(es)	ь	**мя́гкий знак**	(my<u>a</u>khky znak *soft sign*)
						Ээ	**э**	(eh)
Зз	**зэ**	(zeh)	Тт	**тэ**	(teh)	Юю	**ю**	(yoo)
Ии	**и**	(ee)	Уу	**у**	(oo)	Яя	**я**	(ya)
Йй	**и**	**кра́ткое** (ee kr<u>a</u>tkoye *short* **и**)	Фф	**эф**	(ef)			

Glance back through the book, picking a few words at random and spelling them out loud.

 ———————— **Ключевы́е слова́** ————————

Диало́г 1

Одну́ мину́точку	Adn<u>oo</u> min<u>oo</u>tuchkoo	*(Wait) one moment*
Слу́шаю вас	Sl<u>oo</u>shayoo vas	*I'm listening to you*
ко́мната	k<u>o</u>mnata	*room*
но́мер	n<u>o</u>myer	*hotel room/number*
Запо́лните э́тот бланк	Zap<u>o</u>lneetye <u>e</u>tot blank	*Fill in this form*
Мо́жно?	M<u>o</u>zhna?	*Is it possible/Would you mind?*
но	no	*but*
я пишу́	ya peesh<u>oo</u>	*I write*
Мо́жно	M<u>o</u>zhna	*It is possible/I don't mind*
Как э́то пи́шется?	Kak <u>e</u>ta p<u>ee</u>shetsa?	*How is that spelt?*
А́нглия	<u>A</u>ngleeya	*England*
Кто вы по профе́ссии?	Kto vy pa prafy<u>e</u>ssee?	*What are you by profession?*
учи́тельница/учи́тель	ooch<u>ee</u>tyelneetsa/ooch<u>ee</u>tyel'	*teacher(f/m)*
я рабо́таю	ya rab<u>o</u>tayoo	*I work*
в	v	*in*
шко́ла	shk<u>o</u>la	*school*
гражда́нство	grazhd<u>a</u>nstva	*nationality/citizenship*
англича́нка	angleech<u>a</u>nka	*Englishwoman*
бага́ж	bag<u>a</u>sh	*luggage*
чемода́н	chimod<u>a</u>n	*suitcase*
су́мка	s<u>oo</u>mka	*bag*
аккордео́н	akorde<u>o</u>n	*accordion*
ключ	klyooch	*key*

Диало́г 2

душ	doosh	*shower*
ва́нная	v<u>a</u>nnaya	*bathroom*
туале́т	tooaly<u>et</u>	*toilet*
буфе́т	boofy<u>et</u>	*snack bar*
внизу́	vneez<u>oo</u>	*downstairs*

Диало́г 3

Где вы живёте?	Gdye vy zheevy<u>o</u>tye	*Where do you live?*
Где вы рабо́таете?	Gdye vy rab<u>o</u>tayetye?	*Where do you work?*

инжене́р eenzhin**ye**r	*engineer*
не́мец ny**e**myets	*German man*
францу́женка frants**oo**zhenka	*French woman*
я живу́ ya zheev**oo**	*I live*
продаве́ц/продавщи́ца	*shop assistant (m/f)*
pradavy**e**ts/pradavshch**ee**tsa	
коне́чно kany**e**shna	*of course*
ру́сский/ру́сская r**oo**skee/	*Russian man/woman*
r**oo**skaya	
америка́нец amyirik**a**nyets	*American man*
врач vrach	*doctor*
испа́нка eesp**a**nka	*Spanish woman*

Диало́ги

Диало́г 1

Fiona arrives at a hotel where she has reserved a room.

Фио́на	Здра́вствуйте.
Администра́тор	Одну́ мину́точку. Да, слу́шаю вас.
Фио́на	Меня́ зову́т Фио́на Ха́рисон. Я хочу́ ко́мнату, пожа́луйста.
Администра́тор	(*looks through bookings*) Фио́на Ха́рисон? Да, вот ва́ша фами́лия. Ва́ша ко́мната но́мер 38 (три́дцать во́семь).
Фио́на	Спаси́бо.
Администра́тор	Запо́лните э́тот бланк.
Фио́на	(*handing the form to the administrator for help*) Мо́жно, пожа́луйста? Я говорю́ по-ру́сски, но пло́хо пишу́.
Администра́тор	Мо́жно. Как ва́ша фами́лия?
Фио́на	Фами́лия Ха́рисон, и и́мя Фио́на.
Администра́тор	Так, Ха́рисон. Как э́то пи́шется, Фио́на?
Фио́на	Ф - и - о - н - а.
Администра́тор	Како́й у вас а́дрес?
Фио́на	А́нглия, Ше́лтон, у́лица Кро́сли, дом 13 (трина́дцать).
Администра́тор	И кто вы по профе́ссии?

Фиóна	Я учи́тельница. Я рабо́таю в шко́ле в Шéлтоне.
Администра́тор	Како́е у вас гражда́нство?
Фиóна	Я англича́нка.
Администра́тор	Ваш па́спорт, пожа́луйста.
Фиóна	Вот он.
Администра́тор	Спаси́бо. У вас есть бага́ж?
Фиóна	Да, вот мой чемода́н, моя́ су́мка и мой аккордео́н.
Администра́тор	Вот ваш ключ.

Диало́г 2

Fiona is shown to her room.

Администра́тор	Вот ва́ша ко́мната. Вот у вас телеви́зор, телефо́н и балко́н. И в коридо́ре душ, ва́нная и туалéт.
Фиóна	Спаси́бо. Скажи́те, в гости́нице есть рестора́н?
Администра́тор	Да, рестора́н, буфéт и бар. Но рестора́н сейча́с закры́т.
Фиóна	Как жаль! Как попа́сть в буфéт?
Администра́тор	Буфéт напра́во. Э́то недалеко́.
Фиóна	И бар?
Администра́тор	Бар внизу́.

Диало́г 3

As you may have guessed from her luggage, Fiona has come to Moscow to an international conference of accordion players. At their first meeting, Fiona gets the ball rolling by asking everyone to introduce themselves and say where they work.

Фиóна	Кто вы по профéссии? Где вы живёте и где вы рабо́таете?
Карл	Меня́ зову́т Карл. Я инженéр. Я рабо́таю в институ́те в Берли́не. Я нéмец.
Брижи́т	Здра́вствуйте, меня́ зову́т Брижи́т. Я францу́женка. Я учи́тельница и я живу́ в Лио́не. Я там рабо́таю в шко́ле.
Сергéй	Меня́ зову́т Сергéй. Я продавéц и я рабо́таю в магази́не здесь в Москвé. Я, конéчно, ру́сский.
Грег	Здра́вствуйте, я америка́нец и меня́ зову́т Грег. Я

актёр и я живу́ в Нью Йо́рке.

Ири́на	Я врач. Меня́ зову́т Ири́на. Я рабо́таю в поликли́нике в Но́вгороде. Я ру́сская.
Хуани́та	Меня́ зову́т Хуани́та. Я продавщи́ца и рабо́таю в магази́не. Я живу́ в Барсело́не. Я испа́нка.

Numerals 100–1,000

100	сто	sto	600	шестьсо́т	shes-s<u>o</u>t
200	две́сти	dvy<u>e</u>stee	700	семьсо́т	syems<u>o</u>t
300	три́ста	tr<u>ee</u>sta	800	восемьсо́т	vasyems<u>o</u>t
400	четы́реста	chyet<u>i</u>ryesta	900	девятьсо́т	dyevits<u>o</u>t
500	пятьсо́т	pits<u>o</u>t	1000	ты́сяча	t<u>y</u>syacha

1539 ты́сяча пятьсо́т три́дцать де́вять   t<u>y</u>syacha pits<u>o</u>t tr<u>ee</u>tsat dy<u>e</u>vyat

Practise these numbers until you are confident with them, testing yourself with numbers which you see around you every day.

Механи́зм языка́
Mechanics of the language

1 Я рабо́таю в магази́не в Москве́ *How to say* in

You will remember that in unit 5 on page 54 you met the words **в** and **на**, meaning *to*, as in **Как попа́сть в теа́тр)** *How do I get to the theatre?* There the words **в** and **на** triggered the accusative case in the following word. However, when **в** and **на** mean *in* or *at* a certain place, they trigger a different case, known as the *prepositional case*, in the following word. Again, you use **в** unless you see (**на**) next to the word in your vocabulary list. You saw **в** used a good deal in Диало́г 3. Did you notice what happened to the ending of each word following **в**?

Masculine
(институ́т) в институ́т**е**
(теа́тр) в теа́тр**е**
(Но́вгород) в Но́вгород**е**

Feminine
(шко́ла) в шко́л**е**
(поликли́ника) в поликли́ник**е**
(Москва́) в Москв**е́**

Masculine words generally add the ending **-e** and feminine words replace the ending **-a** with **-e**.

2 How to say which one you mean (demonstrative pronouns)

Did you notice in Диало́г 1 that Fiona was told to fill in this form, **Запо́лните э́тот бланк**. **Э́тот** is the word for *this* or *that* which is used to point out masculine words. So, **Да́йте, пожа́луйста, э́тот чемода́н** would mean *Please give me that suitcase*. If you want to refer to a feminine noun, use **э́та** instead. *This girl is my daughter* would be **Э́та де́вушка – моя́ дочь**. For neuter words you need to use **э́то**, as in **Покажи́те, пожа́луйста, э́то ра́дио** *Please show me that radio*. To refer to plural nouns use **э́ти**, as in **Э́ти биле́ты – мои́**. *These tickets are mine.*

3 Гражда́нство *Nationality*

In Диало́г 3 you met people of different nationalities. As you would expect, there are different words in Russian to refer to the male and female of a particular nationality, so a Russian man is **ру́сский** and a Russian woman is **ру́сская**. In the chart below you can see the name of the country, the words for a man and woman of that nationality, and finally the language which they speak. You could make up sentences to practise: **Вы ру́сский? Вы, коне́чно, говори́те по-ру́сски!**

	Country (страна́)	*Man* (мужчи́на)	*Woman* (же́нщина)	*Language* (язы́к)
Russia	Росси́я Rasseeya	ру́сский roosky	ру́сская rooskaya	по-ру́сски pa-roosky
England	А́нглия Angleeya	англича́нин angleechanin	англича́нка angleechanka	по-англи́йски pa-angleesky
America	Аме́рика Amyereeka	америка́нец amereekanyets	америка́нка amereekanka	по-англи́йски pa-angleesky
Japan	Япо́ния Yaponiya	япо́нец yaponyets	япо́нка yaponka	по-япо́нски pa-yaponsky
Spain	Испа́ния Eespaniya	испа́нец eespanyets	испа́нка eespanka	по-испа́нски pa-eespansky
France	Фра́нция Frantsiya	францу́з frantsoos	францу́женка frantsoozhenka	по-францу́зски pa-frantsoozsky
Germany	Герма́ния Germaniya	не́мец nyemyets	не́мка nyemka	по-неме́цки pa-nemyetsky

—————— **Упражне́ния** ——————

1 You are staying in St. Petersburg when a friend calls you asking for the phone numbers of hotels in the city. You look in the directory and read out the names and numbers of the following hotels. The line is poor so you have to spell them out clearly. Read them out loud and check them on your cassette.

(*a*) Асто́рия   311–42–06   (*d*) Оли́мпия   119–68–00
(*b*) Евро́па   312–00–72   (*e*) Санкт-Петербу́рг 542–94–11
(*c*) Каре́лия   226–35–15   (*f*) Коммодо́р   119–66–66

2 Tony, a visiting sports coach, has to fill in a registration form **анке́та** at the hotel reception desk. Match the information required with his personal details. His written Russian is not very good, so he spells out his details for the **администра́тор**. Read the spellings out loud.

```
           Анке́та
(a) Фами́лия _____
(b) И́мя      _____
(c) А́дрес    _____
(d) Гражда́нство _____
(e) Профе́ссия _____
(f) Но́мер па́спорта_____
```

(*i*) Англича́нин (*ii*) Ка́ртер (*iii*) Тре́нер (*iv*) А́нтони (*v*) Р 243569 О (*vi*) А́нглия, Сто́кпорт, Э́дуард Стрит, дом 35.

3 See if you can guess what nationality these people are.

(*a*) шотла́ндец/шотла́ндка (*b*) португа́лец/португа́лка
(*c*) ирла́ндец/ирла́ндка (*d*) норве́жец/норве́жка

4 Below you have a jumbled up table of information about four people. You are told their **и́мя** *name*, **гражда́нство** *nationality*, **профе́ссия** *job* and **где рабо́тает** *where he or she works*. See if you can sort out the information so that it makes sense, i.e. so that a French person with a French name is working in a French city. Make up a sentence about each person. The first one has been done for you: (*a*) Мари́ – францу́женка. Она́ врач. Она́ рабо́тает в больни́це в Пари́же.

	Имя		Гражда́нство		Профе́ссия		Где рабо́тает
(a)	Мари́	(i)	ру́сский	(1)	учи́тель	(A)	в теа́тре в Арха́нгельске
(b)	Ханс	(ii)	францу́женка	(2)	актёр	(B)	в шко́ле в Берли́не
(c)	Бори́с	(iii)	англича́нка	(3)	продавщи́ца	(C)	в больни́це в Пари́же
(d)	Дже́нни	(iv)	не́мец	(4)	врач	(D)	в магази́не в Бирминге́ме

5 Match up the questions and answers so that they make sense.

(a) Где вы рабо́таете? (i) Моя́ фами́лия Бра́дли.

(b) Кто вы по профе́ссии? (ii) Иди́те пря́мо и буфе́т нале́во.

(c) Как попа́сть в буфе́т? (iii) Я рабо́таю в шко́ле.

(d) Вы говори́те по-англи́йски? (iv) Нет, магази́н закры́т.

(e) Как ва́ша фами́лия? (v) Я врач.

(f) Магази́н откры́т? (vi) Меня́ зову́т Серге́й.

(g) Как вас зову́т? (vii) Нет, я говорю́ по-францу́зски.

6 Remembering that after **в** and **на** (meaning *in* or *at*) you have to change the ending of the following word, choose the correct form in these sentences.

(a) Я рабо́таю в больни́ца / больни́це в Арха́нгельске / Арха́нгельск.

(b) –Где футболи́сты? –Футболи́сты на стадио́н / стадио́не.

(c) В гости́нице / гости́ница есть буфе́т?

(b) –Молодо́й челове́к, где здесь бар? –Бар внизу́, в рестора́н / рестора́не.

7 Underline the correct demonstrative form (э́тот, э́та, э́то, э́ти) in the following sentences.

(Э́тот, Э́та, Э́то, Э́ти) кни́га о́чень интере́сная.

Покажи́те, пожа́луйста, (э́тот, э́та, э́то, э́ти) па́спорт.

(Э́тот, Э́та, Э́то, Э́ти) сигаре́ты не мой. Они́ ва́ши.

Да́йте, пожа́луйста, (э́тот, э́та, э́то, э́ти) ра́дио.

8 Read out loud the following selection of international dialling codes from Russia. Try to work out which countries are represented, and match them up with their English equivalents.

(*a*)	Австра́лия	61	(*i*)	*Germany*
(*b*)	Бангладе́ш	880	(*ii*)	*Canada*
(*c*)	Болга́рия	359	(*iii*)	*Fiji*
(*d*)	Гайа́на	592	(*iv*)	*Israel*
(*e*)	Герма́ния	49	(*v*)	*Ethiopia*
(*f*)	Изра́иль	972	(*vi*)	*Australia*
(*g*)	Кана́да	1	(*vii*)	*Bulgaria*
(*h*)	То́нга	676	(*viii*)	*Guyana*
(*i*)	Фи́джи	679	(*ix*)	*Tonga*
(*j*)	Эфио́пия	251	(*x*)	*Bangladesh*

☑ Прове́рьте себя́

The dialogue below, between a hotel administrator and a tourist called Richard Rigby, has been written down in the wrong order. Unscramble it, beginning with the phrase in bold print.

Администра́тор	**Ри́чард Ри́гби**
1 Вы америка́нец?	2 У вас есть ко́мната?
3 Запо́лните э́тот бланк, пожа́луйста.	4 **Здра́вствуйте.**
5 Слу́шаю вас.	6 Нет, я англича́нин.
7 Да. Как вас зову́т?	8 Меня́ зову́т Ри́чард Ри́гби.

Before moving on to the next unit, say your own name with a Russian accent, and then try spelling out the sound of your name in Russian letters. Some sounds are tricky to reproduce, but here are a few clues from common English names.

Carol	Кэ́рол	*George*	Джордж
Catherine	Ка́трин	*Hugh*	Хью
Jane	Джейн	*John*	Джон
Susan	Сью́зан	*Simon*	Са́ймон
Wendy	Уэ́нди	*William*	Уи́льям

8

КОТО́РЫЙ ЧАС?
What time is it?

In this unit you will learn

- to tell the time
- to say the days of the week
- to talk about meals and daily routine
- how to make arrangements

Before you start

If you go to Russia, or meet Russians at home, you need to understand when things are happening and at what time public places open and close. For this, you need to be able to tell the time and know the days of the week. With the structures introduced in this unit you will be able to make arrangements and feel in control.

Информа́ция

За́втрак, обе́д, у́жин *Breakfast, dinner, supper*

За́втрак (za̲ftrak) *breakfast* may be **ка́ша** (ka̲sha) *porridge*, meat, cheese, fish or eggs and tea or coffee. There is nearly always bread on a Russian meal table as well. At midday you may have a second breakfast if your main meal is to be late.

Обéд (ab*ye*t) *dinner* is the main meal and may be eaten at any time from midday to late evening. It may include **закýски** (zak*oo*sky) *starters*, a soup and a main dish, followed by cake and tea or coffee.

Ýжин (*oo*zhin) *supper* is a light meal, served in the evening.

Telling the time

To ask the time, you say:

Котóрый час? (Kat*o*ry chas?) literally *Which hour?* or **Скóлько сейчáс врéмени?** (Sk*o*l'ka syeych*a*s vry*e*myinee?) literally *How much now time?*

Telling the time on the hour is easy.
Сейчáс час. (Syeych*a*s chas)   *Now it's one o'clock.*
Сейчáс два часá. (Syeych*a*s dva chas*a*)   *Now it's two o'clock.*

3.00	**Три часá**	tree chas*a*
4.00	**Четы́ре часá**	chyet*i*rye chas*a*
5.00	**Пять часóв**	pyat' chas*ov*
6.00	**Шесть часóв**	shest' chas*ov*
7.00	**Семь часóв**	syem' chas*ov*
8.00	**Вóсемь часóв**	v*o*syem' chas*ov*
9.00	**Дéвять часóв**	dy*e*vyat' chas*ov*
10.00	**Дéсять часóв**	dy*e*syat' chas*ov*
11.00	**Оди́ннадцать часóв**	ad*ee*natsat' chas*ov*
12.00	**Двенáдцать часóв**	dven*a*tsat' chas*ov*
Пóлдень	P*o*ldyen'	*Midday*
Пóлночь	P*o*lnoch'	*Midnight*

Час means *hour*. A watch or clock is **часы́**, literally *hours*. Notice that **час** has different endings depending on which number it follows. After 1 you use **час**, after 2, 3 and 4 you use **часá** and after 5-20 you use **часóв**. To complete the 24-hour clock, after 21 you use **час**, and after 22, 23 and 24 you use **часá**.

To ask *At what time?* say **В котóром часý?**
To say *At 5 o'clock* say **В пять часóв**.

Telling the time if it is not on the hour can be done in a number of ways, but the easiest is to do it digitally, for example 10.20 is **дéсять часóв двáдцать минýт** and 4.45 is **четы́ре часá сорок пять минýт**.

Ключевы́е слова́

Диало́г 1

когда́ kagd<u>a</u>	*when*
музе́й открыва́ется moozy<u>ey</u> atkriv<u>a</u>yetsa	*the museum opens*
выходно́й день vykhadn<u>oy</u> dyen'	*day off*
вто́рник ft<u>o</u>rneek	*Tuesday*
музе́й-кварти́ра moozy<u>ey</u>-kvart<u>ee</u>ra	*former flat preserved as museum*
среда́ sryid<u>a</u>	*Wednesday*
зоологи́ческий музе́й za-alag<u>ee</u>chesky moozy<u>ey</u>	*zoological museum*
по́здно p<u>o</u>zdna	*late*
пя́тница py<u>a</u>tneetsa	*Friday*

Диало́г 2

конце́рт начина́ется kantsy<u>e</u>rt n<u>a</u>chinayetsa	*the concert begins*
четве́рг chitvy<u>e</u>rk	*Thursday*
ра́но r<u>a</u>na	*early*
ка́ждый день k<u>a</u>zhdy dyen'	*every day*

Диало́г 3

у́тром <u>oo</u>trum	*in the morning*
я встаю́ ya fstay<u>oo</u>	*I get up*
я за́втракаю ya z<u>a</u>ftrakayoo	*I have breakfast*
я иду́ ya eed<u>oo</u>	*I go (on foot in one direction)*
рабо́та (на) rab<u>o</u>ta	*work*
я обе́даю ya aby<u>e</u>dayoo	*I have dinner*
ве́чером vy<u>e</u>chirom	*in the evening*
я у́жинаю ya <u>oo</u>zhinayoo	*I have supper*
я смотрю́ ya smatry<u>oo</u>	*I watch*
я ложу́сь спать ya lazh<u>oos</u>' spat'	*I go to bed*

Диало́г 4

Где мы встре́тимся? Gdye my fstry<u>e</u>timsa?	*Where shall we meet?*
за́л Филармо́нии zal Feelarm<u>o</u>nee	*Philharmonic hall*
Встре́тимся Fstry<u>e</u>timsa	*Let's meet*

Диало́ги

Диало́г 1

Steven is visiting his friend Са́ша in St. Petersburg for a week. They are trying to plan their time. There are several museums which Steven wants to visit, but first he must find out which **выходно́й день** (vykhadn_oy dyen') *day off* each museum has. Са́ша looks through the phone directory to find out details.

Сти́вен **Са́ша, когда́ открыва́ется ру́сский музе́й?**

Са́ша **Ру́сский музе́й открыва́ется в 10 часо́в. Выходно́й день – вто́рник.**

Сти́вен **И музе́й-кварти́ра Пу́шкина?**

Са́ша **Одну́ мину́точку. Да, музе́й-кварти́ра Пу́шкина открыва́ется в 10 часо́в. Выходно́й день – среда́.**

Сти́вен **И когда́ открыва́ется зоологи́ческий музе́й?**

Са́ша **Зоологи́ческий музе́й открыва́ется по́здно, в 11 часо́в. Выходно́й день – пя́тница.**

Диало́г 2

When they have planned their days they think about the evenings. They want to go to a concert and see a film.

Сти́вен **Когда́ начина́ется конце́рт?**

Са́ша **Конце́рт в четве́рг. Он начина́ется ра́но, в 6 часо́в.**

Сти́вен **И когда́ начина́ется фильм?**

Са́ша **Ка́ждый день фильм начина́ется в 4 часа́ и в 7 часо́в.**

Диало́г 3

Steven wants to fit in with Sasha's life, so Sasha tells him about his daily routine.

Са́ша **У́тром я встаю́ в 8 часо́в и за́втракаю в 9 часо́в. Пото́м я иду́ на рабо́ту в библиоте́ку. Библиоте́ка открыва́ется в 10 часо́в. Я там обе́даю, и ве́чером я у́жинаю до́ма в семь часо́в. Пото́м я смотрю́ телеви́зор и по́здно ложу́сь спать.**

Диало́г 4

Before Sasha leaves for work, Steven asks where they should meet before going to the concert.

Сти́вен **Где мы встре́тимся, Са́ша?**

Са́ша **Конце́рт начина́ется в 6 часо́в в за́ле Филармо́нии. Встре́тимся в 5 часо́в в библиоте́ке. Мо́жно, Сти́вен?**

Сти́вен **Мо́жно.**

Механи́зм языка́
Mechanics of the language

1 Days of the week

Note that the days of the week and months are written with lower case letters in Russian.

Monday	**понеде́льник**	panidyel'neek
Tuesday	**вто́рник**	ftorneek
Wednesday	**среда́**	sryida
Thursday	**четве́рг**	chitvyerk
Friday	**пя́тница**	pyatneetsa
Saturday	**суббо́та**	soobota
Sunday	**воскресе́нье**	vaskrisyen'ye

To ask what day it is, say **Како́й сего́дня день?** (Kakoy sivodnya dyen'?) Notice that the word **сего́дня** *today* is not pronounced as it is spelt, the **г** being pronounced as a **в**. To say what day it is, say **Сего́дня суббо́та** (Sivodnya soobota) *today is Saturday.*

If you want to say *on* a day of the week, use **в**. If the day of the week ends in **-a**, change **-a** to **-y**, for example, **в суббо́ту**.

Notice that when you say *on Wednesday* the stress changes from **среда́** to **в сре́ду**.

on Monday	в понеде́льник	fpanidy<u>e</u>l'neek
on Tuesday	во вто́рник	vo vt<u>o</u>rneek
on Wednesday	в сре́ду	fsry<u>e</u>doo
on Thursday	в четве́рг	fchyetvy<u>e</u>rk
on Friday	в пя́тницу	fpy<u>a</u>tneetsoo
on Saturday	в суббо́ту	fsoob<u>o</u>too
on Sunday	в воскресе́нье	v-vaskrisy<u>e</u>n'ye

2 First, second, third . . . ordinal numerals

In the next unit you will be learning the months so that you can say the date in Russian. To prepare for this you need to know the ordinal numerals in Russian, *first, second, third* etc. Once you get past the first few, they are formed quite logically by adding an adjective ending to the numerals you already know. In this unit you will meet the ordinal numerals from *first* to *tenth* in their masculine forms, for use with masculine nouns (деся́тый эта́ж dyesy<u>a</u>ty et<u>a</u>sh *tenth floor*).

✳ When you are in Russia, remember that the ground floor is called пе́рвый эта́ж (py<u>e</u>rvy et<u>a</u>sh), so an English first floor will be второ́й эта́ж (ftar<u>o</u>y et<u>a</u>sh).

In the next unit you will need to become familiar with *first* to *31st* in order to deal with any date which may arise.

1st	пе́рвый py<u>e</u>rvy	5th	пя́тый py<u>a</u>ty	8th	восьмо́й vas'm<u>o</u>y
2nd	второ́й ftar<u>o</u>y	6th	шесто́й shest<u>o</u>y	9th	девя́тый divy<u>a</u>ty
3rd	тре́тий try<u>e</u>ty	7th	седьмо́й syidm<u>o</u>y	10th	деся́тый disy<u>a</u>ty
4th	четвёртый chitvy<u>o</u>rty				

✔ ─────── Упражне́ния ───────

1 Listen to your cassette, and jot down (using numbers) the times that places open and events begin.

(a) Бассе́йн открыва́ется в . . .

(b) О́пера начина́ется в . . .

(c) Буфе́т открыва́ется в . . .

(d) Марафо́н начина́ется в . . .

(e) Галере́я открыва́ется в . . .

(f) Конце́рт начина́ется в . . .

(g) Зоопа́рк открыва́ется в . . .

(h) Моя́ рабо́та начина́ется в . . .

(i) Фильм начина́ется в . . .

2 Кото́рый час? What would you say for these times?

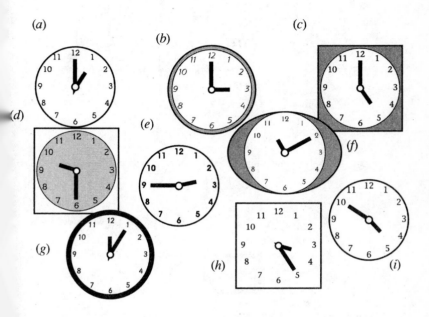

(a) (b) (c) (d) (e) (f) (g) (h) (i)

3 Look at the pictures and fill in the blanks in the captions. If you need to, choose from the verbs below in brackets.

(a) В _____ часо́в я _____ .

(b) В _____ часо́в я _____ .

(c) В _____ часо́в я _____ на рабо́ту.

(d) В час я _____ на рабо́те.

(e) В _____ часо́в я у́жинаю до́ма.
(f) В _____ часо́в я _____ телеви́зор.
(g) В _____ часо́в я ложу́сь спать.

(встаю́ иду́ обе́даю за́втракаю смотрю́)

4 Read the details of these St. Petersburg museums in your English language guide book, and tell your Russian friend out loud at what time they open, on which days they are closed, and what their telephone numbers are.

		Time of opening	*Day off*	*Telephone number*
(a)	*Museum of Anthropology and Ethnography* Музе́й антрополо́гии и этногра́фии	11.00	Sat	218-14-12
(b)	*Museum of Musical Instruments* Музе́й музыка́льных инструме́нтов	12.00	Tues	314-53-55
(c)	*Museum Apartment of A.A. Blok* Музе́й-кварти́ра А.А. Бло́ка	11.00	Wed	113-86-33
(d)	*Museum of the Arctic and Antarctic* Музе́й А́рктики и Анта́рктики	10.00	Mon	311-25-49

5 Below is Anna's diary. Note the usual abbreviations for the days of the week. Each day she is seeing someone different and doing a different activity.

Пн.	Вт.	Ср.	Чт.	Пт.	Сб.	Вс.
Са́ша	Та́ня	О́ля	Юрий	Ма́ша	Ди́ма	Кири́лл
фильм	обе́д	о́пера	футбо́л	экску́рсия	конце́рт	джаз

In the bottom of her bag she has seven scraps of paper on which her friends wrote down where they would meet her. See if you can match each scrap of paper to the right day.

(*a*) Встре́тимся на стадио́не в 3 часа́.

(*b*) Встре́тимся в кинотеа́тре в 7 часо́в.

(*c*) Встре́тимся до́ма в 6 часо́в.

(*d*) Встре́тимся в теа́тре о́перы и бале́та в 7 часо́в.

(*e*) Встре́тимся в за́ле Филармо́нии в 6 часо́в.

(*f*) Встре́тимся в це́нтре джа́зовой му́зыки в 2 часа́.

(*g*) Встре́тимся в авто́бусе в час.

6 Here is a list of departments placed next to the lift in a multi-storey shop.

Шесто́й эта́ж:	Факс.
Пя́тый эта́ж:	Се́йфы. Лино́леум. Сувени́ры.
Четвёртый эта́ж:	Видеомагнитофо́ны, видеопле́йеры, телеви́зоры, видеокассе́ты, тю́неры.
Тре́тий эта́ж:	Музыка́льные инструме́нты. Фо́то.
Второ́й эта́ж:	Парфюме́рия. Косме́тика.
Пе́рвый эта́ж:	Апте́ка. О́птика – конта́ктные ли́нзы.

On which floor would you be likely to find (*a*) contact lenses (*b*) perfume (*c*) a saxophone (*d*) a matryoshka doll (*e*) a safe (*f*) a fax (*g*) a video player (*h*) linoleum (*i*) lipstick?

7 Read the complete meal menus on the following page and decide which one you would be likely to have for за́втрак, обе́д and у́жин.

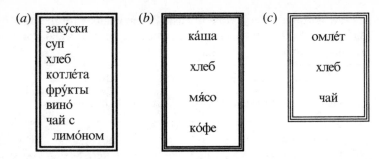

(a)
закуски
суп
хлеб
котлета
фрукты
вино
чай с
    лимоном

(b)
каша

хлеб

мясо

кофе

(c)
омлет

хлеб

чай

8 Remember how the words **в** and **на** may be used in two different ways. The first way you met was in unit 5 **Как попасть в галерею?** *How do I get to the gallery?* Here **в** means *to*, and it changes the ending of following feminine nouns from -а to -у and from -я to -ю. Masculine and neuter nouns do not change. These are called *accusative* endings.

The second way of using **в** and **на** you met in unit 7: **Я работаю в магазине в Москве** *I work in a shop in Moscow.* Here **в** means *in* or *at* and it usually changes the ending of following nouns to -е. These are called prepositional endings.

Choose the correct endings in the following sentences, depending on whether they use **в** and **на** to mean *to* or *in*.

(a) Я работаю в театр / театре в Новгород / Новгороде.

(b) Я иду в библиотеку / библиотеке.

(c) Вы работаете в университет / университете или в школу / школе?

(d) –Куда вы идёте? Я иду в институт / институте.

(e) Извините, пожалуйста. Как попасть в поликлинику / поликлинике.

9 Listen to the cassette. Anna is talking about some of the things she does on each day of the week. Fill in the gaps with the correct day of the week in English, and then say each whole sentence out loud in Russian.

(a) В _____ я работаю в институте.

(b) В _____ я обедаю в ресторане.

(c) В _____ вечером я смотрю телевизор.

(d) В _____ я встаю рано и слушаю радио.

(e) В _____ утром я иду в библиотеку. Потом в 2 часа я иду в институт.

(f) В _____ я ложусь спать очень поздно.

(g) В _____ я встаю и завтракаю поздно.

10 This is a notice you might see on a shop door.

Магазин работает			
Пн	с 9.00	до	19.00
Вт	с 10.00	до	20.00
Ср	с 10.00	до	20.00
Чт	с 10.00	до	20.00
Пт	с 10.00	до	20.00
Сб	с 11.00	до	16.00
Вс	выходной день		
Перерыв на обед 13.00 – 14.00			

   (*a*) On which day does the shop open early in the morning?
   (*b*) When is the lunch break?
   (*c*) On which day does the shop open late in the morning?
   (*d*) On which day does the shop not open?
   (*e*) At what time does the shop close on Saturdays?

11 On which day does the museum not open?

◢ Проверьте себя

1 Say the days of the week in the correct order and then in reverse order.
2 Say what time it is now.
3 How would you ask *When does the bank open?*
4 Ask *When does the film start?*
5 Tell a friend *Let's meet at 7 o'clock at the restaurant.*

9

ВЫ ЛЮБИТЕ СПОРТ?
Do you like sport?

In this unit you will learn

- how to talk about leisure activities
- how to say the date
- how to talk about likes and dislikes
- how to use verbs in different forms
- how to use numerals over 1,000

✳ Before you start

When practising your Russian, do not worry too much about getting the word endings right, as you will still be understood even if you make a mistake. Concentrate on communicating, and with practice you will make fewer errors. Do not let fear of making a mistake stop you from trying to get your message across, as this is how you learn.

Once you make Russian friends you will probably want to express your likes and dislikes and say what you do in your free time. Here are some useful structures:

Я о́чень люблю́ му́зыку	*I really love music*
Я люблю́ смотре́ть телеви́зор	*I love/like watching television*
Я не люблю́ чита́ть	*I don't like reading*
Я совсе́м не люблю́ гуля́ть	*I really don't like walking*
Я игра́ю в бадминто́н	*I play badminton*
Я игра́ю на гита́ре	*I play the guitar*
Я хожу́ в кино́	*I (habitually) go to the cinema*

Информа́ция

Пра́здники *Public holidays*

Here are just a few of the **пра́здники** (pr<u>a</u>zdneeky) *public holidays* which are celebrated in Russia.

Но́вый год	1 января́	(N<u>o</u>vy got)	New Year, 1st January
Рождество́	7 января́	(Razhdyestv<u>o</u>)	Orthodox Christmas, 7th January
Же́нский День	8 ма́рта	(Zh<u>e</u>nsky dyen')	Women's Day, 8th March
День Побе́ды	9 ма́я	(Dyen' paby<u>e</u>dy)	Victory Day, 9th May, end of World War II.

The greeting **С пра́здником** (s pr<u>a</u>zdneekum) means literally *(I congratulate you) with the holiday*, and may be applied to any occasion. To wish someone a *Happy New Year* say **с но́вым го́дом** (s n<u>o</u>vym g<u>o</u>dum). On New Year's Eve, Grandfather Frost **Дед Моро́з** (Dyet Mar<u>o</u>s) with his helper the Snowmaiden **Снегу́рочка** (Snyeg<u>oo</u>rachka) gives out presents by the tree **ёлка** (y<u>o</u>lka). *Happy Birthday* is rather a mouthful, **с днём рожде́ния** (s dnyom razhdy<u>e</u>niya), literally *with the day of birth*.

Months

The names of the months, which are all masculine, are easy to recognise.

January	**янва́рь**	yinva̲r'	*July*	**ию́ль**	eey<u>oo</u>l'
February	**февра́ль**	fyevra̲l'	*August*	**а́вгуст**	a̲vgoost
March	**март**	mart	*September*	**сентя́брь**	syentya̲br'
April	**апре́ль**	aprye̲l'	*October*	**октя́брь**	aktya̲br'
May	**май**	maee'	*November*	**ноя́брь**	naya̲br'
June	**ию́нь**	eey<u>oo</u>n'	*December*	**дека́брь**	dyeka̲br'

Ключевы́е слова́

хо́бби kh<u>o</u>bbee	*hobby*
я о́чень люблю́ чита́ть	*I really love reading*
ya <u>o</u>chen' lyooblyoo cheeta̲t'	
вы чита́ете vy cheeta̲yetye	*you read*
я чита́ю ya cheeta̲yoo	*I read*
газе́та gazye̲ta	*newspaper*
то́же t<u>o</u>zhe	*also*
рома́н rama̲n	*novel*
интере́сно intirye̲sna	*That's interesting*
я совсе́м не люблю́ чита́ть	*I really don't like reading*
ya savsye̲m nye lyooblyoo cheeta̲t'	
я игра́ю в бадминто́н	*I play badminton*
ya eegra̲yoo v badmeento̲n	
гуля́ть goolya̲t'	*to go for a walk*
му́зыка m<u>oo</u>zyka	*music*
я игра́ю на саксофо́не	*I play the saxophone*
ya eegra̲yoo na saksafo̲nye	
ходи́ть на конце́рты	*to go (habitually) to concerts*
khad<u>ee</u>t' na kantsye̲rty	
путеше́ствовать pootyishe̲stvovat'	*to travel*
пя́тое октября́ pya̲tore aktyabrya̲	*5th of October*
Ди́ксиленд D<u>ee</u>kseelend	*Dixieland*
Вы хоти́те пойти́	*Do you want to go?*
Vy khat<u>ee</u>tye paeet<u>ee</u>	

Диало́г

Диало́г

George is introduced to Lyudmila, and they talk about their leisure interests. Listen to the tape or read the dialogue and answer the following questions: What interests does George have? What sports does Lyudmila play? Now listen or read again. What instrument does George play? Where do they decide to go and when?

Людми́ла	**Каки́е у вас хо́бби?**
Джордж	**Я о́чень люблю́ чита́ть.**
Людми́ла	**Чита́ть? Каки́е кни́ги вы чита́ете?**
Джордж	**Ка́ждый день я чита́ю газе́ты, и я то́же люблю́ чита́ть рома́ны.**
Людми́ла	**Интере́сно. Вы лю́бите ру́сские рома́ны?**
Джордж	**Да, о́чень люблю́. А вы, у вас есть хо́бби?**
Людми́ла	**Да, но я совсе́м не люблю́ чита́ть! Я люблю́ спорт. Я игра́ю в бадминто́н и в те́ннис, и я люблю́ гуля́ть.**
Джордж	**Вы лю́бите му́зыку?**
Людми́ла	**Да, я о́чень люблю́ джаз.**
Джордж	**Я то́же. Я игра́ю на саксофо́не. В Ло́ндоне я о́чень люблю́ ходи́ть на конце́рты.**
Людми́ла	**В Ло́ндоне? Скажи́те, вы не ру́сский?**
Джордж	**Нет, я англича́нин. Я живу́ в Ло́ндоне.**
Людми́ла	**Вы хорошо́ говори́те по-ру́сски.**
Джордж	**Спаси́бо. Я говорю́ по-ру́сски и по-францу́зски, и я о́чень люблю́ путеше́ствовать.**
Людми́ла	**Интере́сно. Джордж, вы лю́бите джаз и сего́дня пя́тое октября́. Сего́дня ве́чером я иду́ на конце́рт – Ди́ксиленд. Вы хоти́те пойти́ на конце́рт?**
Джордж	**Да, коне́чно я хочу́. Спаси́бо. Когда́ начина́ется конце́рт?**
Людми́ла	**В семь часо́в. Встре́тимся здесь в шесть часо́в.**
Джордж	**Хорошо́. Спаси́бо, Людми́ла.**
Людми́ла	**Пожа́луйста.**

Numerals 1,000 – 20,000

1,000 **тысяча** tisyacha		6,000 **шесть тысяч** shest' tisyach
2,000 **две тысячи** dvye tisyachee		7,000 **семь тысяч** syem' tisyach
3,000 **три тысячи** tree tisyachee		8,000 **восемь тысяч** vosyem' tisyach
4,000 **четыре тысячи** chyetyrye tisyachee		9,000 **девять тысяч** dyevvyat' tisyach
5,000 **пять тысяч** pyat' tisyach		10,000 **десять тысяч** dyesyat' tisyach
20,000 **двадцать тысяч** dvatsat' tisyach			

Practise these numbers in whichever way has proved successful for you with lower numbers.

Механизм языка
Mechanics of the language

1 Какое сегодня число? *What is the date today?*

In answer to the question **Какое сегодня число?** (Kakoye sivodnya cheeslo?) literally *which today number?*, you need the ordinal numbers which you learned on page 88. This time they need their neuter ending **-oe** to agree with the neuter **число**. This is followed by the month with the ending **-a** or **-я** which gives the meaning *of*.

Ordinal numbers 1st – 31st with neuter endings for forming dates:

1st **первое**	pyervoye	13th **тринадцатое**	treenatsatoye
2nd **второе**	ftaroye	14th **четырнадцатое**	chyetirnatsatoye
3rd **третье**	tryet'ye	15th **пятнадцатое**	pitnatsatoye
4th **четвёртое**	chyetvyortoye	16th **шестнадцатое**	shestnatsatoye
5th **пятое**	pyatoye	17th **семнадцатое**	syemnatsatoye
6th **шестое**	shestoye	18th **восемнадцатое**	vasyemnatsatoye
7th **седьмое**	syed'moye	19th **девятнадцатое**	dyevitnatsatoye
8th **восьмое**	vas'moye	20th **двадцатое**	dvatsatoye
9th **девятое**	dyevyatoye	21st **двадцать первое**	dvatsat' pyervoye
10th **десятое**	dyesyatoye	22nd **двадцать второе**	dvatsat' ftaroye
11th **одиннадцатое**	adeenatsatoye	30th **тридцатое**	treetsatoye
12th **двенадцатое**	dvyenatsatoye	31st **тридцать первое**	treetsat' pyervoye

The months with endings **-а** or **-я** for forming dates:

январ**я́**, феврал**я́**, м**а́**рта, апре́ля, м**а́**я, и**ю́**ня,
и**ю́**ля, **а́**вгуста, сентябр**я́**, октябр**я́**, ноябр**я́**, декабр**я́**

So, **Сего́дня пя́тое а́вгуста** *today is 5th August.*

12/1	двена́дцатое января́	2/12	второ́е декабря́
7/5	седьмо́е ма́я	6/2	шесто́е февраля́
30/9	тридца́тое сентября́	19/3	девятна́дцатое ма́рта

To say *on* a certain date, the ending of the ordinal numeral should change to **-ого**, pronounced -ovo. **Двена́дцатого а́вгуста** – on 12th August.

To say *in* June, you use **в** and change the ending of the month to **-е**.

в январе́, в феврале́, в ма́рте, в апре́ле, в ма́е, в ию́не,
в ию́ле, в а́вгусте, в сентябре́, в октябре́, в ноябре́, в декабре́

---

in spring	**весно́й**	in autumn	**о́сенью**
in summer	**ле́том**	in winter	**зимо́й**

2 Verbs

Verbs are 'doing words' for example, *run, read, talk, sleep.* You have met some Russian verbs in phrases where they are already in their correct form: **Вы говори́те** по-русски? It is hard to say anything without verbs, so to make up sentences yourself you will need to understand how they work. There are two main groups of verbs in Russian, which we will call group 1 and group 2. The infinitive is the form you will find if you look up a verb in the dictionary.

Look at this English verb.

---

to work (*infinitive*)
(*singular*)   (*plural*)
I   work   we   work
you   work   you   work
he/she/it work**s**   they   work

The same verb in Russian **рабо́тать** is a group 1 verb, and it changes its endings more than its English equivalent. You have already met the two forms which are underlined in the box below.

рабо́тать (*infinitive*) *to work*			
(*singular*)		(*plural*)	
я	рабо́таю	мы	рабо́таем
ты	рабо́таешь	вы	рабо́таете
он/она́/оно́	рабо́тает	они	рабо́тают

To make the different forms of a group 1 verb, remove the **-ть** from the infinitive and add the endings in bold type. This applies to other group 1 verbs you have met, for example, **знать**, **понима́ть**, **за́втракать**, **обе́дать**, **у́жинать**, **чита́ть**, **игра́ть**, **гуля́ть**.

You have also met some group 2 verbs for example, **говори́ть**.

говори́ть (*infinitive*) *to speak/talk*			
я	говорю́	мы	говори́м
ты	говори́шь	вы	говори́те
он/она́/оно́	говори́т	они	говоря́т

To make the different forms of a group 2 verb, remove the last three letters from the infinitive and add the endings in bold type. You have also met **люби́ть** which is a group 2 verb. It is slightly unusual in the **я** form, because it inserts an **л** before the ending: **я люблю́**. In future vocabulary lists you will often see 1 or 2 next to a verb indicating which group it belongs to so that you know what to do with it.

Some verbs are irregular, i.e. they do not follow the patterns given above, like **хоте́ть** (khaty<u>et</u>') *to want*.

я	хочу́	мы	хоти́м
ты	хо́чешь	вы	хоти́те
он/она́/оно́	хо́чет	они	хотя́т

Another verb which is unusual is the group 1 verb **жить** (zheet') *to live*.

я	живу́	мы	живём
ты	живёшь	вы	живёте
он/она́/оно́	живёт	они	хиву́т

3 I love to, I want to, I play ...

To say *I love doing something* say **Я люблю** + verb infinitive: e.g. **Я люблю читáть** *I love reading.*

To say *I love something* say **Я люблю** + noun. Remember that the noun is a direct object, so it needs accusative endings. If it is feminine **-a** will change to **-y** and **-я** to **-ю**: e.g. **Я люблю мýзыку** *I love music.* If it is masculine or neuter it will not change: e.g. **Я люблю спорт** *I love sport.*

To say *I want to do something* say **Я хочý** + verb infinitive: e.g. **Я хочý говорúть по-рýсски** *I want to speak Russian.* **Я хочý есть банáн и пить кóфе** *I want to eat a banana and drink some coffee.* (**Пить** is the verb *to drink* and **есть** is the verb *to eat* – spelled exactly like **есть** in **у меня есть**.)

To say *I play a sport* say **Я игрáю в** + sport: e.g. **Я игрáю в бадминтóн/в футбóл** *I play badminton/football.*

To say *I play an instrument* say **Я игрáю на** + instrument, using the prepositional ending **-e**: e.g. **Я игрáю на гитáре/на балалáйке** *I play the guitar/balalaika.*

To say *I (habitually) go somewhere* say **Я хожý в/на** + place. Remember you are going *to* the place, so you need to use an accusative ending. If the place is feminine **-a** will change to **-y** and **-я** to **-ю**: e.g. **Я хожý в больнúцу/на вокзáл** *I go to the hospital/station.*

Упражнéния

1 On a visit to Russia you have a programme of cultural events to choose from. Read it out loud, including the dates, and answer the questions. For the first event, you will say: **Суббóта пéрвое октября. Пьéса. Отéлло.** (**Пьéса** is a *play*).

сб. 1 октября	Пьéса. Отéлло
вс. 2 октября	Пьéса. Три сестрь́
пн. 3 октября	Пьéса. Клаýстрофобия
вт. 4 октября	Óпера. Борúс Годунóв
ср. 5 октября	Концéрт. Дúксиленд «Мúстер Джаз»
чт. 6 октября	Концéрт. Бах, Шýберт и Шýман
пт. 7 октября	Пьéса. Три мушкетéра

(*a*) If you liked classical music, which evening would suit you?
(*b*) If you liked jazz, which evening would interest you?
(*c*) What is the title of the Chekhov play on Sunday?
(*d*) On which evening could you see an opera?

2 Volodya is writing an illustrated letter to his little niece saying what he likes to do at different times of year.

Весно́й я люблю́ путеше́ствовать.
Ле́том я люблю́ игра́ть в те́ннис и чита́ть на пля́же.
О́сенью я люблю́ гуля́ть в па́рке.
Зимо́й я люблю́ игра́ть в хокке́й и смотре́ть телеви́зор.

Now respond by saying what you like doing at different times of year. You could also add what you like doing at different times of day: **у́тром** (<u>oo</u>trum) *in the morning*, **днём** (dnyom) *in the afternoon*, **ве́чером** (v<u>ye</u>chirom) *in the evening*, **но́чью** (n<u>o</u>ch'yoo) *at night*.

3 Listen to the tape, and write down in English which activities the following people like and dislike. You may not catch every word they say, but try to pick out the relevant details.

(*a*) Бори́с (*b*) Ли́за (*c*) Андре́й (*d*) Ни́на

4 Како́е сего́дня число́? Read these dates out loud, and fill in the blanks.

(*a*) 1/1 – но́вый год.

(*b*) 7/1 – рождество́.

(*c*) 8/3 – же́нский день.

(*d*) 9/5 – день побе́ды.

(*e*) Сего́дня _____

(*f*) Мой день рожде́ния (*birthday*) _____.

For the remaining dates, say *on* 13th June **трина́дцатого ию́ня** and so on.

(*g*) 13/6, 24/12, 31/10

(*h*) 6/9, 3/10, 14/2

Pick some more dates at random from a calendar and practise until you feel confident.

5 Below are twelve jumbled sentences. Match the correct halves together.

(*a*) Я игра́ю на

(*b*) Я игра́ю в

(*c*) Я хожу́ в

(*d*) Я рабо́таю в

(*e*) Я хочу́ есть

(*f*) Я гуля́ю в

(*g*) Я говорю́

(*h*) Я хочу́ пить

(*i*) Сего́дня

(*j*) Я о́чень люблю́

(*k*) Я хочу́

(*l*) Каки́е у вас

(*i*) хо́бби?

(*ii*) девя́тое апре́ля.

(*iii*) лимона́д.

(*iv*) по-ру́сски.

(*v*) па́рке.

(*vi*) хокке́й.

(*vii*) сала́т.

(*viii*) му́зыку.

(*ix*) саксофо́не.

(*x*) магази́не.

(*xi*) библиоте́ку.

(*xii*) смотре́ть телеви́зор.

6 What are these numbers? Write down the answers in numerals.

(*a*) шесть ты́сяч

(*b*) четы́рнадцать ты́сяч пятьсо́т

(*c*) два́дцать ты́сяч три́ста во́семьдесят

(*d*) пять ты́сяч три́ста со́рок шесть

(*e*) девятна́дцать ты́сяч девятьсо́т два́дцать три

(*f*) две ты́сячи четы́реста оди́ннадцать

(*g*) ты́сяча две́сти девяно́сто во́семь.

(*h*) де́сять ты́сяч пятьсо́т три́дцать оди́н

Now look at your answers and see if you can say the numbers in Russian without looking at the questions! Good luck!

7 Choose the right endings for these verbs.

(a) Я рабо́таю/рабо́таете в шко́ле.
(b) Вы говорю́/говори́те по-ру́сски?
(c) Я не понима́ете/понима́ю.
(d) Я люблю́/лю́бите чай с лимо́ном.
(e) Вы живу́/живёте в Ло́ндоне?
(f) Ка́ждый день я за́втракаю/за́втракаете до́ма.
(g) О́сенью я гуля́ю/гуля́ете в па́рке.

8 Никола́й Никола́евич has agreed to answer some questions for a survey you are conducting. Can you ask him the following questions in Russian?

(a) What is your name?
(b) Are you Russian?
(c) Where do you live?
(d) What is your profession?
(e) Where do you work?
(f) Do you have any hobbies?
(g) Do you like sport?

Could you answer these questions in Russian if you were asked?

9 **Когда́ мы встре́тимся?** When shall we meet?

You are making arrangements to meet Russian friends. Read out (a) and (b) and jot down the dates and times in English. Then change (c) and (d) into Russian and say them out loud.

(a) В суббо́ту, два́дцать пя́того ма́я, в шесть часо́в.
(b) В четве́рг, три́дцать пе́рвого ию́ля, в де́вять часо́в два́дцать пять мину́т.
(c) On Monday, 8th February, at 7.30.
(d) On Friday, 16th March, at 5 o' clock.

☑ *Прове́рьте себя́*

On the cassette, listen to Андре́й talking about himself. Put ticks in the boxes below to show what he likes and dislikes. If you do not have the cassette, work from the text below.

	Я о́чень люблю́	Я люблю́	Я не люблю́	Я совсе́м не люблю́
(a) Work				
(b) Sport				
(c) Music				
(d) Watching T.V.				
(e) Travel				
(f) Cinema				

Здра́вствуйте! Меня́ зову́т Андре́й. Я живу́ в Москве́. Я – сту́дент в университе́те и в суббо́ту и в воскресе́нье я рабо́таю в рестора́не. Я официа́нт. Я не люблю́ рабо́тать в рестора́не. Я о́чень люблю́ спорт, и игра́ю в хокке́й, в футбо́л, в те́ннис и в бадминто́н. Я люблю́ му́зыку, игра́ю на гита́ре и хожу́ на конце́рты. Я совсе́м не люблю́ смотре́ть телеви́зор. Ле́том я о́чень люблю́ путеше́ствовать и зимо́й я люблю́ ходи́ть в кино́.

Now talk about yourself in Russian, your likes and dislikes. You might like to make a recording. Try to imitate the accent of the people you have heard on the tape.

10

ВХОДИ́ТЕ, ПОЖА́ЛУЙСТА!
Do come in!

In this unit you will learn

- how to talk about home and family (yours and theirs!)
- how to be a guest in a Russian home
- how to read a public transport route plan

Before you start

In the last few units you have built up a lot of vocabulary and new structures. In this unit you should aim to consolidate everything you have learned before moving on to the second section of the book. You now know enough to experiment and make up sentences of your own, and you are able to hold a conversation in Russian. If you don't understand what is being said to you, don't panic. Try to guess what is being said, or ask for an explanation of a particular word or phrase. If you can't think how to express yourself, don't give up, but paraphrase or simplify what you want to say. You learn best by trying things out and building up your skills, just as you build up muscles in physical exercise. You will probably find that people are very willing to help you.

Информа́ция

Семья́ (Sim'y<u>a</u>) *The family*

In many Russian families, three generations share one home. Living space in cities is at a premium, so you may find that the дива́н in the living room is a sofa by day and a bed by night. **Бáбушка** *grandmother* may help to bring up the children and run the home while the parents work. Pre-school children may attend **я́сли** (yạsly) *nursery* and **дéтский сад** (dyẹtskee sat) *kindergarten.* If you visit a Russian home, you may be offered slippers **тáпочки** (tạpochkee) to wear when you arrive, as outdoor shoes are not generally worn inside. Be prepared for warm hospitality from your Russian hosts.

Дáча Dạcha *A country house, but much more besides*

A *dacha* can be anything from a structure like a garden shed to a two-storey hunting lodge in the country. Russian city dwellers fortunate enough to have a да́ча may use it and its plot of land to grow fruit, vegetables and flowers and to rear chickens and pigs, visiting at weekends to enjoy the fresh air and to bring home-grown produce back to the city. They may house the grandparents and children there in the warmer months, and they gather berries and mushrooms in the woods.

Маршру́ты Marshr<u>oo</u>ty *Transport routes*

When finding your way around a Russian city you may need to consult a plan of bus, trolleybus and tram routes. Major roads on the route will be named. You already know у́лица *street*, проспе́кт *avenue*, пло́щадь *square* and мост *bridge*, but here are two more useful words: на́бережная (nabyiry<u>e</u>zhnaya) *embankment* and шоссе́ (shoss<u>ey</u>) *highway*).

Ключевы́е слова́

Диало́г 1

входи́те	vkhad<u>ee</u>tye	come in
сади́тесь	sad<u>ee</u>tyes'	sit down
семья́	sim'y<u>a</u>	family
Да, есть	Da, yest'	Yes, I have/he has/they have,etc.
посмотри́те	pasmatr<u>ee</u>tye	look (imperative)
у меня́ (есть)	oo miny<u>a</u> (yest')	I have
альбо́м	al'b<u>o</u>m	album
жена́	zhen<u>a</u>	wife
де́ти	dy<u>e</u>tee	children
ви́дите	v<u>ee</u>deetye	you see
их зову́т	eekh zav<u>oo</u>t	they are called
маши́на	mash<u>ee</u>na	car
её зову́т	yiy<u>o</u> zav<u>oo</u>t	she is called
да́ча (на)	d<u>a</u>cha	dacha (country house)
мать/оте́ц	mat'/aty<u>e</u>ts	mother/father
на пе́нсии	na py<u>e</u>nsee	on a pension (retired)
их	eekh	them
его́ зову́т	yiv<u>o</u> zav<u>oo</u>t	he is called
зперги́чный	inyerg<u>ee</u>chnee	energetic
дере́вня	dyiry<u>e</u>vnya	countryside/village
дя́дя/тётя	dy<u>a</u>dya/ty<u>o</u>tya	uncle/aunt

Диало́г 2

у́лица Ми́ра	<u>oo</u>leetsa M<u>ee</u>ra	street (of) peace
у нас (есть)	oo nas (yest')	we have
гости́ная	gast<u>ee</u>naya	living room
спа́льня	spal'nya	bedroom
ку́хня	k<u>oo</u>khnya	kitchen (also cookery)
но́вый/ста́рый	n<u>o</u>vy/st<u>a</u>ry	new/old
прекра́сный	prikr<u>a</u>sny	fine
столо́вая	stal<u>o</u>vaya	dining room
на́ша соба́ка	n<u>a</u>sha sab<u>a</u>ka	our dog (на́ш works like ва́ш)
река́ Мо́йка (на)	ryik<u>a</u> M<u>o</u>ika	River Moika
кабине́т	kabeeny<u>e</u>t	study
вид	veet	view
так прия́тно	tak preey<u>a</u>tna	so pleasant

Диало́г 3

почему́?	pachem<u>oo</u>?	Why?
потому́, что	patam<u>oo</u> shta	because
магази́н	magaz<u>ee</u>n	shop
по магази́нам	pa magaz<u>ee</u>nam	round the shops
наш го́род	nash g<u>o</u>rat	our city
истори́ческий	eestar<u>ee</u>cheskee	historical

споко́йно spak<u>o</u>ina		*peaceful*
лес, в лесу́ lyes, vlyes<u>oo</u>		*forest, in the forest*
Приезжа́йте к нам Preeyezh<u>ai</u>tye		*Come and visit us (* literally *Come to us*
в го́сти k nam vg<u>o</u>stee		*as guest)*

*A child who is always asking *Why* ? is called a **почему́чка** (pachem<u>oo</u>chka)!

Диало́ги

Диало́г 1

Sally goes with Ната́ша to visit Никола́й. Once the introductions are over, she asks him if he has any family. He gets out his photos. How many children does he have, and where do his parents live in the summer?

Никола́й **Входи́те, Са́лли! Меня́ зову́т Никола́й.**

Са́лли **О́чень прия́тно, Никола́й.**

Никола́й **О́чень прия́тно, Са́лли. Сади́тесь, пожа́луйста.**

Са́лли (*Sitting down on toy car*) **Извини́те! Скажи́те, у вас есть семья́?**

Никола́й **Да, есть. Посмотри́те, у меня́ здесь альбо́м. Э́то моя́ жена́, и вот де́ти, ви́дите? У меня́ сын и дочь. Их зову́т Алёша и Ли́за. Алёша о́чень лю́бит маши́ны и Ли́за лю́бит спорт. Жена́ - учи́тельница. Её зову́т Га́ля. Жена́ и де́ти сейча́с на да́че.**

Са́лли **На да́че? Как хорошо́.** (*looking at next photo*) **А кто э́то? Мать и оте́ц?**

Никола́й **Да, э́то ма́ма и па́па. Они́ на пе́нсии, и ле́том они́ живу́т на да́че. Я их о́чень люблю́. И вот мой брат. Его́ зову́т Ви́ктор. Он студе́нт, хорошо́ говори́т по-неме́цки и по-англи́йски и хо́чет путеше́ствовать.**

Са́лли **Интере́сно...**

Никола́й **И вот моя́ сестра́. Её зову́т Йра. Она́ о́чень знерги́чная де́вушка, игра́ет в баскетбо́л и лю́бит гуля́ть в дере́вне. И вот дя́дя и тётя. Они́ инжене́ры, рабо́тают на фа́брике в Новосиби́рске.**

Диало́г 2

Серёжа, Tim and Бе́лла are comparing photos of their homes. Match their descriptions to the pictures.

Серёжа **Я живу́ в кварти́ре на у́лице Ми́ра. У нас в кварти́ре гости́ная, спа́льня, ку́хня, ва́нная и балко́н. Кварти́ра но́вая, и у нас есть лифт и телефо́н. А где вы живёте, Тим?**

Тим **Я живу́ в до́ме в Ливерпу́ле. Э́то ста́рый, большо́й дом. У нас больша́я гости́ная, прекра́сная столо́вая, ма́ленькая ку́хня, три спа́льни и ва́нная.**

Серёжа **У вас есть сад?**

Тим **Да, у нас большо́й сад. На́ша соба́ка, Три́кси, лю́бит там игра́ть.**

Бе́лла **У меня́ ста́рая кварти́ра в до́ме на реке́ Мо́йке. Она́ краси́вая. У меня́ в кварти́ре гости́ная, кабине́т, ку́хня и ва́нная. У меня́ прекра́сный вид на ре́ку Мо́йку. Там так прия́тно!**

Диало́г 3

You are conducting interviews again. This time you are asking why people have chosen to live in the city or in the country. Where do Anna and Sasha prefer to live, and why?

Вы   **Почему́ вы лю́бите жить в го́роде?**

А́нна **Я люблю́ жить в го́роде потому́, что мо́жно ходи́ть на концéрты, в теáтр, в кинó, по магази́нам. Наш го́род истори́ческий, краси́вый. Мы живём в цéнтре и у нас есть стáнция метрó недалекó.**

Вы   **Сáша, почему́ вы лю́бите жить в дерéвне?**

Сáша **Я люблю́ жить в дерéвне потому́, что там спокóйно и мóжно гуля́ть в лесý. Приезжáйте к нам в гóсти. В дерéвне óчень прия́тно.**

Механи́зм языка́
Mechanics of the language

1 У вас есть...? *Do you have...?*

You have already met this question, which means literally *by you is there?* The answer is **Да, есть** (Da, yest') *Yes, there is.* Or in full it may be **Да, у меня́ есть. . .** (Da, oo minya yest'. . .) *Yes, by me there is . . .* If you want to make a statement rather than ask a question, simply omit the question mark: **У вас есть брат** *You have a brother.* **У вас есть** does not function like a verb, but is simply a phrase which is used in place of the verb *to have.* To ask or say that different people have something, use these forms:

У когó есть газéта? oo kav<u>o</u> yest' gaz<u>e</u>ta? *Who has a newspaper?*

я	**У меня́** oo min<u>a</u>	*I have*	мы	**У нас** oo nas	*we have*
ты	**У тебя́** oo tib<u>a</u>	*you have*	вы	**У вас** oo vas	*you have*
он/онó	**У негó** oo nyiv<u>o</u>	*he/it has*	они́	**У них** oo neekh	*they have*
онá	**У неё** oo nyiy<u>o</u>	*she has*			

You may choose whether or not to include the word **есть** in your statements. **Есть** adds emphasis: **У меня есть газета** I **do** have a newspaper.

У меня, у тебя etc. may also mean *at my home, at your home*, or even *in my country*. This is a very useful phrase for making comparisons between cultures: **У вас Рождество седьмого января, но у нас рождество двадцать пятого декабря.** *In your country, Christmas is on the 7th January, but in our country, Christmas is on 25th December.*

2 More about verbs

You already know that **я хожу** is used to say: *I go somewhere habitually*, and **я иду** is usually used to say *I am going somewhere now*. Here are the verbs **ходить** and **идти** in full. They both refer to going on foot, not by transport.

ходить *to go habitually*		**идти** *to go on one occasion*	
я хожу	мы ходим	я иду	мы идём
ты ходишь	вы ходите	ты идёшь	вы идёте
он ходит	они ходят	он идёт	они идут

Куда вы ходите каждый день в 7 часов?	*Where do you go every day at 7 o'clock?*
Куда вы идёте?	*Where are you going now?*

3 Points of the compass

You may wish to say in which part of the country your town or city is. The points of the compass are: **север** (syevyir) *North*, **юг** (yook) *South*, **запад** (zapat) *West*, **восток** (vastok) *East*. To say *in the North* etc., use **на** with the prepositional endings, adding **-e** to the end of the following word.

на севере		
на западе	Австралии, Америки, Англии, Ирландии,	
на востоке	России, Уэльса, Шотландии	
на юге	**of** *Australia, America, England, Ireland, Russia,*	
в центре	*Wales, Scotland*	

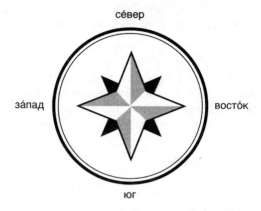

4   Whose is it?

You have already met **мой** and **ваш**, *my* and *your*. Here are the words meaning *your* (if you address someone as **ты**), and *our*. They are **твой** (tvoy) *your* and **наш** (nash) *our*. Remember that **мой** and **ваш** have different forms to agree with the gender of the nouns to which they refer (See page 68). The same is true of **твой** and **наш**.

Masculine	*Feminine*	*Neuter*	*Plural*
твой па́спорт	**твоя́** балала́йка	**твоё** пиани́но	**твои́** кассе́ты
your passport	*your balalaika*	*your piano*	*your cassettes*
наш па́спорт	**на́ша** балала́йка	**на́ше** пиани́но	**на́ши** кассе́ты
our passport	*our balalaika*	*our piano*	*our cassettes*

The words **его́** (yiv<u>o</u>) *his*, **её** (yiy<u>o</u>) *her* and **их** (eekh) *their* are easier to use as they do not change at all. So, **его́** can used with any noun to mean *his*; **его́ па́спорт, его́ балала́йка, его́ пиани́но, его́ кассе́ты**. **Её** *her* is just as simple, as is **их** *their*.

5   Him, her, them: direct object pronouns

As well as meaning *his*, *her* and *their*, the words **его́, её** and **их** have another meaning: *him*, *her* and *them* in phrases where people are the direct object of the verb. To fill in a few gaps, here is the full range of *me, you, him, her, us, you, them*. You have met many of these forms before, for example in the phrase **Как вас зову́т?** literally '*How you do they call?*'

ты лю́бишь **меня́** *You love me* я люблю́ **тебя́** *I love you* она́ лю́бит **его́** *she loves him* он лю́бит **её** *he loves her*	вы лю́бите **нас** *you love us* они́ лю́бят **вас** *they love you* мы лю́бим **их** *we love them*

───── # Упражне́ния ─────

1 Look at these route plans for St. Petersburg public transport. What should you catch to go to the following places?

(*a*) Finland station (*b*) Arsenal embankment (*c*) Revolution Highway (*d*) Moscow Avenue (*e*) Gor'kovskaya metro station (*f*) Tuchkov Bridge (*g*) Kazan Square (*h*) Industrial Avenue

Семна́дцатый тролле́йбус: Каза́нская пло́щадь – Горо́ховая у́лица – Витéбский вокза́л – За́городный проспéкт – Моско́вский проспéкт.

Шестьдеся́т трéтий трамва́й: Финля́ндский вокза́л – Сампсони́евский мост – ста́нция метро́ «Го́рьковская» – Тучко́в мост.

Два́дцать восьмо́й авто́бус: Финля́ндский вокза́л – Арсена́льная на́бережная – шоссé револю́ции – Индустриа́льный проспéкт

2 Listen to these descriptions of people on your cassette. Each description mentions where they live, where they work, their family, their hobbies, and something they want to do. Listen and try to note down something in English in each category for each person.

	А́ня	Пи́тер	Леони́д	Зо́я
живёт				
рабо́тает				
семья́				
хо́бби				
хо́чет				

3 Fill in the blanks in this description of Nadyezhda's home and life, using the words in brackets below.

Надéжда _____ в квартúре в Архáнгельске, на сéвере Росси́и. У неё нóвая квартúра, не óчень краси́вая, но Надéжда лю́бит там жить потому́, что _____ недалекó. В квартúре, у неё большáя гости́ная и мáленькая спáльня, _____ и вáнная. Её муж рабóтает в Москвé. В квартúре живу́т Надéжда, её мáма и ____ дочь. Их зову́т Гали́на и Мáша. У них кот. Егó зову́т Гóрби. Мáша егó óчень _____. Кáждый _____ Надéжда хóдит на фáбрику, где онá рабóтает. Мáша хóдит в шкóлу, и бáбушка _____ по магази́нам.

(лю́бит живёт её день магази́ны хóдит ку́хня)

4 Look at this map of Russia and say where these cities are:

(*a*) Магадáн на _____ Росси́и.   (*i*) сéвере
(*b*) Москвá на _____ Росси́и.   (*ii*) ю́ге
(*c*) Ирку́тск на _____ Росси́и.   (*iii*) востóке
(*d*) Нори́льск на _____ Росси́и.   (*iv*) зáпаде

5 Listen to the tape to find out what these people have. Put a tick in the correct columns when you have understood. When you have finished, you could construct an imaginary interview with each person, asking **У вас есть маши́на?** etc. and improvising answers based on your chart and on what you can remember from the tape.

	Маши́на	Брат	Кот	Кварти́ра	Да́ча
Бори́с					
На́стя					
Ли́за					

6 Choose the correct form of the verb to complete each of these sentences.

(a) –Скажи́те, пожа́луйста. Где здесь банк? –Извини́те, я не зна́ете/зна́ю/зна́ем.

(b) –Куда́ вы иду́/идёшь/идёте? –Я иду́/идёшь/идёте в музе́й.

(c) Я хоти́м/хо́чешь/хочу́ купи́ть сувени́ры.

(d) Он хорошо́ говорю́/говори́т/говоря́т по-ру́сски.

(e) Где ты рабо́таем/рабо́тают/рабо́таешь?

(f) У́тром я за́втракаю/за́втракает/за́втракаете в 7 часо́в.

(g) –У вас есть хо́бби? –Да, я о́чень лю́бит/люблю́/лю́бят чита́ть.

(h) Мы игра́ю/игра́ет/игра́ем в хокке́й.

(i) Они́ у́жинает/у́жинают/у́жинаем по́здно ве́чером.

Прове́рьте себя́

Check how confident you feel with all the material so far by doing this revision test.

1 Choose one appropriate response to each question or remark.

(a) –Как вас зову́т?
(i) –Меня́ зову́т Са́ша. (ii) –Я живу́ в Москве́. (iii) –Я говорю́ по-ру́сски.

(b) –Извини́те, пожа́луйста, э́то банк?
(i) –Иди́те пря́мо. (ii) –Как дела́? (iii) –Нет, э́то по́чта.

(c) –Спаси́бо.
(i) –Пло́хо. (ii) –О́чень прия́тно. (iii) – Не́ за что! (iv) –Я живу́ в дере́вне.

(d) –Как попа́сть в цирк?
(i) –Апте́ка вон там. (ii) –Иди́те напра́во. (iii) –Музе́й закры́т на ремо́нт.

(e) –У вас есть сувени́ры?
(i) –Нет, иди́те нале́во. (ii) –Как жаль. (iii) –Да, вот матрёшки.

(f) –Ско́лько сто́ит?
(i) –Семь часо́в (ii) –Ты́сяча рубле́й. (iii) –Пя́тый авто́бус.

(g) –Что у вас есть?

    (i) –Чай и кófe. (ii) –Я живу́ в Аме́рике. (iii) –Я -ру́сский.

(h) –Когда́ открыва́ется музе́й?

    (i) –Фильм начина́ется в де́сять часо́в. (ii) –Я встаю́ в во́семь часо́в. (iii) –В три часа́.

2 Choose the **least** appropriate phrase from each section.

    (a) You don't understand, so you say:

        (i) –Извини́те, я не понима́ю. (ii) –До́брый ве́чер. (iii) –Ме́дленнее, пожа́луйста. (iv) –Повтори́те, пожа́луйста.

    (b) You ask what someone does for a job, and they say:

    (i) –Я инжене́р. (ii) –Я рабо́таю на фа́брике. (iii) –Я люблю́ смотре́ть телеви́зор.

    (c) You ask someone about their hobbies, and they say:

    (i) –Я о́чень люблю́ чита́ть. (ii) –Я люблю́ спорт. (iii) –Я люблю́ тебя́. (iv) –Я хожу́ в кино́.

3 Choose the correct form of the words below.

    (a) Како́й э́то го́род? Э́то большо́й/больша́я го́род.

    (b) Я иду́ в больни́ца/больни́цу.

    (c) Вот ва́ша/ва́ше ко́мната.

    (d) Я живу́ в Магада́н/Магада́не.

    (e) Он игра́ет в бадминто́н/бадминто́не.

    (f) Она́ игра́ет на гита́ре/гита́ра.

    (g) Сего́дня пя́тый/пя́тое сентября́.

4 How much do you know about Russian life?

    (a) What would you do with a **папиро́са?** (i) eat it (ii) smoke it (iii) put it in a letter box?

    (b) In which city would you find **ГУМ?** (i) St. Petersburg (ii) Magadan (iii) Moscow?

    (c) If you were at a **вокза́л** would you catch (i) a train (ii) a plane (iii) a cold?

    (d) If you were speaking to an **официа́нт** would you be (i) showing your passport (ii) ordering a drink (iii) paying a fine?

    (e) Is **ка́ша** (i) porridge (ii) someone's name (iii) a cash desk?

    (f) Is **пра́здник** (i) a day of the week (ii) a shop assistant (iii) a holiday?

    (g) If you are walking along a **на́бережная** should you look out for (i) a runway (ii) a river (iii) a hospital?

11

НАПИШИ́ТЕ, ПОЖА́ЛУЙСТА!
Write it down, please!

In this unit you will learn

- how to read Russian script
- how to write in Russian

Before you start

Before moving on to the second part of the book you have the chance to meet the handwritten form of the language. At some time you may need to read Russian in script rather than the printed form. You may also want to write some Russian yourself, and if you learn some basic writing skills at this stage, it will help you to monitor your progress as you work through the rest of the book. The exercises in the second half of the book will still require you to read, speak and listen to Russian, but some of them will also give you the opportunity to write a little. However, if you choose not to learn to write in script, you can always print your answers or find alternative ways of answering.

Here are the letters of the Russian alphabet in their handwritten forms. Get used to their appearance, and then try copying them down in pencil until you feel confident with them. Carry on to a blank sheet of paper if necessary.

А	а	*Я а*
Б	б	*Б б*
В	в	*В в*
Г	г	*Г г*
Д	д	*Д д*
Е	е	*Е е*
Ё	ё	*Ё ё*
Ж	ж	*Ж ж*
З	з	*З з*
И	и	*И и*
Й	й	*Й й*
К	к	*К к*
Л	л	*Л л*
М	м	*М м*
Н	н	*Н н*
О	о	*О о*
П	п	*П п*
Р	р	*Р р*
С	с	*С с*

Т	т	*Т̄* *т*	
У	у	*У* *у*	
Ф	ф	*Ф* *ф*	
Х	х	*X* *x*	
Ц	ц	*Ц* *ц*	
Ч	ч	*Ч* *ч*	
Ш	ш	*Ш* *ш*	
Щ	щ	*Щ* *щ*	
	ъ	*ъ*	
	ы	*ы*	
	ь	*ь*	
Э	э	*Э* *э*	
Ю	ю	*Ю* *ю*	
Я	я	*Я* *я*	

When you are happy with the individual letters, move on to looking at some words in handwritten form. Notice that the letters

л *л*

м *м*

and я *я*

must always begin with a little hook, so you cannot join them onto a preceding **o**. *o*

The letter т *т̄*

is often written with a line above it and

the letter ш *ш̱*

with a line beneath it so that they can easily be distinguished from surrounding letters. First read the words out loud to make sure you recognise them and then try writing them yourself. The stress marks do not appear on the handwritten words. Carry on to a blank sheet for more practice.

А	а	А́том	*Атом*	Atom
Б	б	Борщ	*Борщ*	Beetroot soup
В	в	Входи́те	*Входите*	Come in
Г	г	Горбачёв	*Горбачёв*	Gorbachev
Д	д	Диа́гноз	*Диагноз*	Diagnosis
Е	е	Е́льцин	*Ельцин*	Yeltsin
Ё	ё	Ёлка	*Ёлка*	Fir tree
Ж	ж	Жена́	*жена*	Wife
З	з	Здра́вствуйте	*Здравствуйте*	Hello
И	и	Институ́т	*Институт*	Institute
Й	й	Музе́й	*Музей*	Museum
к	к	Ключ	*Ключ*	Key
Л	л	Ле́том	*летом*	In summer
М	м	Маши́на	*Машина*	Car

Н	н	Напра́во	*Направо*	On the right
О	о	Официа́нт	*Официант*	Waiter
П	п	Поэ́т	*Поэт*	Poet
Р	р	Росси́я	*Россия*	Russia
С	с	Сын	*Сын*	Son
Т	т	Тра́нспорт	*Транспорт*	Transport
У	у	У́жин	*Ужин*	Supper
Ф	ф	Фа́брика	*Фабрика*	Factory
Х	х	Хорошо́	*Хорошо*	Good
Ц	ц	Царь	*Царь*	Tsar
Ч	ч	Чай	*Чай*	Tea
Ш	ш	Шесть	*Шесть*	Six
Щ	щ	Щи	*Щи*	Cabbage soup
	ъ	Объе́кт	*Объект*	Object
	ы	Ры́нок	*Рынок*	Market
	ь	Ию́нь	*Июнь*	June
Э	э	Эта́ж	*Этаж*	Floor
Ю	ю	Юг	*Юг*	South
Я	я	Япо́ния	*Япония*	Japan

You have now written all the letters of the Russian alphabet in both their lower case and capital forms where possible. For further practice you could try converting words and phrases from elsewhere in the book into handwriting.

Упражнéния

In the following exercises you will be asked to read and write Russian script. If you decide that writing will not be useful to you, then find another way of responding to the exercises. You may be able to say the answers aloud, or print the words asked for, or group them using numbers or symbols.

1   To test your new skills, see if you can read all the handwritten words in this box. Now sort them into three categories: sport, food and members of the family. If you are going to practise your writing skills, write out the three lists.

котлéта   шоколáд   тéннис

сестрá   бокс   пáпа

баскетбóл   бáбушка   рéгби

салáт   хлеб   дочь

брат   банáн

футбóл   пинг-понг   дя́дя

сын   борщ   хоккéй

мáма

2 Write down or indicate the odd-man-out in each of these groups.

Город
парк
библиотека
музей
гитара
гастроном

Музыка
балалайка
оркестр
саксофон
инженер
опера

Профессия
врач
больница
учитель
футболист
дипломат

For further practice you could copy out the rest of the words in the boxes.

3 Can you complete the words in the grid using the clues in English given below?

(1) Plays are performed here.
(2) He studies at the university.
(3) Underground train system.
(4) You come here to eat out.
(5) This dish is made of eggs.
(6) General weather conditions.
(7) Document for foreign travel.
(8) Do come in!
(9) Farm vehicle.
(10) Capital of the Netherlands.
(11) Tenth month of the year.

(**12**)   Day after Monday.

(**13**)   A means of talking to distant friends.

1	m̄								
2		m̄							
3			m̄						
4				m̄					
5					m̄				
6						m̄			
7							m̄		
8						m̄			
9					m̄				
10				m̄					
11			m̄						
12		m̄							
13	m̄								

4   Write out the following words, not forgetting the little hooks at the start of *л* , *м* , and *я* .

кассета   _____

водка   _____

администратор   _____

ресторан   _____

телевизор   _____

институт   _____

рекорд   _____

атом   _____

Now take the first letter of each word to make another word. What is it? Can you write it?

5   Identify at least one word from each of these labels and tickets, and write it out.

ТРЕСТ СТОЛОВЫХ   РАЙОН   Главное управление
общественного питания
Ленгорисполкома

МЕНЮ

		ЦЕНА	Масса
«__» _____ 198_ года	ПОРЦИОННЫЕ БЛЮДА		

ХОЛОДНЫЕ ЗАКУСКИ	ЦЕНА	МАССА

СЛАДКИЕ БЛЮДА

ПЕРВЫЕ БЛЮДА   НАПИТКИ

ВТОРЫЕ БЛЮДА   ВЫПЕЧНЫЕ ИЗДЕЛИЯ

Директор:
Зав. производством:
Калькулятор:

МИНИСТЕРСТВО   СВЯЗИ СССР   ПЕРЕДАЧА
CLEANDMINE

ТЕЛЕГРАММА

го	ч.	м.
ndal	kell

№ связи
Ohend Nr.

Откуда
Kust

Передал
Andis õie

№

сл.   го   ч.   м.
sn.   ndal   kell

Служеб. отметки
Amet-
märkus

Автотранс
724737

АВТОБУС

10 руб.

Сер. ББ-601

Мтв з.106—93

Санкт-Петербургская
ГОСУДАРСТВЕННАЯ
ОРДЕНА ТРУДОВОГО
КРАСНОГО ЗНАМЕНИ

ФИЛАРМОНИЯ

им. Д. Д. ШОСТАКОВИЧА

БОЛЬШОЙ ЗАЛ

Ул. Бродского, 2

Тел. 110-42-57 (касса)

Серия БЗ

К/№   0077

Ряд 24   Кресло 28

19 ЧАС Цена 1 руб. 60 коп.

1 2 НОЯ 1994 Дата 2000

НОЧЬ
КОНФЕТЫ
КАРНАВАЛЬНАЯ
НОЧЬ

СДЕЛАНО В СССР

6 Read these words and write down or say the missing word in each sequence.

(a) Север, юг, запад и _____.

(b) Брат и сестра, тётя и дядя, бабушка и _____.

(c) Май, июнь, июль, _____, сентябрь, октябрь

(d) Десять, двадцать, _____, сорок, пятьдесят

(e) Англия, англичанин. Франция, француз. _____, русский.

Continue to practise your writing little and often, and refer back to this unit frequently to make sure that you are not learning any bad habits!

12

В АЭРОПОРТУ
At the airport

In this unit you will learn

- what to do and say on the plane
- what to do and say at the airport

Before you start, revise

- greetings, page 31
- numbers, times and dates, pages 235, 84, 98
- *my* and *your*, page 68 and *whose is it?* page 114
- how to use the verb **хотéть**, page 100

Now that you have reached the second half of the book, you should need less help with reading Russian, so the transliteration of words will no longer be shown. There will still be lots of listening and speaking, and in many exercises you can choose whether to write in Russian or not. To test your reading skills, there will be exercises and anecdotes both in print and script. The Russian anecdote has a long tradition, and by reading anecdotes from the Soviet era and the modern day you can learn a lot about the history, culture and humour of the Russian people. Some of the anecdotes appear on your cassette.

Пáспорт, вíза и декларáция
Passport, visa and declaration

When you arrive in Russia you will have to show your **пáспорт, вíза** and **деклара́ция**. The visa is a document from which a sheet is removed on entry and exit. The declaration is a form declaring any foreign currency and valuables you are taking into Russia. This is stamped on entry, and you should show it again on exit, declaring what you are taking out and showing receipts for goods purchased and money exchanged.

В самолёте
In the aeroplane

If you travel on a Russian plane you will feel that you are on Russian territory from the moment you board, and you may want to try out your Russian immediately. Here are some signs that you may see:

Не кури́ть   No smoking
Застегни́те ре́мни   Fasten your seat belts

Learn the key words, some of which you already know, and then listen to or read the dialogue.

самолёт	aeroplane	**пи́во**	beer
стюарде́сса	stewardess	**журна́лы**	magazines
ме́сто	seat/place	**гра́дус**	degree (temperature)
обе́дать	to have dinner		

Диало́г 1   Где моё ме́сто?

Вы	**Где моё ме́сто?**
Стюарде́сса	**Покажи́те, пожа́луйста, биле́т.**
Вы	**Вот он.**
Стюарде́сса	**Спаси́бо. Шестна́дцатое «а». Напра́во, пожа́луйста.**

Once you are in the air, the stewardess asks you a question.

Стюарде́сса	**Вы хоти́те обе́дать?**
Вы	**Обе́дать? Да, коне́чно, о́чень хочу́.**
Стюарде́сса	**И что вы хоти́те пить? У нас минера́льная вода́, вино́, пи́во, ко́фе и чай.**
Вы	**Да́йте, пожа́луйста, бе́лое вино́.**
Стюарде́сса	**Хоти́те журна́лы, газе́ты?**
Вы	**Да, пожа́луйста. У вас есть англи́йские газе́ты?**

Стюардесса **Да, англи́йские и америка́нские.**

Just before landing, the pilot gives you some information.

Пило́т **В Москве́ сейча́с восемна́дцать часо́в три́дцать пять мину́т, температу́ра – пятна́дцать гра́дусов.**

Упражне́ние 1

Say in English and Russian:

(а) your seat number (б) what you chose to drink (в) the time using the 24-hour clock, and the temperature in Moscow.

Упражне́ние 2

Read through the dialogue aloud, altering the information as follows:

(а) Your seat number is now 9 «б» on the left. (б) The stewardess offers you lemonade, fruit juice, and coffee with milk. (в) You choose fruit juice. (г) You ask for a Russian magazine.

Упражне́ние 3

Listen to the cassette and note down, using a numeral and a Russian letter, the seat numbers as the stewardess reads them out:

(а)
(б)
(в)
(г)

and the time and temperature in these cities.

(д) В Краснода́ре
(е) В Арха́нгельске
(ж) В Петербу́рге

——— Аэропо́рт *The airport* ———

Once you arrive at the airport in Russia, you may see these signs. The first group you will already recognise.

аэропóрт	*буфéт*	сувенúры

НЕ КУРИ́ТЬ   ПАРФЮМЕ́РИЯ

спрáвочное бюрó	кáсса	ТУАЛЕ́Т

✅ Упражнéние 4

The following groups of words you have not seen before. Work out what they mean.

(а) вы́ход   вы́хода нет   вы́ход на посáдку
(б) тамóженный контроль   вы́дача багажá   транзи́т
    пáспортный контрóль   № рéйса
(в) регистрáция   крáсный коридóр   зал ожидáния   вход
    exit/boarding gate (exit to embarkation)/no exit/luggage
    reclaim/passport control/flight number/customs control/transit/
    red channel/check-in/entrance/waiting room

Па́спортный контрóль
Passport control

Upon arrival at the airport, you will first go through passport control, and then on to customs – **тамóженный контрóль**.

Отку́да вы?	Where are you from?	**то́лько**	only
нарко́тик	narcotics	**до́ллар**	dollar
фунт сте́рлингов	pound sterling	**доро́жный чек**	traveller's cheque

Диало́г 2 Отку́да вы?

Де́вушка	**Да́йте, пожа́луйста, па́спорт.**
Джеймс	**Вот он.**
Де́вушка	**Спаси́бо. А где ва́ша ви́за?**
Джеймс	**Извини́те. Вот она́.**
Де́вушка	**Вы тури́ст и́ли бизнесме́н?**
Джеймс	**Я тури́ст.**
Де́вушка	**Вы англича́нин?**
Джеймс	**Да, англича́нин.**
Де́вушка	**Отку́да вы?**
Джеймс	**Я живу́ в Пре́стоне, на се́вере А́нглии.**
Де́вушка	**Хорошо́. Вот ваш па́спорт.**
Джеймс	**Спаси́бо.**

James moves on to customs.

Молодо́й челове́к	**Э́то ваш бага́ж?**
Джеймс	**Да, э́то мой чемода́н и моя́ су́мка. И вот моя́ деклара́ция.**
Молодо́й челове́к	**Спаси́бо. У вас в багаже́ есть нарко́тик?**
Джеймс	**Нет.**
Молодо́й челове́к	**У вас есть фунты сте́рлингов?**
Джеймс	**Нет, то́лько до́ллары и доро́жные че́ки.**
Молодо́й челове́к	**Хорошо́. Вот ва́ша деклара́ция. До свида́ния.**

Listen to the dialogue several times, then work on it by covering up James' lines and answering the questions yourself, altering information as you choose.

Упражне́ние 5

In the **деклара́ция** you are asked to declare any foreign currency, weapons, drugs and valuables. Underline the items in this handwritten list which you think you should declare.

доллары
план
компьютер

книга
фунты стерлингов
французские франки

пистолет
виза

дорожные чеки
камера

минеральная вода   *газета*

 Упражнéние 6

Last week you rang your friend, **Валентúн**, to tell him when you would be arriving in Moscow. Read through what he says first, and familiarise yourself with the new words. Then complete your side of the conversation.

ты бýдешь	you will be	понятно	understood
Áнна бýдет	Anna will be	так	so

(а) You *Hello. Valentin?*
Валентúн **Аллó! Стив, э́то ты?**
(б) You *Yes. How are you?*
Валентúн **Хорошó, спасúбо. Стив, когдá ты бýдешь в Москвé?**
(в) You *On Friday.*
Валентúн **Шестóго ию́ля?**
(г) You *Yes, on the 6th of July.*
Валентúн **В котóром часý?**
(д) You *At 18:40.*
Валентúн **И Áнна тóже бýдет на самолёте.**
(е) You *Yes, of course.*
Валентúн **И какóй нóмер рéйса?**
(ж)You *The flight number is SU242.*
Валентúн **SU двéсти сóрок два. Понятно. Так, мы встрéтимся в аэропортý шестóго ию́ля в восемнáдцать часóв сóрок минýт. До свидáния, Стив.**
(з) You *Goodbye, Valentin.*

Well done! Did you notice the unusual ending on **аэропо́рт** when Valentin says *at the airport?* You would expect to see **-e**, but instead you see **-у**. This happens with a few masculine nouns, including **сад** *garden*, and **лес** *forest*: **в саду́** *in the garden*, **в лесу́** *in the forest*.

The verb **быть** *to be* in the future tense (i.e. not what is happening now, but what *will* happen in the future), which you also met in this dialogue, is very useful when making arrangements, so here it is:

я бу́ду	I will be	**мы бу́дем**	we will be
ты бу́дешь	you will be	**вы бу́дете**	you will be
он/она́ бу́дет	he/she will be	**они́ бу́дут**	they will be

Упражне́ние 7

You are flying to St. Petersburg, and you need to ring your Russian friend with the details. Prepare what you will say on the phone.

Flight no. BA 878
Arrival in St. Petersburg: 19.40
Date of travel: Thursday 26 Jan.

At last you have completed the formalities, and you see Валенти́н waiting for you.

наконе́ц	at last
Как долете́ли?	How was your flight?
прекра́сно	fine
Как вы пожива́ете?	How are you (getting on)?
пожива́ть [1]	to get on
немно́жко	a little
уста́л/уста́ла/уста́ли	tired (*m f pl*)
как всегда́	as always
ждать [1] (я жду, ты ждёшь, они́ ждут)	to wait

Диало́г 3   Здра́вствуй, Валенти́н!

Валенти́н	**Здра́вствуй, Стив! Здра́вствуй, А́нна! Наконе́ц!**
А́нна	**Здра́вствуй, Валенти́н! Как прия́тно тебя́ ви́деть!**
Валенти́н	**Как долете́ли?**
Стив	**Прекра́сно, спаси́бо.**

Валентин	Как вы поживаете? Хотите есть, пить?
Анна	Спасибо нет, Валентин. Я немножко устала.
Стив	Я тоже немножко устал. Но я, как всегда, очень хочу есть и пить.
Валентин	Хорошо, мы скоро будем дома. Ирина там ждёт.

☑ Упражнение 8

Listen to the dialogue or read it and find the Russian for:

(a) How lovely to see you!
(б) How are you?
(в) I am a little tired.
(г) as always
(д) We will soon be at home.

☑ Упражнение 9

Read out loud the arrival dates and times of these travellers.

(a) Салли будет в Сочи   16/8, в 22,30.
(б) Станислав будет в Мурманске   5/11, в 10,15.
(в) Люба будет в Москве   29/5, в 13,50.
(г) Алла будет в Иркутске   10/2, в 15,20.

Обмен валюты
Currency exchange

Now that you are through passport control and customs, you may need to change some money into roubles. To do this you need to find a sign saying **обмен валюты** *exchange of currency*. Check the exchange rate – **курс** – and don't forget to get your **декларация** stamped and keep your receipt.

☑ Упражнение 10

Look at these numerals 1 – 10 written by hand, and copy them until you can write them authentically without looking at the original.

1
2
3
4
5

6
7
8
9
10

Упражнéние 11

At the information office **спрáвочное бюрó** of the airport you overhear people asking where the check-in **регистрáция** is for various flights **рéйсы:** Скажи́те, пожáлуйста, где регистрáция, рейс вóсемьсот сéмьдесят дéвять (879) в Лóндон?

For practice, you decide to note down the flight numbers. Listen to the cassette and fill in the numbers as a Russian would write them.

(а) Рейс _____ в Дéли.
(б) Рейс _____ в Амстердáм.
(в) Рейс _____ в Цю́рих.
(г) Рейс _____ в Пари́ж.
(д) Рейс _____ в Нью-Йóрк.

Упражнéние 12

Rearrange the words in these questions so that they make sense. You could choose to say the sentences out loud, number the words, or write them.

(а) пить вы что хоти́те?
(б) вáша как фами́лия?
(в) мéсто моё где?
(г) вас фу́нты есть стéрлингов у?
(д) вáша чемодáн э́то и сýмка ваш?

☑ Упражнёние 13

Match up the questions and answers.

а.) Где моё место?

б) Где ваша виза?

в) Вы бизнесмен?

г.) Это ваш багаж?

д) У вас есть доллары?

е.) Что вы хотите пить?

ж) У вас есть русские газеты?

1) Нет, я турист.

2) Нет, это не мой багаж.

3) Нет, у меня есть фунты.

4) Чай, пожалуйста.

5) Пятое "г", налево.

6) Да, русские и английские.

7) Вот она.

👤 Анекдо́т

This anecdote from pre-glasnost days is about a Russian emigré in America recalling life in the Soviet Union. He explains why he chose to emigrate. There is one key phrase you need before you begin: **Нельзя́ пожа́ловаться** *Mustn't grumble.*

Интервьюёр	**Проду́кты есть в Москве́?**
Ру́сский эмигра́нт	**Нельзя́ пожа́ловаться.**
Интервьюёр	**И как тра́нспорт в Москве́?**
Ру́сский эмигра́нт	**Нельзя́ пожа́ловаться.**
Интервьюёр	**Как там больни́цы?**
Ру́сский эмигра́нт	**Нельзя́ пожа́ловаться.**
Интервьюёр	**И как там шко́лы?**
Ру́сский эмигра́нт	**Нельзя́ пожа́ловаться.**
Интервьюёр	**Почему́ вы сейча́с живёте в Аме́рике?**
Ру́сский эмигра́нт	**Потому́, что здесь мо́жно пожа́ловаться.**

1 Which four aspects of Soviet life was the emigré questioned about?

2 What was his reason for emigrating?

Congratulations on successfully negotiating the airport! Now it's time to look at other situations in which you might find yourself if visiting Russia or entertaining Russian guests at home.

13

КАК ПОПА́СТЬ НА МОСКО́ВСКИЙ ВОКЗА́Л?

How do I get to Moskovsky station?

In this unit you will learn

- how to use public transport
- more about asking directions

Before you start, revise

- directions, Unit 5
- numbers and telling the time, pages 84
- how to say *to* Moscow and *in* Moscow, page 54, 78

Russian distinguishes between going somewhere on foot and by some means of transport, so two verbs which will be useful to you are **идти́** *to go on foot* (page 00) and **е́хать** *to go by transport*.

идти́ *to go on foot*		**е́хать** *to go by transport*	
я иду́	мы идём	я е́ду	мы е́дем
ты идёшь	вы идёте	ты е́дешь	вы е́дете
он/она́ идёт	они́ иду́т	он/она́ е́дет	они́ е́дут

Городско́й тра́нспорт
Public transport

To find the stop for a bus, trolleybus or tram, look out for these signs.

A for a bus **авто́бус**, **П** for a trolleybus **тролле́йбус**, **Т** for a tram

трамва́й. The signs for buses and trolleybuses are usually attached to a wall, but tram signs are suspended from cables over the road.

To travel on any of these vehicles you need a ticket **тало́н**. These may be bought from kiosks or from the bus driver, singly or in strips of ten called a little book **кни́жечка**. Plain clothes inspectors fine people travelling without a ticket. Some people prefer to buy a season ticket **еди́ный биле́т** which covers all forms of transport including the metro. When you get on, you should get your ticket punched at one of the little contraptions mounted in the vehicle. If it is too crowded to reach one, ask someone to do it for you: **Пробе́йте тало́н, пожа́луйста**. If someone is trying to get off when the vehicle is crowded they will say: **Вы сейча́с выхо́дите?** *Are you getting off now?* If you are not, you should try to let them past.

авто́бус	bus
тролле́йбус	trolleybus
трамва́й	tram
остано́вка (на)	stop
остано́вка авто́буса	bus stop
остано́вка тролле́йбуса	trolleybus stop
остано́вка трамва́я	tram stop
тало́н	ticket (bus, trolleybus and tram)
кни́жечка	little book (strip of 10 tickets)
еди́ный (биле́т)	season ticket for all forms of transport
пешко́м	on foot
мину́та	minute
Как попа́сть в...?	How do I get to ...?
Сади́тесь на пя́тый авто́бус	Get on to bus no. 5
Пробе́йте тало́н, пожа́луйста	Punch my ticket, please
Когда́ мне выходи́ть?	When do I need to get off?
Че́рез три остано́вки	after 3 stops
Вы сейча́с выхо́дите?	Are you getting off now?

Диало́г 1 Как попа́сть в цирк?

Robert has arranged to meet Slava at the circus, but he doesn't know how to get there.

Ро́берт	Де́вушка, извини́те, пожа́луйста, как попа́сть в цирк?
Де́вушка	В цирк? Сади́тесь на четы́рнадцатый трамва́й.
Ро́берт	Где остано́вка?
Де́вушка	Там, напра́во. Ви́дите?
Ро́берт	Да. А мо́жно пешко́м?

Дéвушка **Мóжно.**
Рóберт **Скóлько минýт пешкóм, и скóлько на трамвáе?**
Дéвушка **Пешкóм двáдцать – трúдцать минýт. А на трамвáе дéсять.**

On the tram

Рóберт **Извинúте, я éду в цирк. Когдá мне выходúть?**
Бáбушка **Чéрез три останóвки.**
Рóберт **Пробéйте талóн, пожáлуйста.**

Three stops later

Рóберт **Вы сейчáс выхóдите?**
Молодóй человéк **Да.**

Упражнéние 1

Listen to the dialogue above, and say (a) which tram Robert has to catch (б) where the tram stop is (в) how long it would take on foot (г) how long it would take by tram (д) how many stops he has to travel.

Now work through the dialogue playing the parts of дéвушка and бáбушка, and altering these details: (е) Robert needs bus no. 8 (ж) the bus stop is straight ahead (з) it will take 30 – 40 minutes on foot and 15 on the bus (и) he needs to get off after 4 stops.

Упражнéние 2

В АВТОБУСЕ НЕЛЬЗЯ КУРИТЬ!

You see this sign on a bus. What must you not do?

МЕТРÓ *The metro*

To spot a metro station **стáнция метрó** look out for a big red letter **M**. To enter the metro, you buy a token **жетóн** from the window at the station, insert it into the automatic barrier, pass through the turnstile and you are free to travel as far as you want. The metro generally runs from at least 6 a.m. to midnight. At each station an announcement is made. The order varies, but it will usually include the name of the station you are at, **Стáнция «Лубя́нка»**, the name of the next station, **Слéдующая стáнция – «Китáй Гóрод»**, and a warning to be careful because the doors are shutting, **Осторóжно. Двéри закрывáются**.

стáнция метрó	*metro station*
жетóн	*token*
автомáт	*slot*
турникéт	*turnstile*
пересáдка	*change*
без пересáдки	*without a change*
с пересáдкой	*with a change*
дéлать пересáдку	*to make a change*
доéдете до стáнции ...	*go as far as station ...*

Look out for these signs:

ВХОД	*entrance*
ВЫ́ХОД	*exit*
НЕТ ВХÓДА	*no entrance*
НЕТ ВЫ́ХОДА	*no exit*
К ПОЕЗДÁМ	*to the trains*
ПЕРЕХÓД НА СТÁНЦИЮ	*Transfer to station 'Theatre Square'*
«ТЕАТРÁЛЬНАЯ ПЛÓЩАДЬ»	

 Диалóг 2 На метрó

Martin has heard that the view over Moscow from the University is worth seeing. He has left his plan of the metro at the hotel so he stops Valya and asks her the way.

Мáртин	**Скажи́те пожáлуйста, как попáсть в университéт?**
Вáля	**На метрó?**
Мáртин	**Да, на метрó.**
Вáля	**Хорошó. Там налéво стáнция метрó. «Парк Культýры».**

Мáртин	**Поня́тно.**
Вáля	**На метро́ дое́дете до ста́нции «Университе́т».**
Мáртин	**Э́то далеко́?**
Вáля	**Нет, четы́ре остано́вки.**
Мáртин	**Спаси́бо.**

Упражне́ние 3

(a) In the dialogue above, which station does Martin go from?
(б) Which station must he go to?
(в) How many stops does he have to go?

Упражне́ние 4

You are staying with Lydia in Moscow, but she has to work today. She writes you out a list of places you could visit and how to get there.

станция метро

Кремль — *Александровский сад*
Ботанический сад — *Ботанический сад*
Рынок — *Пушкинская*
Дом книги — *Арбатская*
ГУМ — *Площадь Революции*

Which metro station do you need for (a) Red Square (б) the market (в) the book shop (г) the botanical gardens (д) the department store *GUM*?

Another friend wants to meet you later. Arrange which metro station to meet at and write it down so you don't forget. (You choose which one!)

Now make up questions and answers based on the information above, for example – Скажи́те, пожа́луйста, как попа́сть в Кремль? – Дое́дете до ста́нции «Алекса́ндровский сад».

—— ВОКЗА́Л   *The train station* ——

Russian trains offer differing degrees of comfort: **мя́гкий** *soft* (*seated*), **жёсткий** *hard* (*seated*) and **спа́льный** *sleeper*. Each train has a **проводни́к** or **проводни́ца** *conductor*, who checks tickets and supplies bedding and tea on long journeys. The names of main-line stations refer to the places to and from which trains travel, so **Ки́евский вокза́л** in Moscow is where you would catch a train to Kiev, and **Моско́вский вокза́л** in St. Petersburg is where you would catch a train to Moscow. If Russian friends are going to see you off on a long journey, you may find that before leaving home, everyone sits down for a moment in silence. This is a tradition meant to bring the traveller safely back home.

вокза́л (на)	station
по́езд (*pl* поезда́)	train(s)
ско́рый по́езд	express train
электри́чка	suburban electric train
ваго́н	carriage
купе́	compartment
ме́сто	seat
ваго́н-рестора́н	dining car
расписа́ние	timetable
отправле́ние	departure
платфо́рма	platform
обра́тный биле́т	return ticket
биле́т в оди́н коне́ц	single ticket
мя́гкий ваго́н	soft (seated) carriage
жёсткий ваго́н	hard (seated) carriage
спа́льный ваго́н	sleeper carriage
По́езд отхо́дит в 7 часо́в	The train leaves at 7 o'clock
проводни́к, проводни́ца	conductor
касси́р	ticket office cashier
пассажи́р	passenger
для куря́щих	for smokers
для некуря́щих	for non-smokers

Look out for these notices:

ВЫ́ХОД В ГО́РОД	exit to the town
ЗАЛ ОЖИДА́НИЯ	waiting room
БУФЕ́Т	snack bar
КА́ССА	ticket office

🔊 Диало́г 3 Когда́ отхо́дит по́езд?

Trevor wants to travel to Moscow by train to see Konstantina. First he goes to the **ка́сса** to get a ticket.

Тре́вор	**Да́йте, пожа́луйста, оди́н обра́тный биле́т в Москву́ на шесто́е а́вгуста.**
Касси́р	**Одну́ мину́точку... Хорошо́. По́езд семь, ваго́н трина́дцать.**
Тре́вор	**Когда́ отхо́дит по́езд?**
Касси́р	**У́тром, в де́сять часо́в три́дцать мину́т.**

Шесто́го а́вгуста. На платфо́рме:

Тре́вор	**Э́то трина́дцатый ваго́н?**
Проводни́ца	**Да. Ваш биле́т, пожа́луйста.**
Тре́вор	**Вот он.**
Проводни́ца	**Второ́е ме́сто. Иди́те в пе́рвое купе́, пожа́луйста.**
Тре́вор	**Скажи́те, в по́езде есть ваго́н-рестора́н?**
Проводни́ца	**Есть.**
Тре́вор	**Когда́ он открыва́ется?**
Проводни́ца	**В оди́ннадцать часо́в.**

Упражне́ние 5

Re-read the dialogue above and find out (a) on which date Trevor wants to travel (б) the number of his train and carriage (в) the departure time (г) the seat number (д) the opening time of the dining car.

– Мя́гкий ваго́н ищу́.

ищу́	I am looking for

☑ Упражне́ние 6

Read this timetable and give out information about it, for example, **По́езд но́мер пятьсо́т оди́ннадцать в Петербу́рг отхо́дит в де́вять часо́в три́дцать шесть.**

РАСПИСА́НИЕ

ПО́ЕЗД		ОТПРАВЛЕ́НИЕ
№ 511	ПЕТЕРБУ́РГ	9.36
№ 96	НО́ВГОРОД	12.55
№ 716	ИВА́НОВО	20.47
№ 82	ТУ́ЛА	23.05

Now look back to Trevor's dialogue at the ticket office and substitute the St. Petersburg train for Trevor's train, altering the dialogue accordingly. Perhaps you could change other details as well, or write down part of the conversation in English or Russian.

——— ТАКСИ́ *Taxi* ———

Official taxis are black Volgas with a chequered pattern and the letter **T** on the door, and the fare is supposed to be metered. There are also private unmetered taxis, but some Russians prefer to hitch a lift with a passing vehicle and negotiate a fare.

такси́	taxi
маршру́тное такси́	fixed-route minibus taxi
маши́на	car
автомоби́ль (*m*)	car
стоя́нка такси́ (на)	taxi rank
Такси́! Свобо́дно?	Taxi! Are you free?
Куда́ пое́дем?	Where are we going?
Не волну́йтесь	Don't worry!

Диало́г 4 Такси́!

Lorna is in a hurry to catch a train at **Моско́вский вокза́л** so she flags down a taxi.

Ло́рна	**Такси́! Свобо́дно?**
Такси́ст	**Сади́тесь. Куда́ пое́дем?**
Ло́рна	**На Моско́вский вокза́л, пожа́луйста.**
Такси́ст	**Когда́ отхо́дит ваш по́езд?**
Ло́рна	**В де́вять часо́в со́рок мину́т.**
Такси́ст	**Не волну́йтесь. Мы ско́ро бу́дем на вокза́ле.**

Упражне́ние 7

(а) At what time does her train leave?

(б) Will she be in time to catch it?

(в) Now put yourself in Lorna's position. You are going to Kiev, so you need to go to **Ки́евский вокза́л** and your train leaves at 10 o'clock. What will you say to the taxi driver?

Now that you know all the forms of transport, here is a summary of how to say *I am going to the university* **on the bus** etc. **Я е́ду в университе́т на авто́бусе.**

авто́бус		авто́бусе
тролле́йбус		тролле́йбусе
трамва́й		трамва́е
такси́	**на**	такси́
метро́		метро́
маши́на		маши́не
автомоби́ль		автомоби́ле
по́езд		по́езде

Упражне́ние 8

Would you understand these instructions and signs?

(а) **Сади́тесь на пя́тый тролле́йбус** means

    (i)   Get on trolleybus no. 15

    (ii) Get on trolleybus no. 5

    (iii) Get on trolleybus no. 50

(б) **ВЫ́ХОД В ГО́РОД** means

   (i)   To the trains
   (ii) No exit
   (iii) Exit to the town

(в) **Да́йте, пожа́луйста, обра́тный биле́т** means

   (i)   Please give me a return ticket.
   (ii) Please give me a single ticket.
   (iii) Please give me a metro token.

Упражне́ние 9

How would you say:

(а) How do I get to the Kremlin?
(б) Where is the bus stop?
(в) Are you getting off now?
(г) I am going to the Botanical Gardens on the metro.
(д) What time does the train leave?

Анекдо́т 1

This anecdote is about a man and a little boy on a bus. The words below will help you to understand it, but you need only learn **е́сли** *if* for active use. Notice that the man is addressed as **дя́дя** *uncle*, meaning that he is probably too old to be called **молодо́й челове́к**.

вхо́дит	*(he) gets on*
пробива́ет (тало́н)	*punches (a ticket)*
ма́льчик	*boy*
е́сли я теря́ю	*if I lose*
е́сли вы теря́ете	*if you lose*
дура́к	*fool*

Челове́к вхо́дит в авто́бус и пробива́ет три тало́на.

Ма́льчик **Дя́дя, почему́ у вас три тало́на?**
Челове́к **Е́сли я теря́ю пе́рвый тало́н, у меня́ второ́й есть.**
Ма́льчик **А е́сли вы теря́ете второ́й тало́н?**
Челове́к **У меня́ тре́тий есть.**

Ма́льчик **А е́сли вы теря́ете тре́тий тало́н?**
Челове́к **Я не дура́к! У меня́ еди́ный биле́т.**

1 Why does the man punch the third **тало́н** *ticket*?
2 Why does he not need any **тало́ны** *tickets* at all?

Анекдо́т 2

This anecdote is set in a train and is about someone who can't find his way back to his carriage from the dining-car. Again, you do not need to learn the vocabulary for active use, although **Что вы!**, or **Что ты!**, *What?!* is excellent for expressing amazement!

я не по́мню	*I can't remember*
что вы!	*What on earth?!*
за окно́м	*through the window*
был	*there was*

В по́езде е́дет дура́к. Он обе́дает в ваго́н-рестора́не.

Дура́к **Извини́те, де́вушка, я не по́мню, где мой ваго́н.**
Проводни́ца **Что вы! Вы не зна́ете, где ваш ваго́н?**
Дура́к **Нет, не зна́ю. Но за окно́м лес был.**

1 Who does he ask to solve his problem?
2 What does he remember seeing through his carriage window?

14

ГДЕ МО́ЖНО КУПИ́ТЬ САМОВА́Р?
Where can I buy a samovar?

In this unit you will learn

- more about shopping
- what to buy and where

Before you start, revise

- shopping vocabulary from unit 6, pages 63–4
- numbers, page 235; times, page 84; directions, page 54; days of the week, page 87.

— Где плати́ть? *Where do I pay?* —

As mentioned before, the system of shopping in many state-owned shops involves quite a bit of queueing. The word for a queue is **о́чередь**. First you queue to find out the availability and price of what you want, then queue a second time at the **ка́сса** to pay for the goods and collect the **чек**. At the cash desk you will need to say for which number department **отде́л** you need the receipt. Finally you queue for a third time to hand over the receipt and collect the goods. This system, and the fact that many shops sell an unpredictable variety of goods, can make shopping a long process. However, for the language learner the queues and transactions are an opportunity not to be missed! This sort of shopping is far more interesting than using the many Western-style shops and supermarkets where you simply take your goods to the till, or where the prices are so high that the queues have melted away!

Сувениры *Souvenirs*

A samovar **самовар** is an urn, usually powered by charcoal or electricity, in which water is heated. Very strong tea is made in a tiny tea pot which stands on top of the samovar to keep warm. A little strong tea is poured into a glass and topped up with water from the samovar. Tea may be taken with sugar **сахар**, lemon **лимон** or fruit preserves **варенье**.

Other popular souvenirs which you have encountered in earlier units include the balalaika **балалайка**, which is a triangular stringed musical instrument used for playing Russian folk music, and the *matryoshka* doll **матрёшка**. The name means *little mother* and these dolls are made of wood, brightly painted, and when they are opened they reveal a whole series of smaller dolls hidden inside each other.

In this unit there are inevitably a lot of key words, but some of them you already know, and some you will not need to learn for active use. When you have learned as many of them as possible, test yourself by covering up first the English side and then the Russian, saying out loud the words which are hidden.

Ключевы́е слова́

What you say

Мо́жно посмотре́ть?	*May I have a look?*
Покажи́те, да́йте...	*Show me, give me...*
Ско́лько сто́ит? Ско́лько сто́ят?	*How much is it? How much are they?*
Напиши́те, пожа́луйста, ско́лько сто́ит	*Please write down how much it is*
Повтори́те, пожа́луйста, ме́дленнее	*Repeat that more slowly please*
У вас есть кни́ги о спо́рте?	*Do you have any books about sport?*
Пожа́луйста, да!	*Yes please.*
Спаси́бо, нет!	*No thank you.*
Ско́лько с меня́?	*How much do I owe?*
До́рого/недо́рого (d<u>o</u>ruga, ned<u>o</u>ruga)	*That's expensive/not expensive*
Всё? Да, всё.	*Is that all? Yes, that's all.*
Где плати́ть? В ка́ссу?	*Where do I pay? At the cash desk?*
Где ка́сса? Напро́тив.	*Where is the cash desk? Opposite.*
Пять ты́сяч рубле́й на второ́й отде́л	*5,000 roubles for department 2*
Магази́н откры́т/закры́т	*The shop is open/closed*
Я хочу́ купи́ть... Куда́ мне пойти́?	*I want to buy... Where should I go?*
Где продаю́тся газе́ты?	*Where are newspapers sold?*

☑ Упражне́ние 1

What does this shop sell?

What the shop assistant says

Слу́шаю вас	I'm listening (May I help)
Вам помо́чь?	May I help you?
Что вы хоти́те?	What do you want?
Ско́лько вы хоти́те?	How much do you want?
Сыр сто́ит 15,000 рубле́й килогра́мм	Cheese costs 15,000 roubles a kilo

Где мо́жно купи́ть проду́кты?
Where can you buy food?

Универса́м *Supermarket*

суперма́ркет	supermarket
гастроно́м	grocer's
Здесь продаю́тся...	Here you can buy...
проду́кты	provisions
мя́со	meat
ры́ба	fish
колбаса́	sausage (salami)
соси́ска	sausage (frankfurter)
ко́фе, чай, са́хар	coffee, tea, sugar
конфе́ты	sweets
торт	cake
вино́, пи́во, во́дка	wine, beer, vodka

Моло́чные проду́кты *Dairy produce*

молоко́	milk
смета́на	sour cream
сыр	cheese
ма́сло	butter

Бу́лочная *Bakery*

Чёрный/бе́лый хлеб	black/white bread
бато́н	long loaf
бу́лка	sweet bread roll
су́шка	dry ring-shaped biscuit

Ры́нок *Market*

свѐжие фру́кты/о́вощи/цветы́	*fresh fruits/vegetables/flowers*
я́блоко (*pl.* я́блоки)	*apple(s)*
гру́ша	*pear*
апельси́н	*orange*
карто́шка	*potato*
помидо́р	*tomato*
огуре́ц (*pl.* огурцы́)	*cucumber(s)*

Ско́лько вы хоти́те?
How much do you want?

You will find that after any expression of quantity (kilo, litre, packet, etc.) the next word will change its ending: **кило́ бана́нов** *a kilo of bananas*. This is called the *genitive case*. It is not essential for you at this stage to know how this works. Not knowing the endings will not prevent you from understanding or being understood.

кило́	*kilo*
грамм	*gram*
литр	*litre*
метр	*metre*
ба́нка	*jar, tin*
буты́лка	*bottle*
па́чка	*packet*
сто грамм/пятьсо́т грамм	*100 grams/500 grams*

🔊 Диало́г 1 В гастроно́ме

Nick is looking for some cheese. Read the dialogue and answer the questions below.

Продавщи́ца	Слу́шаю вас.
Ник	У вас есть сыр?
Продавщи́ца	Сыр у нас есть? Да, коне́чно. Вот он.
Ник	Како́й э́то сыр? Мо́жно посмотре́ть, пожа́луйста?

Продавщи́ца	Мо́жно. Э́то эсто́нский сыр. Сто́ит пятна́дцать ты́сяч рубле́й кило́.
Ник	Повтори́те, пожа́луйста, ме́дленнее.
Продавщи́ца	Пятна́дцать ты́сяч рубле́й.
Ник	Э́то до́рого?
Продавщи́ца	Нет, недо́рого. Ско́лько вы хоти́те?
Ник	Пятьсо́т грамм. Ско́лько с меня́?
Продавщи́ца	Семь ты́сяч пятьсо́т рубле́й. Всё?
Ник	Да, всё. Где плати́ть?
Продавщи́ца	В ка́ссу.
Ник	А где ка́сса?
Продавщи́ца	Напро́тив. Ви́дите?
Ник	Да. Спаси́бо. Како́й здесь отде́л?
Продавщи́ца	Четвёртый.

Упражне́ние 2

(а) Where do you think the cheese is from, and how much does it cost? Find the Russian for (б) Could I have a look? (в) How much do you want? (г) Is that all? (д) Opposite.

Now put yourself in Nick's place and work through the dialogue covering up his lines and saying his part.

Bear in mind that any prices quoted in this book may be out of date, as the economic situation in Russia makes prices unpredictable.

Упражне́ние 3

Lists of food prices are printed in newspapers to keep consumers up to date. Read this list, identify the products, and answer the questions.

Майоне́з
Сыр Эда́мский, Голла́ндия
Киви́, Гре́ция
Лимо́ны, Испа́ния
Мандари́ны, Испа́ния
Ке́тчуп, Болга́рия
Чай инди́йский
Ко́фе, Брази́лия
Шокола́д, Герма́ния
Во́дка, «Столи́чная», «Смирнофф», «Абсолют»

(a) Which two fruits from Spain can you buy?
(б) What sort of cheese is there?
(в) What has been imported from Bulgaria?
(г) What sort of tea can you buy?
(д) Which brands of vodka are listed?

☑ Упражнéние 4

You are in a **гастронóм**. Listen on your cassette to people asking for things. Underline the items on the list which you hear requested. For further practice, you could copy the list.

чай
огурец
сосиски
банка кофе
кило помидоров
рыба

сахар
колбаса
конфеты
торт
мясо
бутылка пива

Упражнéние 5

Find five drinks and six types of food in this box.

кофе
ФРУКТОВАЯ ВОДА
ВОДКА
шоколад
ЛАНЧЕН МИТ
чай фруктовый
СОУСЫ И КЕТЧУПЫ
КАРАМЕЛЬ
конфеты
шампанское

☑ Упражне́ние 6

Ask in the **гастроно́м** if they have:

(a) salami sausage (б) tea (в) cake (г) fish (д) milk (e) oranges
(ж) cucumbers

Ходи́ть по магази́нам
Going round the shops

Универма́г *Department store*

пода́рок (pl пода́рки)	*present(s)*
оде́жда	*clothes*
джи́нсы	*jeans*
ша́пка	*fur hat*

Сувени́ры *Souvenirs*

матрёшка	*stacking* matryoshka *doll*
электри́ческий самова́р	*electric samovar*
плато́к (pl платки́)	*shawl(s)*
деревя́нная игру́шка	*woooden toy*

Кио́ск *Kiosk*

газе́та, журна́л, план	*newspaper, magazine, plan*
откры́тка	*postcard*
моро́женое	*ice cream*

Апте́ка *Chemist's*

аспири́н	*aspirin*
лека́рство	*medicine*

Диало́г 2 Ру́сские сувени́ры

Chris is asking Oleg to help organise her day. Read the dialogue several
times and then answer the questions below it.

Крис Я сего́дня хочу́ ходи́ть по магази́нам.

Оле́г Что ты хо́чешь купи́ть?

Крис Пода́рки и сувени́ры. Я хочу́ купи́ть кни́ги, деревя́нные игру́шки, откры́тки и самова́р. Я о́чень люблю́ ру́сский чай с лимо́ном.

Оле́г Поня́тно. Кни́ги и откры́тки продаю́тся в магази́не «Дом Кни́ги». Э́то недалеко́.

Крис А где продаю́тся самова́ры и игру́шки?

Оле́г В магази́не «Ру́сский сувени́р». Кото́рый сейча́с час?

Крис Де́вять часо́в.

Оле́г Хорошо́. «Дом Кни́ги» открыва́ется в де́вять часо́в.

Крис Как попа́сть в «Дом Кни́ги»?

Оле́г Три остано́вки на авто́бусе. Остано́вка там, напро́тив.

Later, in «Ру́сский сувени́р»:

Де́вушка Вам помо́чь?

Крис Пожа́луйста, да! Покажи́те, пожа́луйста, э́тот самова́р. Нет, вот э́тот. Оле́г, како́й э́то краси́вый самова́р! Де́вушка, э́то электри́ческий самова́р?

Де́вушка Да, электри́ческий. Отку́да вы?

Крис Я англича́нка, живу́ в Ло́ндоне.

Дéвушка	Не волнýйтесь. Моя́ тётя живёт в Лóндоне, и она́ говори́т, что на́ши самова́ры хорошó там рабóтают.
Крис	Поня́тно. Покажи́те, пожа́луйста, э́ти деревя́нные игру́шки. Да, кра́сные и зелёные. И вот э́ти жёлтые.
Дéвушка	Вот э́ти?
Крис	Да. Спаси́бо. Напиши́те, пожа́луйста, скóлько они́ стóят.

☑ Упражнéние 7

(а) What does Chris want to do today?
(б) What four things does she want to buy?
(в) Is it far to the book shop?
(г) Where is the bus stop?
(д) What is the Russian for *she says that*?
(е) How does Chris know that the samovar will work in England?
(ж) What colours are the toys she wants to look at?

Now you could make up your own dialogue, buying things which you would particularly like.

☑ Упражнéние 8

Read the shopping list on the left and match up the items with an appropriate shop on the right. You could then rewrite the list correctly.

аспири́н	ки́оск
ма́сло	сувени́ры
са́хар	ры́нок
вино́	молóчные продýкты
морóженое	универса́м
цветы́	апте́ка
хлеб	универма́г
самова́р	бýлочная
ша́пка	гастронóм

☑ Упражне́ние 9

Listen to the three conversations on your cassette. Note down in Russian or English what Sasha wants to buy, the shop he needs and the directions he is given.

Са́ша хо́чет купи́ть ...	Магази́н	Куда́?
(а)		
(б)		
(в)		

☑ Упражне́ние 10

Here is an alphabetical list of the types of shops you could find in a major Russian city. You have met many of the words, and the rest you can probably work out.

Автомоби́ли
Антиквариа́т
А́удио-Видеоте́хника
Бу́лочная
Гастроно́м
Диети́ческие проду́кты
Кни́ги
Колбаса́
Косме́тика
Моло́чные проду́кты
Музыка́льные инструме́нты

Мя́со
О́вощи-фру́кты
О́птика
Пода́рки
Ры́ба
Спорти́вные това́ры
Сувени́ры
Таба́к
Цветы́
Часы́

Read the list and underline where you think you could buy (а) spectacles (б) a watch (в) a bread roll (г) antiques (д) food for a special diet (е) a herring (ж) a trombone (з) a video player (и) a car.

☑ Упражне́ние 11

How would you say:

(a) I want to buy some bread, cheese, tomatoes and tea.
(б) Where can I buy a newspaper?
(в) That's all.
(г) Repeat that, please.
(д) Do you have any white wine?
(е) How much is it?

🙂 Анекдо́т

This anecdote from the times of food shortages is set in an empty butcher's shop opposite an empty fish shop. How would you say the punch-line in English?

Ба́бушка	**У вас есть мя́со?**
Продаве́ц	**Нет.**
Ба́бушка	**У вас есть колбаса́?**
Продаве́ц	**Нет.**
Ба́бушка	**У вас есть соси́ски?**
Продаве́ц	**Нет.**
Ба́бушка	**У вас есть ры́ба?**
Продаве́ц	**Нет. Ры́бы нет в магази́не напро́тив.**

And finally, here is a tongue twister for you to learn by heart to practise the letters **с** and **ш**. It means *Sasha walked along the road and sucked a biscuit.* (lit. *walked Sasha along road and sucked biscuit*).

Шла Са́ша по шоссе́ и соса́ла су́шку.

—————15—————

В ЧЁМ ДЕ́ЛО?
What's the matter?

In this unit you will learn

- how to book a hotel room
- how to complain
- how to sort out problems

Before you start, revise

- vocabulary and structures from unit 7
- у вас есть . .? unit 10, page 112

When learning new vocabulary, decide which words it will be most useful to learn and which you only need to recognise. Test yourself by covering up the English words first and then the Russian words, and see how many you can remember.

————— В гости́нице *At the hotel* —————

Like hotels the world over, you will find that Russian hotels vary, but many will provide these facilities: a restaurant **рестора́н**, bar **бар**, café **кафе́**, shops **магази́ны**, post office **по́чта**, service desk **бюро́ обслу́живания**, bureau de change **обме́н валю́ты**, lost property office **бюро́ нахо́док**, cloakroom **гардеро́б**, lifts **ли́фты** and hairdresser's **парикма́херская**.

ОТ СЕБЯ/К СЕБЕ *PUSH/PULL*

От себя and **к себе** mean literally *away from yourself* and *towards yourself*. This is what you will see on doors in public buildings to tell you when to push and when to pull.

Заказáть нóмер *Booking a room*

У вас есть свобóдный нóмер/ свобóдная кóмната?	Do you have a free room?
нóмер на одногó с вáнной	a room for one with a bath
нóмер на двои́х с ду́шем	a room for two with a shower
нóмер на день	a room for a day
нóмер на 2,3,4 дня	a room for 2, 3, 4 days
нóмер на 5,6 дней	a room for 5, 6 days
нóмер на недéлю	a room for a week
день, недéля, мéсяц, год	day, week, month, year
Скóлько стóит нóмер в день?	How much is a room per day?
Мóжно заказáть нóмер?	Could I book a room?
нóмер на одногó на четы́рнадцатое мáя	a room for one for 14th May
к сожалéнию	unfortunately
к счáстью	fortunately
зáвтрак начинáется/кончáется в . . .	breakfast starts/finishes at . . .
Когдá нáдо заплати́ть?	When do I have to pay?
вчерá, сегóдня, зáвтра	yesterday, today, tomorrow
счёт	the bill
прáвильно/непрáвильно	that's right/that's not right

Диалóг 1 У вас есть свобóдный нóмер?

Steve has just arrived at a hotel without having made a reservation. Listen to or read the dialogue. When you have got the gist of the conversation, look at the questions below and answer them.

Стив	**У вас есть свобóдный нóмер на сегóдня?**
Администрáтор	**Да, есть. Какóй нóмер вы хоти́те?**
Стив	**Нóмер на одногó с вáнной, пожáлуйста.**
Администрáтор	**К сожалéнию, у нас тóлько большóй нóмер на двои́х с ду́шем.**
Стив	**Скажи́те, пожáлуйста, скóлько стóит нóмер на двои́х?**
Администрáтор	**Сто двáдцать дóлларов в день.**
Стив	**Это дóрого. Когдá нáдо заплати́ть?**

Администра́тор	**За́втра.**
Стив	**В кото́ром часу́ начина́ется за́втрак?**
Администра́тор	**В семь часо́в. И конча́ется в де́вять часо́в.**
Стив	**Мо́жно обе́дать в гости́нице?**
Администра́тор	**Коне́чно, мо́жно. В гости́нице о́чень хоро́ший рестора́н. Вот ваш ключ. Ваш но́мер – 104.**
Стив	**Спаси́бо. А как попа́сть в но́мер 104? У меня́ чемода́н и больша́я су́мка.**
Администра́тор	**Лифт пря́мо и напра́во.**

✅ Упражне́ние 1

(а) What sort of room does Steve want? (б) What is he offered? (в) How much does it cost per day? (г) When does he have to pay? (д) What is the earliest he may have breakfast? And the latest? (е) Can he have dinner in the hotel? (ж) What luggage does he have? (з) Where is the lift?

✅ Упражне́ние 2

Steve decides to go out and explore the town, but first he must give his key to the woman on duty on his landing.

Дежу́рная	**Молодо́й челове́к, где ваш ключ?**
Стив	**Вот он. Скажи́те, в кото́ром часу́ но́чью закрыва́ется вход?**
Дежу́рная	**В по́лночь.**
Стив	**Спаси́бо. А где здесь бар?**
Дежу́рная	**Внизу́. Нале́во.**

(а) At what time does the entrance to the hotel close? (б) Where is the bar?

✅ Упражне́ние 3

Listen to these customers. What sort of rooms do they want, and for how long?

(а)

(б)

(в)

✅ Упражнéние 4

Complete your part of this dialogue.

(а)	You	*Do you have a free room?*
	Администрáтор	**Да. Какóй нóмер вы хотúте?**
(б)	You	*A double room with a bath, please.*
	Администрáтор	**Однý минýточку. Да, у нас есть нóмер на двоúх с вáнной. Стóит сто дóлларов в день.**
(в)	You	*Good. What time is dinner?*
	Администрáтор	**Обéд начинáется в шесть часóв.**
(г)	You	*Is there a lift here? I have a big suitcase.*
	Администрáтор	**Да, лифт прямо, вúдите?**
(д)	You	*Yes, I see.*
	Администрáтор	**Вот ваш ключ. Ваш нóмер – 34.**
(е)	You	*Thank you. Room number 34. Is that right?*
	Администрáтор	**Да. прáвильно. Нóмер 34.**
(ж)	You	*Thank you very much. Goodbye.*

—— В нóмере *In the hotel room* ——

окнó	*window*	**вáнная**	*bathroom*
дверь (f)	*door*	**туалéт**	*toilet*
стол	*table*	**душ**	*shower*
стул	*chair*	**вáнна**	*bath*
крéсло	*armchair*	**кран**	*tap*
шкаф	*cupbord*	**одеяло**	*blanket*
кровáть (f)	*bed*	**подýшка**	*pillow*
лáмпа	*lamp*	**полотéнце**	*towel*
телефóн	*telephone*	**мыло**	*soap*
телевúзор	*television*	**шампýнь** (m)	*shampoo*
часы	*clock*	**зéркало**	*mirror*

To help you learn this vocabulary you could make labels for your furniture at home.

✅ Упражнéние 5

The vocabulary list above is a checklist of things which should be in each hotel room. Look at the pictures and make a list in Russian (written or spoken) of those things which Simon has in his room. Or you could underline the items in the vocabulary list. Make another list of what is missing in his room.

В номере холодно *It's cold in my room*

жарко	it's hot	тихо	it's quiet
тепло	it's warm	грязно	it's dirty
холодно	it's cold	мне холодно	I'm cold
шумно	it's noisy	мне плохо	I feel bad

Упражнение 6

Choose appropriate words from the list above to describe what it is like in these places.

(a) На пляже _____ и _____.
(б) В Антарктике _____ и _____.
(в) На концерте _____ и _____.
(г) В больнице _____ и _____.

(д) В бассе́йне _____ и _____.

Чем я могу́ вам помо́чь?
How may I help you?

Мо́жно ещё одея́ло, пожа́луйста	*Could I have another blanket, please?*
Я хочу́ заказа́ть биле́т в теа́тр на за́втра	*I want to book a theatre ticket for tomorrow*
Я хочу́ заказа́ть такси́ на за́втра на 10 часо́в	*I want to book a taxi for tomorrow at ten*
Куда́ вы пое́дете?	*Where are you going?*
Я хочу́ позвони́ть домо́й в Австра́лию	*I want to call home to Australia*
код в Австра́лию	*the code for Australia*
Мо́жно принести́ за́втрак в но́мер?	*Could you bring breakfast to my room?*

Диало́г 2 Алло́!

Your friend Katya is a hotel administrator. You go to work with her one day, and overhear the following conversations at her desk and while she is on the phone. To say *hello* on the phone you say **Алло́!**

Клайв	Извини́те, я хочу́ позвони́ть домо́й в Австра́лию. Мо́жно?
Ка́тя	Мо́жно. Код в Австра́лию 61.
А́нна	Алло́, э́то рестора́н?
Ка́тя	Нет, э́то администра́тор.
А́нна	Мо́жно принести́ за́втрак в но́мер, пожа́луйста? Мне пло́хо.
Ка́тя	Мо́жно. Что вы хоти́те?
А́нна	Чай с лимо́ном и фру́кты, пожа́луйста.
Тре́вор	Алло́, администра́тор?
Ка́тя	Да, слу́шаю.
Тре́вор	Я хочу́ заказа́ть такси́ на за́втра на 10 часо́в.
Ка́тя	Куда́ вы пое́дете?
Тре́вор	На вокза́л.
Ка́тя	У вас есть бага́ж?
Тре́вор	Да, чемода́н.

Упражнéние 7

(а) Where does Clive want to phone, and what code does he need?

(б) What does Anna want the restaurant to send to her room, and why?

(в) Where does Trevor want to go, and when?

To practise your writing, you could pretend to be the administrator and jot down notes in English or Russian to remind you what your customers wanted.

——— Проблéмы! *Problems!* ———

Всё хорошó?	*Is everything all right?*
В чём дéло?	*What's the matter?*
кáжется, мы потерáли ключ	*It seems we have lost the key*
горáчая/холóдная водá не идёт	*The hot/cold water is not running*
окнó выхóдит на плóщадь	*The window looks out onto the square*
окнó не открывáется/закрывáется	*The window won't open/shut*
телефóн не рабóтает	*The telephone doesn't work*
Как это мóжет быть?	*How can that be?*
У меня пропáл бумáжник/ фотоаппарáт/кошелёк (*m*)	*I have lost my wallet/camera/ purse*
У меня пропáла сýмка (*f*)	*I have lost my bag*
У меня пропáло пальтó (*n*)	*I have lost my coat*
У меня пропáли дéньги/ докумéнты (*pl*)	*I have lost my money/documents*
я, ты, он не/довóлен (*m*)	*I am, you are, he is un/happy*
я, ты, онá не/довóльна (*f*)	*I am, you are, she is un/happy*
мы, вы, они́ не/довóльны (*pl*)	*We, you, they are un/happy*
Спаси́бо большóе	*Thank you very much*

Диалóг 3 Извини́те

Read these dialogues, imagining you are the administrator.

(а)

Эдна   **Извини́те, в нóмере жáрко.**

Кáтя   **Окнó откры́то?**

Эдна   **Нет, закры́то. Окнó выхóдит на плóщадь, и там óчень шýмно.**

(б)

Марк   **Извини́те, мне хóлодно. Мóжно ещё одеáло, пожáлуйста?**

| Катя | Можно. Какой ваш номер? |
| Марк | Номер 73. Там холодно, кран не закрывается и телевизор плохо работает. |

(в)

Ванесса	Извините, кажется, мы потеряли ключ.
Катя	Какой ваш номер?
Ванесса	Шестнадцать.
Катя	Вот ваш ключ.
Ванесса	Здесь? У вас? Как это может быть? Спасибо большое.

(г)

Билл	Дайте, пожалуйста, счёт.
Катя	Вот счёт. Номер на двоих на неделю. Правильно?
Билл	Да, правильно.
Катя	Всё хорошо?
Билл	Да, здесь очень приятно. В номере тепло и тихо. Спасибо большое. Мы очень довольны.

(д)

| Катя | В чём дело? Вы недовольны? |
| Гари | Мы очень недовольны. Горячая вода не идёт, телефон не работает и в номере грязно. |

☑ Упражнение 8

Make brief notes in English of the conversations above.

☑ Упражнение 9

On the next page you will find a list of repair work for a hotel. What needs putting right in these rooms? Read the list out loud including the numbers, before summarising the problems in English.

номер 9, телевизор не работает
номер 14, телефон плохо работает
номер 23, кран не закрывается
номер 31, холодно, окно не закрывается
номер 35, жарко, окно не открывается
номер 40, шумно
номер 52, грязно
номер 55, радио не работает

Упражне́ние 10

You have been put in a room which is cold, dirty and noisy. The television doesn't work, the tap won't turn off and the window looks out onto the station. Bad luck! What will you say to the hotel administrator?

Упражне́ние 11

Listen to the cassette, and describe what these four people have lost.

(а)
(б)
(в)
(г)

Упражне́ние 12

On page 172 is a page from a hotel brochure. What facilities are there in this hotel, on which floor are they and when are they open? Where telephone numbers are provided, read them out in Russian. Don't forget that the first floor in Russian is the ground floor in English!

Пе́рвый эта́ж	
Гардеро́б	(переры́в на обе́д 14.00 – 15.00)
Бюро́ нахо́док	10.00 – 16.00
Рестора́н	8.00 – 23.00 тел. 229-02-31
Второ́й эта́ж	
Дире́ктор	тел. 229-569-28
Администра́тор	тел. 229-899-57
Бюро́ обслу́живания	8.00 – 22.00 тел. 229-08-46
Газе́тный кио́ск	8.00 – 16.00
Буфе́т	8.00 – 22.00
Тре́тий эта́ж	
По́чта	8.00 – 20.00 тел. 229-33-13
Парикма́херская	8.00 – 20.00 тел. 229-29-09
Бар	14.00 – 24.00

And finally, remembering that the word **гости́ница** comes from **гость** *a guest*, here is a proverb – the equivalent of *there's no place like home.* (Lit. *Being a guest is good, but being at home is better.*)

> **В гостя́х хорошо́, а до́ма лу́чше.**

16

ПРИЯ́ТНОГО АППЕТИ́ТА!
Bon appétit! Enjoy your meal!

In this unit you will learn

● how to read a menu and order a meal
● how to buy a snack, ice creams or drinks
● what to say if you are eating at a friend's home

Before you start, revise

● likes and dislikes, page 101
● prices, page 66
● unit 6, dialogue 3, page 65

Хочу́ есть и пить
I'm hungry and thirsty

As a visitor to Russia, you will find a variety of options if you want to eat out, varying from high class restaurants to bars and kiosks selling food and drinks on the street. Many museums, train stations and department stores may have a stand-up snackbar **буфе́т**. If you are opting for a full meal you will start with appetisers **заку́ски**, followed by a soup, or first course **пе́рвое блю́до**, which may be beetroot soup **борщ** or cabbage soup **щи**. Then will come a main, or second, course **второ́е блю́до**, usually based on meat or fish with side dishes **гарни́р**, and finally dessert **сла́дкое**. Much Russian cuisine contains meat, but if you are a vegetarian then salads and dishes with mushrooms **грибы́** can usually be found, and are very good. If it is a special occasion, the meal may be accompanied by vodka **во́дка**, wine **вино́** and champagne **шампа́нское**.

The verbs to eat есть *and to drink* пить

есть (irregular)	*to eat*		
я ем	I eat	**мы еди́м**	we eat
ты ешь	you eat	**вы еди́те**	you eat
он ест	he eats	**они́ едя́т**	they eat

пить (1)	*to drink*		
я пью	I drink	**мы пьём**	we drink
ты пьёшь	you drink	**вы пьёте**	you drink
он пьёт	he drinks	**они́ пьют**	they drink

— В рестора́не   *At the restaurant* —

Ключевы́е слова́

Я о́чень хочу́ есть/пить!	*I'm really hungry/thirsty*
Мы хоти́м стол на пять/ шесть челове́к	*We want a table for five/ six people*
Официа́нт/ка, иди́те сюда́, пожа́луйста	*Waiter/waitress, come here please*
Да́йте, пожа́луйста, меню́	*Please give me/us the menu*
Слу́шаю вас	*Can I help you? (I'm listening)*
Что вы хоти́те заказа́ть?	*What do you want to order?*
Что вы хоти́те есть/пить	*What do you want to eat/drink?*
Что вам?	*What would you like?*
Что вы рекоменду́ете?	*What would you recommend?*
На заку́ску, на пе́рвое, на второ́е, на сла́дкое	*For a starter, for 1st/2nd course, for dessert*
Я хочу́ заказа́ть шашлы́к	*I want to order kebab (shashlik).*
Да́йте мне, пожа́луйста, хлеб с колбасо́й	*Please give me bread with salami sausage*
Вот вам бутербро́д	*Here's your sandwich*
чай с лимо́ном, с са́харом, с молоко́м	*tea with lemon, sugar, milk*
чай без лимо́на, без са́хара, без молока́	*tea without lemon, sugar, milk*
Прия́тного аппети́та! (Priyatnuva appiteeta!)	*Bon appétit!*
Да́йте, пожа́луйста, счёт	*Please give me the bill*
Ско́лько с меня́?	*How much do I owe?*
С вас ...	*You owe ...*

Диало́г 1 В кафе́

Henry visits a small café for a snack.

Хе́нри	**Официа́нтка! Да́йте, пожа́луйста, меню́.**
Официа́нтка	**Здра́вствуйте. Вот меню́. Слу́шаю вас. Что вы хоти́те?**
Хе́нри	**Чай, пожа́луйста.**

Официантка	С лимóном?
Хéнри	Да, с лимóном и с сахарóм.
Официантка	Это всё?
Хéнри	Нет. У вас есть бутербрóды?
Официантка	Есть.
Хéнри	Дáйте, пожáлуйста, хлеб с колбасóй.
Официантка	Вот вам чай с лимóном и с сáхаром, и хлеб с кол- басóй.
Хéнри	Скóлько с меня?
Официантка	С вас четы́ре ты́сячи рублéй.

☑ Упражнéние 1

Listen to the dialogue above. (a) How does Henry like his tea? (б) What does he want to eat?

☑ Упражнéние 2

Now complete your part of a dialogue in the café.

(а) You   *You would like to see the menu.*
Официáнт   **Вот вам меню́. Что вы хоти́те?**
(б) You   *You ask for coffee and ice cream.*
Официáнт   **Кóфе без молокá?**
(в) You   *No, you want your coffee with milk and sugar.*
Официáнт   **Вы хоти́те шоколáдное морóженое или вани́льное?**
(г) You   *You don't understand. Ask the waiter to repeat it.*
Официáнт   **Что хоти́те? Шоколáдное морóженое и́ли вани́льное?**
(д) You   *You understand now. Ask for vanilla ice cream.*
Официáнт   **Вот вам кóфе и вани́льное морóженое. Прия́тного аппети́та!**
(е) You   *Thank the waiter. Ask him how much it all costs.*
Официáнт   **С вас пять ты́сяч рублéй.**

Overleaf is a dinner menu from the Hotel Ukraine. Study the headings, and see how many dishes you can work out. Find those which you don't know from the vocabulary list below and learn them, testing yourself by covering up first the English words and then the Russian. You could then see how many dishes you can remember from each category.

Гости́ница «Украи́на»

Меню́

Заку́ски

Сала́т моско́вский
Грибы́ в смета́не
Икра́ чёрная – НЕТ
Икра́ кра́сная
Сыр голла́ндский

Пе́рвые Блю́да

Щи
Борщ украи́нский – НЕТ
Суп с гриба́ми

Вторы́е блю́да

Шашлы́к
Беф-стро́ганов
Ку́рица

Гарни́р

Рис
Грибы́

Сла́дкие блю́да

Компо́т
Шокола́дное моро́женое
бана́ны – НЕТ
апельси́ны

Напи́тки

Кра́сное вино́
Бе́лое вино́
Ко́фе
Чай индийский
Чай с лимо́ном
Тома́тный сок
Газиро́ванная вода́ – НЕТ
Минера́льная вода́
Во́дка
Конья́к

грибы́	mushrooms	ку́рица	chicken
смета́на	sour cream	рис	rice
икра́	caviar	компо́т	stewed fruit
сыр	cheese	напи́тки	drinks
щи	cabbage soup	сок	juice
борщ	beetroot soup	газиро́ванная вода́	sparkling water
шашлы́к	kebab		

Using the menu above as a guide, write out a meal which you would like to order, or underline the dishes which you would select. Now make up a conversation with a waiter, ordering what you have chosen. The waiter begins: **Слу́шаю вас. Что вы хоти́те заказа́ть?**

☑ Упражнéние 3

In a hotel you see a notice telling you at what time and on which floor you may get your meals. A Russian standing next to you is trying to read the notice as well, but he has just broken his spectacles. Explain the details to him.

На пéрвом этажé рабóтает ресторáн.

Зáвтрак – с 8.00 до 10.00
Обéд   – с 13.00 до 15.00
Ýжин   – с 18.00 до 20.00

На вторóм этажé рабóтает гриль-бáр. Здесь мóжно заказáть кóфе и бутербрóды.

——— За столóм   *At the table* ———

стол	*table*		хлеб	*bread*
стул	*chair*		мáсло	*butter*
блюдо	*dish*		нож	*knife*
тарéлка	*plate*		вúлка	*fork*
чáшка	*cup*		лóжка	*spoon*
стакáн	*glass*		соль (f)	*salt*
рюмка	*wine glass*		пéрец	*pepper*
салфéтка	*serviette*			

◗ Диалóг 2 В ресторáне

Victoria is ordering a meal in a restaurant. Read the dialogue before answering the questions below.

Виктóрия   **Молодóй человéк! Я хочý заказáть, пожáлуйста.**
Официáнт   **Слýшаю вас.**
Виктóрия   **На закýски у вас есть салáт москóвский?**
Официáнт   **Извинúте, нет.**
Виктóрия   **Жаль. Что вы рекомендýете?**
Официáнт   **Я рекомендýю грибы́ в сметáне.**
Виктóрия   **Хорошó, на закýски – грибы́ в сметáне. На пéрвое, у вас есть борщ?**
Официáнт   **Нет, сегóдня у нас есть тóлько щи.**
Виктóрия   **Так, на пéрвое – щи, на вторóе – шашлы́к с рúсом, и на слáдкое – фрýкты.**

Официант	Понятно, на закуски – грибы в сметане, на первое – щи, на второе – шашлык с рисом, и на сладкое – фрукты. А что вы хотите пить?
Виктория	У вас есть вино?
Официант	Да, какое вино вы хотите?
Виктория	Дайте белое вино, и чай, пожалуйста.
Официант	Чай с сахаром?
Виктория	Нет, чай с лимоном без сахара.
Официант	Это всё?
Виктория	Да, это всё, спасибо. Нет! Вот идёт мой брат! Дайте, пожалуйста, ещё рюмку и тарелку. Здравствуй, Николай. Что ты хочешь есть и пить?

☑ Упражнение 4

(а) What two things are not available today?

(б) What does Victoria order, and how does she like her tea?

(в) She sees someone come into the restaurant. Who is it, and what does Victoria ask for on his behalf?

☑ Упражнение 5

Did you notice how Victoria asked for *another* **ещё** glass and plate? – **Дайте, пожалуйста, ещё рюмку и тарелку.** Don't forget to change -**a** to -**y** and -**я** to -**ю** if you are asking for a feminine object. How would you ask for an extra cup, spoon, knife and chair?

☑ Упражнение 6

Now imagine you are a bilingual waiter in the Кафе «Тбилиси» taking down a Russian customer's order. Listen to the cassette and jot down in English or Russian what the customer wants.

☑ Упражнение 7

Look at this picture. Make sure that you know how to say everything on the table in Russian. Then cover the picture and try to remember everything. You could try writing a list in Russian.

Упражнéние 8

How would you ask for: Moscow salad, mushroom soup, beef stroganoff, rice, chocolate ice cream, white wine and coffee with milk? Now ask for the bill.

Упражнéние 9

See if you can unscramble the dialogue below. It is set in a **буфéт**. The first sentence is in bold type.

(а) Дáйте, пожáлуйста, хлеб, сыр и кóфе.
(б) Что у вас есть сегóдня?
(в) С вас три тысячи рублей.
(г) Да, дáйте чай без сáхара.
(д) Извинйте, у нас нет кóфе. Вы хотйте чай?
(е) Спасйбо. Скóлько с меня?
(ж) **Слýшаю вас.**
(з) У нас сегóдня хлеб, сыр, колбасá, шоколáд и фрýкты.
(и) Вот вам хлеб, сыр и чай.

Упражнéние 10

Imagine that you are running a restaurant in Russia. Fill out the menu below, putting at least two items in each column, and don't forget the date at the top.

МЕНЮ́

_____ 199_____ гóда

Закýски	Пéрвое блю́до	Вторóе блю́до	Слáдкое	Напи́тки

☑ Упражнéние 11

Кáша is any sort of porridge dish cooked with grains and liquid. There is a Russian saying: **Щи да кáша – пи́ща нáша** *Cabbage soup and porridge are our food.* What ingredients do you need to make a milky rice pudding? See if you can read them out loud from the recipe below, including the numerals.

Каша рисовая молочная

рис	100 грамм
масло	25 грамм
сахар	20 грамм
соль	5 грамм
молоко	260 миллилитров
вода	200 миллилитров

У друзей
With friends at their home

You can now cope with anything which is likely to occur in a restaurant, but what about visiting friends at their home? Here are some phrases which may help.

Входите, раздевайтесь!	*Come in, take your coat off!*
розы	*roses*
нормально	*fine, OK*
Угощайтесь!	*Help yourself!*
вкусно	*It's tasty*
За ваше здоровье!	*Cheers! Your health!*
Берите ещё ...	*Take some more ...*
Спасибо большое за всё	*Thanks very much for everything*
Уже поздно	*It's late already*
Пора идти	*It's time to go*
Спокойной ночи	*Good night*
До завтра	*Until tomorrow*

Диалог 3 В квартире
Упражнение 12

You have been invited to Yulia and Volodya's for supper. Read the dialogue, and say: (a) what you take as a gift (б) how Volodya is feeling (в) what is for starters (г) whether you like it (д) what you have to drink (е) why you have to leave.

Юлия   Добрый вечер. Входите, раздевайтесь!

Вы   Добрый вечер. Вот вам маленький подарок – шампанское и цветы.

Юлия   Спасибо большое. Я так люблю розы. Вот идёт Володя.

Вы   Здравствуйте, Володя. Как дела?

Володя   Нормально, спасибо. Всё хорошо. Садитесь, пожалуйста.

Вы   Спасибо. Ой, какие прекрасные закуски. Я очень люблю грибы в сметане и икру.

Юлия   Вот вам тарелка. Угощайтесь!

Вы   Мм! Всё очень вкусно, Таня.

Воло́дя	И вот вам во́дка. За ва́ше здоро́вье!
Вы	За ва́ше здоро́вье!
Ю́лия	Бери́те ещё заку́ски.
Вы	Спаси́бо большо́е.

Later that evening, in the entrance hall.

Вы	Уже́ по́здно. Пора́ идти́.
Воло́дя	Споко́йной но́чи. До за́втра.
Вы	Спаси́бо за всё. Споко́йной но́чи.

☑ Упражне́ние 13

How would you say:

(а) I really love champagne.
(б) Cheers.
(в) What lovely wine glasses!
(г) How are you?

😀 Анекдо́т

To finish off the unit, here is an anecdote set in a bar. Why does the waiter tell the customer it is now safe to drink beer?

| Официа́нт | Что вам? Вы хоти́те пи́во? |
| Бори́с | Нет, я на велосипе́де. Да́йте, пожа́луйста, сок. |

Че́рез мину́ту ...

| Официа́нт | Вы мо́жете сейча́с пить пи́во. Ваш велосипе́д кто́-то укра́л. |

| велосипе́д | bicycle |
| кто́-то укра́л | someone has stolen |

17

НА ПО́ЧТЕ
At the post office

In this unit you will learn

- how to send a letter, postcard, parcel, telegram
- how to make a phone call

Before you start, revise

- numerals, page 235
- telling the time, page 84
- filling in forms, unit 15

Информа́ция

Телефо́нная и а́дресная кни́га
Telephone directory

Until recently, there was no system of public telephone directories in Russia. If you wanted to find a number, you had to ask at an enquiry office **спра́вочное бюро́**, giving at least the name, patronymic, surname and address of the person you wished to contact. This is why many Russians carry round a little handwritten book with every phone number they are ever likely to need. However, there are now directories available for many cities, mostly giving administrative and commercial numbers rather than private ones, but invaluable nonetheless. Some of them give tourist information, and many have foreign language sections.

On the first page of most directories you will find the emergency phone numbers you might need:

01 **пожа́р** fire
02 **мили́ция** police
03 **ско́рая медици́нская по́мощь** ambulance
04 **газ** gas

Learning the Russian alphabet in the correct order will save a lot of time when using a directory. Remember too that Russian directories will boast that they provide everything you need to know not from A to Z, but from **А** to **Я** «**от А до Я**».

Я хочу́ позвони́ть домо́й *I want to call home*

Many Russians use the phone a lot, making long, late calls from the comfort of an armchair. If you want to use the phone, you have several choices. The easiest and cheapest way to make a call is by private telephone, but if this is not possible, you will need to use a pay phone **телефо́н-автома́т** or **таксофо́н** for local calls, using a token **жето́н**. If the number you want to call is abroad, you will need to book a call through your hotel, which may be expensive, or at the telephone section of a main post office **по́чта**, or at the special telephone and telegraph offices **телефо́н – телегра́ф**. Don't forget the time difference with the country you are calling. If you choose the post office, you book a call at the counter for a certain number of minutes at a certain time and wait for the staff to call out your booth number over the public address system. Then you dash to the right booth (practise your numerals beforehand) and start your call, which is counted from the moment of the announcement. The whole thing can be a little flustering!

—— По телефо́ну *On the phone* ——

Я хочу́ позвони́ть в А́нглию/ в Австра́лию	*I want to call England/ Australia*
Мо́жно заказа́ть разгово́р на за́втра на 3 мину́ты?	*Can I book a 3 minute call for tomorrow?*
Како́й но́мер телефо́на?	*What's the phone number?*
Како́й код?	*What's the code?*
Ско́лько мину́т вы хоти́те заказа́ть?	*How many minutes do you want to book?*

2, 3, 4 мину́ты, 5, 6, 7, 8, 9, 10, мину́т	*2, 3, 4 minutes, 5–10 minutes*
Когда́ вы хоти́те говори́ть?	*When do you want to talk?*
разгово́р	*conversation*
чек	*bill, chit*

Диало́г 1 Мо́жно заказа́ть разгово́р?

Wendy has a call to make, so she goes to the post office to make a booking.

Уэ́нди	**Извини́те, пожа́луйста. Я хочу́ позвони́ть в А́нглию.**
Де́вушка	**Да. Како́й но́мер телефо́на?**
Уэ́нди	**987–25–55.**
Де́вушка	**И како́й код?**
Уэ́нди	**0115.**
Де́вушка	**Ско́лько мину́т вы хоти́те заказа́ть?**
Уэ́нди	**Четы́ре мину́ты, пожа́луйста.**
Де́вушка	**Когда́ вы хоти́те говори́ть?**
Уэ́нди	**Мо́жно заказа́ть разгово́р на сего́дня на восемна́дцать часо́в?**
Де́вушка	**Нет, уже́ по́здно на сего́дня.**
Уэ́нди	**Мо́жно на за́втра, у́тром?**
Де́вушка	**Одну́ мину́точку ... Да, мо́жно заказа́ть разговор на за́втра на де́вять часо́в. Вот вам чек. Всё поня́тно?**
Уэ́нди	**Да, поня́тно.**

Упражне́ние 1

Choose the correct phrase to complete each sentence.

(a) Уэ́нди хо́чет позвони́ть
  (*i*) в Москву́.
  (*ii*) в больни́цу.
  (*iii*) в А́нглию.

(б) Уэ́нди хо́чет заказа́ть разгово́р
  (*i*) на восемна́дцать мину́т.
  (*ii*) на сего́дня на восемна́дцать часо́в.
  (*iii*) по́здно ве́чером.

(в) Уэ́нди не мо́жет заказа́ть разгово́р на сего́дня потому́, что
  (*i*) по́чта закры́та.

(*ii*) де́вушка не понима́ет.

(*iii*) уже́ по́здно.

☑ Упражне́ние 2

You have to fill in a form at the post office to request a call to another city. You guess that the title of the form **Зая́вка на междугоро́дный разгово́р** probably means *Request for inter-city conversation*. **Ме́жду** means *between*, so **междугоро́дный** means *inter-city* and **междунаро́дный** means *international* (between nations). Now you have to decide where to put the rest of the details which you assume are being asked for.

Зая́вка на междугоро́дный разгово́р

(а) С го́родом	(*i*) How many minutes.
(б) Телефо́н и́ли а́дрес	(*ii*) Which city.
(в) Да́та и вре́мя вы́зова.	(*iii*) Telephone number and address.
(г) Коли́чество мину́т	(*iv*) Signature.
(д) По́дпись	(*v*) Date and time of call.

☑ Упражне́ние 3

Listen to the cassette and jot down details of where and when people are calling.

To which city   Phone number   At what time   For how many minutes

(а)

(б)

(в)

☑ Упражне́ние 4

An independent telecommunications company is advertising its products and services. What is it offering to its customers? Cover up the right hand column while you try to work it out.

(а) 24 часа́ междунаро́дная телефо́нная связь.	(*i*) E-mail
(б) Междунаро́дные би́знес-ли́нии.	(*ii*) fax, telex
(в) Ка́рточные таксофо́ны.	(*iii*) mobile phones

(г)	Электро́нная по́чта.	(*iv*)	tele-conferences
(д)	Телеконфере́нции.	(*v*)	24-hour international phone-link
(е)	Моби́льные радиотелефо́ны.	(*vi*)	telephone modems
(ж)	Телефо́нные мо́демы.	(*vii*)	five-year guarantee
(з)	Факс, те́лекс.	(*viii*)	international business lines
(и)	Гара́нтия – 5 лет.	(*ix*)	public card phones

На по́чте *At the post office*

Письмо́, окрты́тка, посы́лка
Letter, postcard, parcel

If you want to send something by post **по по́чте** you will need to visit the post office again, unless you already have the stamps and can use a letter box **почто́вый я́щик**. The post office is usually open from Monday to Saturday from 9.00 till 21.00 and on Sunday from 10.00 till 20.00. If you only need a stamp **ма́рка** then it may be quicker to buy it from your hotel. At the post office, as well as buying stamps, you may buy an envelope **конве́рт**, and send parcels and telegrams. Some post offices now also deal with faxes, as do telephone and telegraph offices and hotels. To send a parcel, take the contents only to the post office, where they will be inspected, weighed and wrapped for you. There is usually a long list on the wall of items which may not be sent by post, such as liquids and perishable goods; but if you like buying books, for example, you might find that sending them home by post is cheaper, although less reliable, than paying excess luggage charges on the plane.

письмо́	letter
откры́тка	postcard
посы́лка	parcel
междунаро́дная телегра́мма	international telegram
конве́рт	envelope
ма́рка	stamp
авиаписьмо́	airmail letter
почто́вый я́щик	letter box
Что на́до де́лать?	What do I need to do?
На́до запо́лнить бланк	You need to fill in a form
Где мо́жно купи́ть ма́рки, конве́рты, откры́тки?	Where can I buy stamps, envelopes, postcards?
Ско́лько сто́ит посла́ть письмо́ в Великобрита́нию?	How much is it to send a letter to the UK?
Ско́лько сто́ит ма́рка на письмо́ в Герма́нию?	How much is a stamp for a letter to Germany?
Три ма́рки по 500 (пятьсо́т) рубле́й	3 stamps at 500 roubles each
Я хочу́ посла́ть посы́лку в А́нглию	I want to send a parcel to England
Напиши́те а́дрес вот здесь	Write the address right here
Ку́да, кому́, а́дрес отправи́теля, вес	Where to, to whom, address of sender, weight
Я хочу́ посла́ть телеграмму в Англию	I want send a telegram to England
Напиши́те текст здесь	Write the text here
500 рубле́й за сло́во	500 roubles per word

🔊 Диало́г 2 Я хочу́ посла́ть письмо́ в Великобрита́нию

Dan has a lot of things to do at the post office. He goes to a small branch so that everything can be done at one counter, instead of queueing at different windows in the main post office.

Дэн	Извини́те, де́вушка, где мо́жно купи́ть ма́рки?
Де́вушка	Здесь у меня́ мо́жно всё купи́ть: ма́рки, конве́рты, откры́тки. Каки́е ма́рки вы хоти́те?
Дэн	Я хочу́ посла́ть э́то письмо́ в Великобрита́нию. Ско́лько сто́ит ма́рка на письмо́?
Де́вушка	Две ты́сячи рубле́й. Вот четы́ре ма́рки по пятьсо́т рубле́й.
Дэн	Спаси́бо. И я хочу́ посла́ть телегра́мму домо́й. Ско́лько сто́ит?
Де́вушка	Пятьсо́т рубле́й за сло́во.
Дэн	Что на́до де́лать?
Де́вушка	На́до запо́лнить бланк. Напиши́те здесь текст.

Дэн	**Спаси́бо. И мо́жно то́же посла́ть э́ти кни́ги и журна́лы в А́нглию?**
Де́вушка	**Коне́чно мо́жно. На́до запо́лнить бланк. Напиши́те а́дрес вот здесь.**
Дэн	**А́дрес в Великобрита́нии?**
Де́вушка	**Да, пра́вильно. И напиши́те ваш а́дрес в Москве́ здесь.**
Дэн	**Поня́тно. Спаси́бо.**
Де́вушка	**Э́то всё?**
Дэн	**Да, всё. Спаси́бо вам большо́е. До свида́ния.**

◢ Упражне́ние 5

(а) What does the girl sell at her counter? (б) What stamps does Dan buy, and what for? (в) What does he have to do to send a telegram? (г) What does he want to send home in a parcel?

◢ Упражне́ние 6

Without looking at the dialogue above, can you remember how to say the following phrases in Russian?

(а) three stamps at 300 roubles (б) What do I need to do? (в) Of course you can. (г) That's right. (д) Thanks very much.

And can you fill in these blanks? Write or say your answers.

(е) Где _____ купи́ть ма́рки?
(ж) Каки́е ма́рки вы _____?
(з) На́до _____ бланк.
(и) _____ всё? Да, всё.
(к) До _____.

Упражне́ние 7

Choose a suitable question word to fill in the blanks. Question words which you already know are кто? что? где? когда́? куда́? как? почему́? ско́лько?

(а) _____ попа́сть на по́чту?
(б) _____ здесь почто́вый я́щик?
(в) _____ мне пойти́?

(г) _____ вы по профéссии?
(д) _____ сейчáс врéмени?
(е) _____ вас зовýт?
(ж) _____ у вас есть?
(з) _____ открывáется пóчта?

☑ Упражнéние 8

You have just arrived in Moscow and are staying in room 331 at the hotel Россúя on ýлица Варвáрка. You can't find Andrei Ivanov's phone number, so you decide to send him a telegram to tell him where you are. His address is flat 9, block 26 on Проспéкт Мúра. (Don't forget that Russian addresses begin with the name of the city and work down to the number of the flat and the person's name.) Fill in this form at the post office.

Телегрáмма

Кудá, комý _____

_____

Текст_____

_____

_____

_____

Фамúлия и áдрес отправúтеля _____

_____

_____

☑ **Упражне́ние 9**

Match up the words which go together.

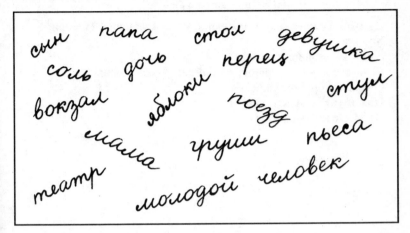

сын папа стол де́вушка
соль дочь пе́рец
вокза́л я́блоки по́езд стул
теа́тр ма́ма гру́ши пье́са
молодо́й челове́к

◪ **Упражне́ние 10**

Your friend has received an unexpected letter from Russia, but is unable
to read the name and address on the envelope in order to reply. Look at
the envelope and find out who has sent it.

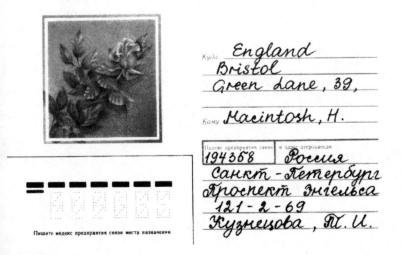

Куда: England
Bristol
Green Lane, 39,
Кому: Macintosh, H.

Индекс предприятия связи и адрес отправителя
194358 Росси́я
Санкт - Петербу́рг
Проспе́кт Энге́льса
121 - 2 - 69
Кузнецо́ва, П. И.

Пишите индекс предприятия связи места назначения

👤 Анекдо́т

Finally, here is an anecdote set in a doctor's office in a busy hospital. The phone rings. It's an enquiry about a patient.

– До́ктор, скажи́те, как пожива́ет Ива́н Ива́нович Ивано́в?
– Хорошо́.
– А когда́ он пойдёт домо́й?
– Е́сли всё пойдёт хорошо́, он пойдёт домо́й за́втра.
– О́чень интере́сно. Спаси́бо.
– Пожа́луйста. А кто говори́т?
– Ива́н Ива́нович Ивано́в.

18

КАКА́Я СЕГО́ДНЯ ПОГО́ДА?
What's the weather like today?

In this unit you will learn

- how to talk about the weather
- how to talk about your holidays
- how to use a tourist brochure
- how to book an excursion

Before you start, revise

- free time in unit 9, page 101
- finding your way around town in unit 5, page 54

Информа́ция

Зи́мний спорт *Winter sports*

From west to east, Russia stretches around 10,000 kilometres, taking in eleven time zones, and its climatic zones from north to south include arctic tundra, forest, steppe and southern deserts, so no generalisations may be made about the climate or weather! This means that whatever you learn to say about the weather will be useful somewhere at some time! However, it would be true to say that in those parts of Russia where the climate permits, many Russians love to participate in winter sports. From a young age they learn to ski **ката́ться на лы́жах**, to skate **ката́ться на конька́х** and to sledge **ката́ться на саня́х**.

Óтпуск *Holidays*

In the past it was difficult for Russians to visit non-Communist countries, but now travel agents can offer a holiday or time-share **тайм-шер** anywhere in the world for those who can afford them. Popular destinations include America **Амéрика**, the Bahamas **Багáмы**, Cyprus **Кипр**, Egypt **Егúпет**, Greece **Грéция**, Jamaica **Ямáйка**, Korea **Корéя**, Malta **Мáльта**, Tenerife **Тенерúф**, Thailand **Таилáнд**, Tunisia **Тунúс** and Turkey **Тýрция**. Below is a typical advert for a holiday. Read it and check anything you don't understand in the **Answers** section at the back of the book.

Майорка (Испания)

Рейсы «Аэрофлота» Москва - Барселона - Москва.

Отель *** : 2 -местные номера, бар, кафе, дискотеки, теннис, бассейн, гольф-клуб, шоп-тур, казино, экскурсия по Барселоне. Персонал говорит по-русски.

Одна неделя (включая завтраки) $745.

Погóда *The weather*

Какáя сегóдня погóда?	*What's the weather like today* (sivodnya)*?*
Сегóдня хóлодно	*Today it's cold*
прохлáдно	*It's cool*
теплó	*It's warm*
слúшком жáрко	*It's too hot*
дýшно	*It's close*
вéтрено	*It's windy*
тумáнно	*It's foggy*
пáсмурно	*It's overcast*
идёт дождь	*It's raining*
идёт снег	*It's snowing*
сóлнце свéтит	*The sun is shining*
морóз	*It's frosty*

температу́ра во́здуха	air temperature
температу́ра воды́	water temperature
плюс 5 гра́дусов тепла́	+ 5 degrees of warmth (5 above)
ми́нус оди́н гра́дус моро́за	- 1 degree of frost (1 below)
ве́тер ю́го-за́падный	The wind is south-westerly
Како́й прогно́з пого́ды на за́втра?	What is the weather forecast for tomorrow?
За́втра бу́дет хо́лодно, тепло́	Tomorrow it will be cold, warm
За́втра бу́дет дождь, снег	Tomorrow there will be rain, snow
весно́й, ле́том, о́сенью, зимо́й	in spring, in summer, in autumn, in winter
весна́, ле́то, о́сень, зима́	spring, summer, autumn, winter
зи́мний спорт	winter sport
Како́й твой люби́мый сезо́н?	Which is your favourite season?
Мой люби́мый сезо́н-весна́	My favourite season is spring
Что де́лать?	What is to be done?

🎧 Диало́г 1 Сего́дня хо́лодно

Rosemary is spending her first winter in Russia and is determined to make the most of the snow. But her friend Maxim is not so keen.

Ро́узмэри Макси́м, ты хо́чешь сего́дня ката́ться на лы́жах в лесу́?

Макси́м Нет, не о́чень хочу́. Сего́дня хо́лодно.

Ро́узмэри Коне́чно хо́лодно! Зима́! Но сего́дня так прекра́сно, Моро́з и со́лнце све́тит.

Макси́м Да, но по ра́дио говоря́т, что температу́ра во́здуха сего́дня ми́нус де́сять гра́дусов. Сли́шком хо́лодно. Я хочу́ смотре́ть телеви́зор и чита́ть до́ма, где тепло́.

Ро́узмэри Смотре́ть телеви́зор? Макси́м, что ты! Как э́то мо́жет быть? Ты совсе́м не лю́бишь зи́му?

Макси́м Нет, я люблю́ ле́то, когда́ жа́рко. Мо́жно гуля́ть на пля́же и есть моро́женое.

Ро́узмэри Поня́тно. Я то́же о́чень люблю́ ле́то. Но я так хочу́ сего́дня ката́ться на лы́жах. Жаль. Что де́лать?

Макси́м Мо́жно позвони́ть А́ндрю. Он о́чень лю́бит зи́мний спорт.

Ро́узмэри Пра́вильно. На́до позвони́ть А́ндрю. Како́й у него́ но́мер телефо́на?

Макси́м Семьсо́т три́дцать де́вять, пятна́дцать, со́рок два.

☑ Упражне́ние 1

(а) What does Rosemary want to do? (б) What is the weather like?
(в) What does Maxim want to do? (г) What is his favourite season and
why? (д) What does Rosemary decide to do? (е) What is Andrew's
phone number?

☑ Упражне́ние 2

Match up the captions with the pictures.

(а) идёт дождь   (г) ве́трено
(б) тума́нно   (д) со́лнце све́тит
(в) идёт снег

☑ Упражне́ние 3

 Listen to the weather forecast and tick the features of the weather which
you hear mentioned.

(а) Rain   (е) Temperature -7^0
(б) Snow   (ж) Frost
(в) Warm   (з) Sun
(г) Cold   (и) Temperature -17^0
(д) Northerly wind

Упражне́ние 4

Look at this weather map for today and play the part of the weather fore-caster on television. You could try writing down your script, and check it with the suggested script in the back of the book. Don't forget the points of the compass: *in the north* **на се́вере**, *in the south* **на ю́ге**, *in the west* **на за́паде**, *in the east* **на восто́ке**.

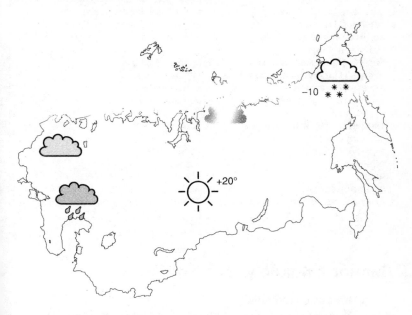

Что ты де́лаешь в свобо́дное вре́мя? *What do you do in your free time?*

де́лать [1]	to do
свобо́дное вре́мя?	free time
лови́ть [2] ры́бу (я ловлю́, ты ло́вишь)	to go fishing
собира́ть [1] ма́рки, грибы́	to collect stamps, mushrooms
гото́вить [2] (я гото́влю, ты гото́вишь)	to cook

ката́ться на лы́жах, на конька́х, на саня́х	to ski, skate, sledge
ката́ться на велосипе́де, на ло́шади, на ло́дке	to cycle, ride a horse, go boating
отды́ха́ть [1] за грани́цей, на берегу́ мо́ря	to holiday abroad, at the seaside
купа́ться в мо́ре	to swim in the sea
загора́ть [1] на пля́же	to sunbathe on the beach
гуля́ть [1] в лесу́	to walk in the woods
ходи́ть [2] в теа́тр, кино́, (я хожу́, ты хо́дишь)	to go to the theatre, cinema
ходи́ть [2] по магази́нам	to go shopping
игра́ть [1] в футбо́л, в ша́хматы	to play football, chess
игра́ть [1] на гита́ре	to play the guitar
рисова́ть [1] (я рису́ю, ты рису́ешь)	to draw
танцева́ть [1] (я танцу́ю, ты танцу́ешь)	to dance
акти́вный челове́к	active person
обы́чно	usually
ча́сто	often
с удово́льствием	with pleasure
идёт бале́т, о́пера, фильм, пъе́са	There is a ballet, opera, film, play on
ты хо́чешь пойти́ в/на ..?	Do you want to go to ..?

🗪 Диало́г 2 Каки́е у тебя́ хо́бби?

Хе́лен **Каки́е у тебя́ хо́бби?**

Ю́ра **Я о́чень акти́вный челове́к. Зимо́й я люблю́ игра́ть в хокке́й и ката́ться на лы́жах, а ле́том я ча́сто гуля́ю в дере́вне и игра́ю в те́ннис. Я то́же люблю́ купа́ться в мо́ре. О́сенью я собира́ю грибы́ в лесу́. А у тебя́ есть хо́бби?**

Хе́лен **Да, но я не о́чень акти́вный челове́к. Я люблю́ слу́шать ра́дио, игра́ть в ша́хматы, чита́ть кни́ги, смотре́ть фи́льмы и ходи́ть на конце́рты.**

Ю́ра **В Ланка́стре есть теа́тр?**

Хе́лен **Коне́чно есть. Но я не о́чень ча́сто хожу́ в театр в Ланка́стре, потому́, что до́рого сто́ит.**

Ю́ра **Да, поня́тно. Здесь в Краснода́ре у нас хоро́шие теа́тры. Ты хо́чешь пойти́ в теа́тр за́втра ве́чером?**

Хе́лен **Да, с удово́льствием!**

✅ Упражнéние 5

From the dialogue above, find out where Helen and Yura are from and what their interests are.

✅ Упражнéние 6

You are working at a sports complex in a resort on the shores of the Black Sea **Чёрное мóре**. You answer an enquiry about what is available for the active holidaymaker. You consult your list of symbols for help and begin: **Здесь мóжно ...**

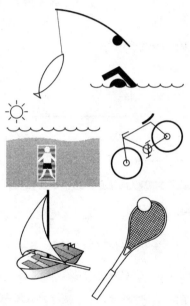

Упражнéние 7

Below are three mini-dialogues. Read or listen to them and match them up with their titles: (а) At the kiosk (б) An invitation to the theatre (в) At the theatre.

(i)

Дéвушка	**Вáши билéты, пожáлуйста.**
Вáня	**Однý минýточку. Вот они́.**
Дéвушка	**Хоти́те прогрáмму?**

Ваня   Да. Дайте, пожалуйста, три программы.

(ii)
Лара   Скажите, пожалуйста, когда идёт балет «Жизель»?
Киоскёр   Восьмого, девятого и десятого апреля.

(iii)
Галя   У меня есть билеты в Большой театр. Вы свободны?
Чарльс   Конечно. Как хорошо! Билеты на сегодня?
Галя   Да, на сегодня на вечер.
Чарльс   Где мы встретимся?
Галя   У меня в квартире в шесть часов.

☑ Упражнение 8

Read this postcard from Sveta to Lena.

(а) Where is she staying?
(б) What is the weather like?
(в) What does she do every day?

Здравствуй, Лена.
Мы отдыхаем в Сочи и живём в гостинице на берегу моря. Солнце светит и жарко. Каждый день я ем мороженое и играю в волейбол на пляже.

         Света.

Why not write a postcard describing your ideal holiday?

☑ Упражне́ние 9

You want to book an excursion to Novgorod.

(а) When do you want to go?
(б) How many are there in your group?
(в) When does the tour guide **экскурсово́д** tell you to be ready to set off?

Вы	**Мо́жно заказа́ть экску́рсию на за́втра в Но́вгород?**
Экскурсово́д	**Мо́жно. Ско́лько вас челове́к?**
Вы	**Во́семь.**
Экскурсово́д	**Хорошо́. В авто́бусе есть свобо́дные места́. Встре́тимся здесь за́втра у́тром в во́семь часо́в.**

☑ Упражне́ние 10

Now you are in Novgorod, you have lost the tour guide and you are the only one who speaks any Russian. Help your friends out with this list of facilities in the Russian guide book. You may not understand every word but you should be able to work out most things. The only word you have to look up is **па́мятник** *a monument.*

1	Спра́вочное бюро́
2	Тури́стский ко́мплекс
3	Гости́ница
4	Ке́мпинг
5	Па́мятник архитекту́ры
6	Музе́й
7	Археологи́ческий па́мятник
8	Теа́тр, конце́ртный зал
9	Стадио́н
10	Рестора́н, кафе́, бар
11	Универса́льный магази́н
12	Ры́нок
13	Стоя́нка такси́
14	Автозапра́вочная ста́нция
15	Железнодоро́жный вокза́л
16	Пляж
17	Сад, парк

☑ Упражне́ние 11

You are a very uncooperative person. Whatever Liza suggests, whatever the season, you use the weather as an excuse. Find a suitable phrase to get you out of these activities.

(а) Хо́чешь пойти́ на пляж?

(б) Хо́чешь ката́ться на велосипе́де?

(в) Хо́чешь пойти́ на конце́рт?

(г) Хо́чешь пойти́ в лес собира́ть грибы́?

(д) Хо́чешь ката́ться на конька́х?

(е) Хо́чешь купа́ться в мо́ре?

(ж) Хо́чешь пойти́ на стадио́н на футбо́л?

(i) Нет, сего́дня идёт дождь.

(ii) Нет, сего́дня сли́шком хо́лодно.

(iii) Нет, сего́дня сли́шком жа́рко.

(iv) Нет, сего́дня тума́нно.

(v) Нет, сего́дня ве́трено.

(vi) Нет, сего́дня ду́шно.

(vii) Нет, сего́дня со́лнце све́тит.

☑ Упражне́ние 12

Browse through this TV programme listing and use all your powers of deduction to say at what time you would watch television if you were interested in (а) sport (б) politics (в) children's programmes (г) games of chance (д) news.

ТЕЛЕВИДЕНИЕ

6.00	Телеутро	16.55	Чемпионат России по футболу. Полуфинал. ЦСКА - «КамАЗ»
8.30	Олимпийское утро		
9.20	Новости Эй-би-си	18.00	Астрология
9.55	Парламентская неделя	18.20	Лотто «Миллион»
10.10	Утренний концерт	19.20	Гандбол. Чемпионат мира.
10.25	Утренняя почта	20.00	Новости
10.45	«Санта -Барбара»	20.40	Спокойной ночи, малыши!
11.10	Русское лото	21.00	Спортивный карусель
11.30	«Живём и любим»	21.40	Москва - Кремль
12.05	Милицейская хроника	22.00	Кинотеатр «Си-би-эс»
12.30	Футбол «Динамо» - «Спартак»	22.50	Что? Где? Когда?
14.00	Новости и погода	23.50	Футбол «Ювентус» - «Парма»
14.20	Винни-Пух		
14.30	Наш сад		
16.30	Кенгуру		

⚡ Упражне́ние 13

(а) Как попа́сть на зи́мний стадио́н?
(б) Как попа́сть в цирк?

Иди́те (i) напра́во (ii) нале́во (iii) пря́мо.

⚡ Упражне́ние 14

Answer these questions about your favourite things.

Како́й твой люби́мый сезо́н?	Мой люби́мый сезо́н _____
Како́й твой люби́мый спорт?	Мой _____
Кака́я твоя́ люби́мая кни́га?	Моя́ люби́мая кни́га _____
Кака́я твоя́ люби́мая маши́на?	_____
Каки́е твои́ люби́мые фи́льмы?	Мои́ люби́мые фи́льмы _____
Каки́е твои́ люби́мые композиторы/спортсме́ны?	_____

Now you could continue making up questions and answers.

Анекдо́т

На у́лице, по́здно ве́чером.
–Куда́ ты идёшь так по́здно?
–Пора́ идти́ домо́й.
–Почему́ так ра́но?

And finally, a Russian proverb about making the most of your time. **Ленивцы** means *lazy people*.

> **За́втра, за́втра, не сего́дня - так ленивцы говоря́т.**

19

У МЕНЯ́ БОЛИ́Т ГОЛОВА́
I've got a headache

In this unit you will learn

- what to do if you feel ill
- how to say what is hurting
- how to say someone's age

Before you start, revise

- how to say *I have* **у меня́**, etc., page 112

Информа́ция

Ба́ня *The bath house*

The Russian health service provides free emergency medical care for everyone, and there are now also many private clinics using imported equipment and drugs, which offer their services for hard currency. Many Russians prefer to use natural cures involving herbs and often vodka. Suggested remedies for a cold may include taking a cold shower, chewing garlic, using nose-drops made from the juice of an onion, and going to bed warmly dressed with extra blankets and a restorative tumbler of pepper vodka and frequent glasses of tea. All of these treatments are sure to leaving you feeling 'as fresh as a little gherkin' **све́жий как огу́рчик** the next morning! Another favourite cure is a visit to the bath house **ба́ня**. The bath house operates on a single sex system, and offers a cold pool, a steam room, bunches of birch twigs to help the circulation, tea and a massage. A visit may take the best part of a day and is extraordinarily relaxing and convivial. Even if you are no better by the end of it, you will hardly care!

Что с вáми?
What's the matter with you?

мне плóхо	I'm ill
Я чýвствую себя хорошó/невáжно/ плóхо	I feel good/not so good/ bad
я плóхо сплю	I'm sleeping badly
у меня температýра	I've got a temperature
меня тошнúт	I feel sick/nauseous
мне то жáрко, то хóлодно	I'm feeling hot and cold
у меня грипп	I've got flu
Что у вас болúт?	What's hurting?
у меня болúт головá/ýхо/ зуб/живóт	my head/ear/tooth/ stomach aches
у меня болúт гóрло/глаз/нос	my throat/eye/nose hurts
у меня болúт рукá/ногá/ спинá/сéрдце	my arm/leg/back heart hurts
у меня болят зýбы/ýши/глазá	my teeth/ears/eyes hurt

☑ Упражнéние 1

Listen to Vadim, Tanya and Anton describing their symptoms. Decide which of them: (a) has just run a marathon (б) has flu (в) has food poisoning.

☑ Упражнéние 2

Look at this picture and number the words below correctly.

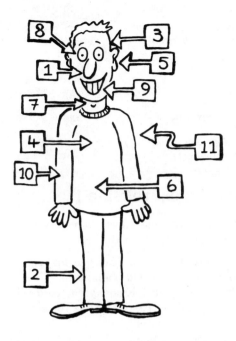

| [ ] голова́ | [ ] глаз | [ ] у́хо | [ ] нос | [ ] зу́бы | [ ] го́рло |
| [ ] рука́ | [ ] нога́ | [ ] спина́ | [ ] живо́т | [ ] се́рдце | |

В кабине́те
In the consulting room

кабине́т	*consulting room*
поликли́ника	*health centre*
больни́ца	*hospital*
апте́ка	*pharmacy*
ско́рая по́мощь	*ambulance*
врач, до́ктор	*doctor*
медсестра́	*nurse*
консульта́ция	*consultation*
симпто́м	*symptom*
диа́гноз	*diagnosis*

реце́пт	prescription
идти́ к врачу́	to go to the doctor's
принима́ть (1) лека́рство	to take medicine
табле́тка	tablet
раз, 3 ра́за в день	once, 3 times a day
откро́йте рот	Open your mouth
я слома́л/а ру́ку	I've (m/f) broken my arm
ле́вый, пра́вый	left, right
серьёзно, несерьёзно	It's serious, not serious
ду́мать [1]	to think
вы́звать ско́рую по́мощь	to send for an ambulance
Не беспоко́йтесь!	Don't worry

🔊 Диало́г 1 Скажи́те а-а-а-!

Listen to this conversation in a doctor's surgery and answer the questions below.

Врач	Входи́те. Сади́тесь. Как вас зову́т?
Бра́йан	Меня́ зову́т Бра́йан Уи́лкинсон.
Врач	Что у вас боли́т? Каки́е у вас симпто́мы?
Бра́йан	У меня́ боли́т голова́. Мне то жа́рко, то хо́лодно, и у меня́ температу́ра.
Врач	У вас боли́т го́рло?
Бра́йан	Да, немно́жко.
Врач	Пожа́луйста, откро́йте рот и скажи́те а-а-а.
Бра́йан	А-а-а-а-а.
Врач	Вы ку́рите?
Бра́йан	Нет.
Врач	Я ду́маю, что у вас начина́ется грипп. Э́то не о́чень серьёзно. На́до отдыха́ть до́ма и принима́ть лека́рство три ра́за в день. Поня́тно?
Бра́йан	Да, поня́тно.
Врач	Вот реце́пт.
Бра́йан	Спаси́бо. До свида́ния.

📝 Упражне́ние 3

(a) What is the patient's name? (б) What are his symptoms? (в) Does he smoke? (г) What does the doctor advise?

🎵 Диало́г 2 Это серьёзно!

Leaving the surgery, poor Brian falls down the stairs. He is in some pain, but he still manages to speak Russian!

Врач	**Что с ва́ми?**
Бра́йан	**Ой, мне пло́хо. У меня́ боли́т нога́.**
Врач	**Кака́я нога́? Ле́вая и́ли пра́вая?**
Бра́йан	**Пра́вая.**
Врач	**Покажи́те, пожа́луйста. Мо́жно посмотре́ть?**
Бра́йан	**Да, мо́жно. Ой, я ду́маю, что я слома́л но́гу.**
Врач	**Да, пра́вильно. Это серьёзно! На́до вы́звать ско́рую по́мощь.**
Бра́йан	**Да́йте, пожа́луйста, аспири́н.**
Врач	**Нет, нельзя́. Не беспоко́йтесь. Ско́рая по́мощь ско́ро бу́дет здесь.**

🎵 Упражне́ние 4

(a) What has Brian done? (б) What does the doctor send for? (в) What will he not let Brian do?

🎵 Диало́г 3 Ско́рая по́мощь

Meanwhile, back at the hotel, Caroline has found the administrator collapsed on the floor. She phones for an ambulance.

Кэ́ролайн	**Алло́, «Ско́рая по́мощь»?**
Телефони́ст	**Да, слу́шаю вас. В чём де́ло?**
Кэ́ролайн	**Я не зна́ю, но администра́тор чу́вствует себя́ пло́хо.**
Телефони́ст	**Како́й у вас а́дрес?**
Кэ́ролайн	**А́дрес? Извини́те, я не по́мню.**
Телефони́ст	**Вы в гости́нице?**
Кэ́ролайн	**Да, в гости́нице «Изма́йлово».**
Телефони́ст	**Хорошо́. Я зна́ю а́дрес. Так, администра́тор чу́вствует себя́ пло́хо. А что у него́ боли́т?**
Кэ́ролайн	**Не зна́ю, но я ду́маю, что у него́ боли́т се́рдце.**
Телефони́ст	**Не беспоко́йтесь. Мы ско́ро бу́дем у вас. Че́рез три мину́ты.**

☑ Упражне́ние 5

Caroline is in a bit of a panic, but she is able to tell the switchboard operator everything he needs to know. (a) Where is she staying? (б) What is the matter with the administrator? (в) When will the ambulance be there?

☑ Упражне́ние 6

Read what people say is wrong with them, and underline the most advisable course of action.

(a) У меня́ боли́т голова́	Я принима́ю табле́тку/я чита́ю газе́ту/я иду́ к врачу́.
(б) У меня́ грипп.	Я иду́ на рабо́ту/я иду́ в бассе́йн/ я иду́ к врачу́.
(в) Я слома́ла но́гу.	Я игра́ю в футбо́л/я е́ду в больни́цу/я пью чай.
(г) Меня́ тошни́т.	Я ем котле́ты с ри́сом/я принима́ю лека́рство/я игра́ю в волейбо́л.

☑ Упражне́ние 7

Your medical expertise is called for again! Study the chart below, and fill in the blanks with ticks or crosses to show whether you think certain activities are advisable for your patients. Then tell them what they may and may not do. For example, you might say to Leonid: **Нельзя́ игра́ть в те́ннис, но мо́жно чита́ть газе́ту.** *You must not play tennis, but you may read the paper.*

	Леони́д (слома́л но́гу)	Ири́на (боля́т глаза́)	Арка́дий (тошни́т)	Мариа́нна (боли́т се́рдце)
(a) игра́ть в те́ннис				
(б) чита́ть газе́ту				
(в) пить вино́				
(г) купа́ться в мо́ре				

☑ Упражнéние 8

Many private hospitals advertise their specialist services in the telephone directories. Which heading would you look under if you wanted:

(а) a diagnostic service
(б) specialised laboratories
(в) Tibetan medicine
(г) express analysis

(д) advice on preventive medicine
(е) physiotherapy
(ж) advice on your infectious disease?

(i)   Тибéтская медицúна
(ii) центр превентúвной медицúны
(iii) инфекциóнная больнúца
(iv) специализирóванные лаборатóрии
(v)   экспрéсс-анали́зы
(vi) физиотерапевти́ческая больнúца
(vii) диагнóстика

Скóлько вам лет?
How old are you?

возраст	age
Скóлько вам/ему́/ей лет?	*How old are you/is he/is she?*
мне два́дцать оди́н год	*I am 21 years old*
ему́ три́дцать три гóда	*He is 33 years old*
ей сóрок шесть лет	*she is 46 years old*

In Russian, you choose a different word for *year* depending on the number.

1 – оди́н **год**
2, 3, 4 – два, три четы́ре **гóда**
5, 6, 7 etc., up to 20 – пять, шесть, семь, два́дцать **лет**

For numbers over 20, look at the last digit, and if it is 1 use **год**, if it is 2-4, use **гóда**, and if it is 5, 6, 7, 8, 9, or a multiple of 10, use **лет**.

☑ Упражнéние 9

Choose the correct word for year to complete these phrases. Don't forget to read the numbers out loud!

(а) Мне 53 _____ .
(б) Ему́ 18 _____ .
(в) Ей 2 _____ .
(г) Ему́ 85 _____ .
(д) Ей 61 _____ .

Упражне́ние 10

Listen to the cassette and make a note of these patients' names, ages and symptoms.

	И́мя	О́тчество	Во́зраст	Симпто́мы
(а)				
(б)				
(в)				

Упражне́ние 11

Look at this family photograph, invent names and relationships for the people on it and say how old they are. For example, you might say Э́то мой де́душка. Его́ зову́т Станисла́в и ему девяно́сто де́вять лет. Or Э́то моя́ дочь. Её зову́т Лю́да и ей три го́да.

Упражне́ние 12

Find these words in Russian in the wordsearch grid. Words may be written in any direction, vertically, horizontally or diagonally.

flu	leg	doctor (врач)	eye
arm	prescription	back	ears
head	throat	heart	tooth
mouth		stomach	

р	щ	ф	я	н	г	т	г
е	ю	й	о	л	р	о	г
щ	е	с	а	п	л	в	в
е	щ	з	п	о	э	и	р
п	д	и	в	з	ш	ж	а
т	р	а	к	у	р	г	ч
г	е	ж	ы	б	о	о	б
ч	с	п	и	н	а	х	т

Анекдо́т

Why is this elderly patient unimpressed by the doctor's advice?

вы проживёте до ...	*You will live to ...*

Врач	**Éсли вы не ку́рите и не пьёте, вы проживёте до девяно́ста лет.**
Ба́бушка	**Э, до́ктор, уже́ по́здно!**
Врач	**Почему́?**
Ба́бушка	**Мне уже́ девятно́сто три го́да!**

And finally, read this Russian proverb and see if you can work out what the first line means.

> Кто не ку́рит и не пьёт,
> Тот здоро́веньким умрёт.

The whole saying could be translated as *Whoever neither smokes nor drinks will die healthy.*

20

КАКÓЙ ОН?
What's he like?

In this unit you will learn how to

- say what people are wearing
- say what people look like
- describe someone's character
- express your opinions and preferences

Before you start, revise

- how to say *my*, *your*, *his*, *her* etc. page 114
- singular adjective endings, page 44

Одéжда и óбувь
Clothes and footwear

In the Soviet era, fashionable clothes and footwear were often in short supply in the shops. There was a joke at the time that Adam and Eve must have been Soviet citizens because in the garden of Eden they were naked, barefoot, with one apple between them, and they believed they were living in paradise! In spite of, or because of, the shortages of this time, many Russians became excellent at designing and making their own clothes, and managed to look elegant whatever the circumstances and climate. The image of the country **бáбушка** dressed in padded coat, shawl **платóк** and felt boots **вáленки** has never applied to the younger generation, who have always been as fashion-conscious as young people anywhere.

— **215** —

Expressing your opinion

Showing your pleasure, surprise, agreement or regret is something you will want to do as you talk to Russian friends. Don't forget the verbs **люби́ть** *to love*, and **хоте́ть** *to want*. And here is another useful verb, **мочь** *to be able*.

люби́ть [2]		хоте́ть [*irregular*]		мочь [1]	
я люблю́	мы лю́бим	я хочу́	мы хоти́м	я могу́	мы мо́жем
ты лю́бишь	вы лю́бите	ты хо́чешь	вы хоти́те	ты мо́жешь	вы мо́жете
он лю́бит	они́ лю́бят	он хо́чет	они́ хотя́т	он мо́жет	они́ мо́гут

Он в костю́ме *He's wearing a suit*

Как он оде́т? Как она́ оде́та?	*How is he/she dressed?*
брю́ки/он в брю́ках	*trousers/He's wearing trousers*
джи́нсы/она́ в джи́нсах	*jeans/She's wearing jeans*
ю́бка/она́ в ю́бке	*skirt/She's wearing a skirt*
руба́шка/он в руба́шке	*shirt/He's wearing a shirt*
блу́за/она́ в блу́зе	*blouse/She's wearing a blouse*
сви́тер/он в сви́тере	*sweater/He's wearing a sweater*
костю́м/он в костю́ме	*suit/He's wearing a suit*
га́лстук/он при га́лстуке	*tie/He's wearing a tie*
пла́тье/она́ в пла́тье	*dress/She's wearing a dress*
пальто́/он в пальто́	*coat/He's wearing a coat*
ша́пка/он в ша́пке	*hat (fur)/He's wearing a hat*
ту́фли/она́ в туфля́х	*shoes/She's wearing shoes*
боти́нки/она́ в боти́нках	*ankle boots/She's wearing ankle boots*
очки́/он но́сит очки́	*glasses /He wears glasses*
он бу́дет в ша́пке	*He will be wearing a hat*

☑ Упражне́ние 1

Listen to or read the dialogues below.

(а) Where do you think Nikita and Alan are? (б) Describe Nikita's sister.
(в) Where and when are Monica and Victor meeting? (г) How will Monica recognise him?

💬 Диало́г 1 Как она́ оде́та?

Ники́та Áлан, вот моя́ сестра́ Ма́ша на платфо́рме. Она́ нас
ждёт.
Áлан А я её не зна́ю. Как она́ оде́та?
Ники́та Она́ но́сит очки́, и она́ в пальто́, в боти́нках и ша́пке.
Áлан Да, ви́жу. Она́ краси́вая. Ско́лько ей лет?
Ники́та Два́дцать три го́да.

💬 Диало́г 2 Я бу́ду в костю́ме

Мо́ника Где мы встре́тимся?
Ви́ктор В рестора́не «Восто́к», в семь часо́в.
Мо́ника Хорошо́. Я бу́ду в пла́тье, а вы?
Ви́ктор Я бу́ду в костю́ме. Мне со́рок лет и я ку́рю сига́ры.

Как она́ вы́глядит?
What does she look like?

мужчи́на/же́нщина	*man/woman*
брюне́т (ка)/блонди́н (ка)	*brunette/blonde (m/f)*
высо́кий/невысо́кий	*tall/short*
по́лный/стро́йный	*chubby/slim*
то́лстый/худо́й	*fat/thin*
краси́вый/некраси́вый	*good looking /not good looking*
молодо́й/пожило́й	*young,elderly*
све́тлые, ры́жие, тёмные во́лосы	*light, red, dark hair*
дли́нные, коро́ткие во́лосы	*long, short hair*
голубы́е, ка́рие, се́рые, зелёные глаза́	*blue, brown, grey, green eyes*
с бородо́й	*bearded*
лы́сый	*bald*

☑ Упражне́ние 2

Tick the correct statements.

Ва́ня

Га́ля

(а) Ва́ня невысо́кий.
(б) Он худо́й.
(в) Он пожило́й.
(г) Он краси́вый.
(д) Он лы́сый.
(е) Он в костю́ме.
(ж) Он в джи́нсах.
(з) У него́ дли́нные во́лосы.
(и) У него́ све́тлые во́лосы.
(к) Он но́сит очки́.

(а) Га́ля невысо́кая.
(б) Она́ стро́йная.
(в) Она́ молода́я.
(г) Она́ некраси́вая.
(д) Она́ блонди́нка.
(е) Она́ в ю́бке и блу́зе.
(ж) Она́ в пальто́.
(з) У неё коро́ткие во́лосы.
(и) У неё тёмные во́лосы.
(к) Она́ но́сит очки́.

☑ Упражне́ние 3

You see someone behaving suspiciously, so you ring the police and give them a description. Fill in your half of the conversation. To give the suspect's approximate age, change the order of the words: **ему́ лет два́дцать** *he's about 20* instead of **ему́ два́дцать лет** *he's 20*.

Милиционе́р	**Как он вы́глядит?**
Вы	*It's a young man.*
Милиционе́р	**Ско́лько ему́ лет?**
Вы	*He's about 19.*
Милиционе́р	**Како́й он? Высо́кий?**
Вы	*Yes, he's tall and thin.*

Милиционе́р	**Каки́е у него́ во́лосы?**
Вы	*He has short, dark hair.*
Милиционе́р	**Как он оде́т?**
Вы	*He's wearing jeans and a shirt.*
Милиционе́р	**Спаси́бо.**

Како́й у него́ хара́ктер?
What is his personality like?

симпати́чный	*nice-looking*
интере́сный	*interesting*
энерги́чный	*energetic*
весёлый	*cheerful*
до́брый	*good*
ми́лый	*sweet*
тала́нтливый	*talented*
у́мный	*clever*
глу́пый	*stupid*
лени́вый	*lazy*
ску́чный	*boring*
неприя́тный	*unpleasant*
проти́вный	*revolting*
Он не челове́к, а мо́края ку́рица	*He is not a man, but a wet hen (i.e. a wimp).*

Упражне́ние 4

Kostya and Kolya are like chalk and cheese. Read this description of Kostya and then fill in the missing words in the description of Kolya.

Ко́стя о́чень интере́сный, энерги́чный челове́к. Он высо́кий, худо́й, и о́чень лю́бит игра́ть в бадминто́н. Он симпати́чный и у́мный студе́нт и тала́нтливый актёр. У него́ коро́ткие, све́тлые во́лосы и он но́сит очки́. Он всегда́ весёлый, и по суббо́там он хо́дит в кино́.

Ко́ля о́чень (*boring, lazy*) челове́к. Он (*short*) и (*fat*) и (*doesn't like*) спорт. Он (*unpleasant*) и (*stupid*) студе́нт. У него́ (*long, dark*) во́лосы (*and green eyes*). По суббо́там он хо́дит в кино́.

☑ Упражнéние 5

Read these excerpts from the 'lonely hearts' column in a newspaper. Which advertisement would you reply to if you were looking for (a) a cheerful, good-looking man who enjoys the theatre (б) an older woman with a family (в) a young blonde Ukrainian woman, good-natured (г) a music loving man?

(i) **ВАЛÉРИЙ** Молодóй человéк, 30 лет, рост 184 см., вес 98 кг., рýсский, не пью, не кýрю. Люблю́ мýзыку, спорт.

(ii) **СЛÁВИК** 35 лет, 174 см., 65 кг., стрóйный брюнéт, краси́вый, спорти́вный. Живý в гóроде Нóвгороде. Дóбрый, весёлый харáктер. Люблю́ теáтр, кни́ги.

(iii) **ТАМÁРА** Симпати́чная дéвушка, 25 лет, рост 165 см., вес 65 кг., блонди́нка, украи́нка, люблю́ цветы́ и сóлнце. По харáктеру дóбрая.

(iv) **ЛЮДМИ́ЛА** Жéнщина, лет 53, рýсская, рост 153 см., вóлосы свéтлые, глазá зелёные, энерги́чная. Сын и дочь.

Упражнéние 6

Match up the descriptions below with the pictures.

Лев Толстóй   Ю́рий Гагáрин   Áнна Пáвлова

(a) Молода́я же́нщина, краси́вая, стро́йная, энерги́чная. Лю́бит бале́т.

(в) Пожило́й челове́к с бородо́й, энерги́чный, у́мный. Лю́бит кни́ги.

(в) Молодо́й челове́к, краси́вый. весёлый. Коро́ткие, тёмные во́лосы. Лю́бит путеше́ствовать.

── По-мо́ему. . . *In my opinion*. . . ──

Here are some expressions to use in conversation to express your opinions and feelings.

к сожале́нию/к сча́стью	*unfortunately/fortunately*
как ужа́сно/интере́сно/ску́чно	*how awful/interesting/boring*
наве́рно	*probably*
мо́жет быть	*possibly, maybe*
ка́жется	*it seems*
по-мо́ему	*in my opinion*
совсе́м	*quite (completely)*
дово́льно	*quite (fairly)*
немно́жко/мно́го	*a bit/ a lot*
пра́вильно/непра́вильно	*That's right/not right*
лу́чше/ху́же	*better/worse*
я о́чень люблю́	*I really love*
я бо́льше люблю́	*I prefer (love more)*
бо́льше всего́ я люблю́	(bol'she vsyiv<u>o</u>) *more than anything I love*
я совсе́м не люблю́	*I really don't like*
вот почему́	*That's why*
бо́же мой!	*my God!*
как жаль!	*what a pity!*
кошма́р!	*what a nightmare!*
чуде́сно!	*wonderful!*
смешно́!	*that's funny!*
то́чно так!	*exactly!*
ла́дно	*OK*

✆ Диало́г 3 Как жаль!

✅ Упражне́ние 7

Read these brief dialogues and decide in which one Anatoly expresses
(a) disappointment (б) horror (в) agreement.

(i)   Anatoly is visiting Deena at her flat.

Анато́лий	**Ди́на, мо́жно смотре́ть футбо́л по телеви́зору?**
Ди́на	**Извини́, к сожале́нию, телеви́зор сего́дня не рабо́тает.**
Анато́лий	**Как жаль! Бо́льше всего́ я люблю́ смотре́ть футбо́л. А по́чему телеви́зор не рабо́тает?**
Ди́на	**Я не зна́ю. Наве́рно потому́, что он ста́рый.**
Анато́лий	**По-мо́ему, на́до купи́ть но́вый телеви́зор.**
Ди́на	**Мо́жет быть. Но ску́чно смотре́ть телеви́зор днём.**

(ii) Anatoly and Leonid are making plans for the evening.

Анато́лий	**Что ты хо́чешь де́лать сего́дня ве́чером?**
Леони́д	**Не зна́ю, но в университе́те идёт хоро́ший конце́рт.**
Анато́лий	**Но ты зна́ешь, что я совсе́м не люблю́ му́зыку. Лу́чше идти́ в кино́, да?**
Леони́д	**Нет, дово́льно ску́чно. Я бо́льше люблю́ теа́тр. Пойдём на пье́су «Три сестры́». Ла́дно?**
Анато́лий	**Ла́дно.**

(iii) Vika rings Anatoly with a problem about tickets for their trip.

Анато́лий	**Алло́! Ви́ка?**
Ви́ка	**Да, э́то я. Анато́лий, извини́, но я не могу́ сего́дня купи́ть на́ши биле́ты на по́езд.**
Анато́лий	**Как не мо́жешь, Ви́ка?**
Ви́ка	**Я в больни́це, слома́ла ру́ку.**
Анато́лий	**Бо́же мой! Рука́ боли́т?**
Ви́ка	**Коне́чно, ужа́сно боли́т.**
Анато́лий	**Кошма́р! Что де́лать? Кто мо́жет купи́ть биле́ты, е́сли ты в больни́це?**

☑ Упражне́ние 8

Match up each problem with a solution.

(а) Зал закры́т! Что де́лать?	(i)	Не волну́йтесь. Он слома́л ру́ку. Вот почему́ он в больни́це.
(б) В маши́не совсе́м гря́зно!	(ii)	Вот идёт экскурсово́д. Он, наве́рно, зна́ет.
(в) Я не зна́ю, как рабо́тает телефо́н!	(iii)	Вот вода́ и мы́ло.
(г) Я чу́вствую себя́ ху́же!	(iv)	Вот жето́н на телефо́н.
(д) Я не зна́ю, как попа́сть в гости́ницу!	(v)	Мо́жет быть, ва́ши биле́ты в су́мке?
(е) Како́й кошма́р! Мы потеря́ли биле́ты!	(vi)	Вот табле́тки. Ско́ро бу́дет лу́чше.
(ж) Как ужа́сно! Почему́ Ива́н в больни́це?	(vii)	Вот ключ.

☑ Упражне́ние 9

Read this letter written by a Russian in Minsk, Belarus. He is seeking a penfriend. Make brief notes in English, or write a reply in Russian.

Здра́вствуйте!
Меня́ зову́т Са́ша Никола́евич Ивано́в, мне 18 лет, у меня́ сестра́ и брат. Их зову́т Оля (10 лет) и Ми́ша (3 го́да). Мы живём в кварти́ре в Ми́нске. Мой па́па рабо́тает в поликли́нике. Он - врач. Моя́ ма́ма - учи́тельница. Оля хоро́шая спортсме́нка и лю́бит игра́ть в те́ннис.

Миша ещё не ходит в школу.

Я высокий, у меня тёмные волосы и чёрные глаза. Вы хотите фотографию? Я люблю читать и играть в шахматы, но я больше всего люблю ходить в театр. Зимой я люблю кататься на лыжах. Пожалуйста, напишите. Где вы живёте? Что вы любите делать в свободное время? У вас есть брат или сестра? Вы живёте в квартире или в доме?

Ваш Саша

Анекдо́т

У́тром мать говори́т:
–Пора́ идти́ в шко́лу, сын.
–Не хочу́, мама. На́до идти́?
–На́до, сын, ты учи́тель.

And finally, a rhyming toast **тост** to congratulate you on finishing *Teach Yourself Beginner's Russian*.

Пора́ и вы́пить!	It's time to drink up!
В до́брый час!	Good luck!
За всех госте́й!	To all the guests!
За всех за вас!	To all of you!

You are now a competent speaker of basic Russian. You should be able to handle most everyday situations on a visit to Russia and to communicate with Russian people sufficiently to make friends. If you would like to extend your ability so that you can develop your confidence, fluency and scope in the language, whether for social or business purposes, why not take your Russian a step further with *Teach Yourself Russian* or *Teach Yourself Business Russian?*

ОТВЕТЫ

Answers

Unit 1

1 (a) ii (b) iv (c) i (d) v (e) iii **2** (a) iii (b) iv (c) ii (d) v (e) i **3** (a) iii (b) i (c) ii **4** (a) ii (b) i (c) iv (d) iii **5** snooker, cricket, tennis, stadium, start, knockout, trainer, record, athletics, sport, sportsman **6** (a) vi (b) i (c) viii (d) vii (e) iii (f) iv (g) ix (h) v (i) ii **7** visa, tractor, passport, taxi **8** diplomat, tourist, cosmonaut, chemist, student, administrator, doctor, tractor driver, captain **9** Ivan <u>Nina</u> Alexander Vladimir <u>Ekaterina</u> <u>Liza</u> Lev <u>Irina</u> Valentin <u>Larisa</u> **11** atom, comet, meteor, climate, mechanism, microscope, sputnik, kilo, litre, planet, moon, kilometre **12** television, cassette, monitor, cinecamera, <u>lemonade</u>, radio, printer **13** park, kiosk, grocer's, zoo, stadium, café, telephone, institute, university **15** lamp, chair, corridor, sofa, mixer, vase, toaster, gas, lift **16** saxophone, composer, guitar, piano, orchestra, soloist, opera, pianist, compact disc, heavy metal rock **17** piano **18** omelette, salad, <u>whisky</u>, fruit, <u>coffee</u>, muesli, cutlet, <u>wine</u>, <u>pepsi-cola</u>, minestrone soup

Unit 2

1 (a) iii (b) vi (c) iv (d) i (e) v (f) ii **2**

(a) stewardess (b) platform (c) excursion (d) bus (e) tram (f) airport (g) express (h) signal (i) Aeroflot (j) trolleybus **3** football, volleyball, badminton, marathon, boxing, ping-pong, surfing, final, rugby, hockey, basketball **4** symphony, ballerina, poet, actress, bestseller, actor, ballet, thriller **5** energy, kilowatt, atmosphere, kilogram, electronics, experiment **6** America, Mexico, Africa, Pakistan, Argentina, England, Russia, Ukraine, Canada, India, Australia, Norway **8** (a) bar (b) Melody (music shop) (c) Pizza Hut (d) museum (e) circus (f) bank (g) library (h) Kremlin (i) post office (j) Bolshoi Theatre **9** (a) souvenir (b) militia (c) information (d) pizza (e) provisions **10** (a) cheeseburger (b) banana (c) cappuccino coffee (d) pizza 'super supreme' **11** (a) manager (b) fax (c) briefing (d) marketing (e) floppy disc (f) businessman (g) know-how (h) broker (i) week-end (j) computer **13** (a) Chekhov (b) Tolstoy (c) Pushkin (d) Tchaikovsky (e) Rachmaninov (f) Shostakovich (g) Lenin (h) Gorbachev (i) Yeltsin **14** (a) temperature (b) bacterium (c) antibiotic (d) massage (e) tablet (f) diagnosis (g) penicillin (h) infection **15** (a) iv (b) iii (c) v (d) ii

(e) i **16** Игорь – футболист. Антон – турист. Лариса – студентка. Борис – теннисист. Наташа – балерина. **18** (a) m (b) f (c) m (d) n (e) f (f) m (g) m (h) f (i) n (j) f (k) m (l) n **19** сестра/стадион/саксофон **20** суп омлет салат (masculine) **21** (a) сестра (b) симфония (c) Аргентина (d) библиотека (e) температура

Unit 3

1 (a) iii (b) i (c) ii (a) i (b) iii (c) ii Vladimir Boris **2** (a) доброе утро (b) добрый день (c) добрый вечер **3** Меня зовут Стюарт. Очень приятно. **4** (e) **5** (a) iii (b) iv (c) i (d) ii. **6** (a) Hello (b) Thank you (c) I speak English (d) Good (e) Where is Boris? (f) I don't know (g) Slower, please (h) Excuse me/Sorry **7** (a) iii (b) v (c) ii (d) i (e) iv **8** (a) зовут (b) Добрый (c) не (d) говорите (e) человек **9** (a) iii (b) ii (c) iii **10** (a) iv (b) v (c) ii (d) iii (e) i

END OF UNIT REVISION

1 Здравствуйте. **2** До свидания. **3** Извините. **4** Как вас зовут? **5** Вы говорите по-английски? **6** Я не понимаю.

Unit 4

BEFORE YOU START

автобус (*m*) опера (*f*) пианино (*n*) метро (*n*) мама (*f*) банк (*m*) **2** (a) boulevard (b) avenue (c) campsite (d) taxi rank (e) café-bar (f) tourist hotel (g) botanical garden (h) first aid post (i) yacht club (j) tourist club (k) canal (l) Red Square **3** (a) он (b) она (c) он (d) оно (e) она (f) он (g) она (h) оно **5** 2-6, 7-5, 3-4, 8-1, 10-0, 9-10 **6** (a) bus no. 5 (b) trolleybus no. 8 (c) tram no. 3 (d) bus no. 9 **7** (a)

Вот оно./Оно вон там. (b) Извините, я не знаю. (c) Нет, это почта. (d) Не за что! **8** (b) (d) (e) (c) (a) **9** красное вино, белая таблетка, зелёный салат, жёлтый банан, чёрный кот

ПРОВЕРЬТЕ СЕБЯ
(d) (c) (a) (e) (b)

Unit 5

2 (a) i (b) ii (c) i (d) i *1* в ресторан *2* в институт *3* в универмаг *4* в бассейн *5* в кафе *6* в библиотеку *7* в школу *8* на площадь *9* в поликлинику *10* в церковь *11* в больницу *12* в музей *13* в театр *14* в аптеку *15* в цирк *16* на станцию метро *17* на почту *18* в парк *19* на стадион *20* в кино *21* в гастроном *22* в банк *23* на фабрику *24* в справочное бюро *25* в гостиницу *26* на вокзал **3** Use same endings as ex. 2, 1-26. **4** (a) Игорь хороший футболист. (b) Лена красивая балерина. (c) Хард-Рок американское кафе. (d) Лондон большой город. (e) Правда русская газета. **5** Tick (*a*) and (*d*) **6** (a) vi (b) iii/iv (c) i (d) iii (e) ii (f) v **7** бананы фрукты таблетки сигареты папиросы цветы конфеты **8** (a) 12-24-18 (b) 25-30-17 (c) 14-32-11 (d) 15-03-24 (e) 20-19-12 **9** (a) ix (b) xi (c) vii (d) i (e) viii (f) iv (g) vi (h) iii (i) x (j) ii (k) v **10** (a) v theatre (b) iv library (c) ii grocer's (d) iii station (e) vi restaurant (f) vii hotel (g) i café

ПРОВЕРЬТЕ СЕБЯ
1 (*ii*) **2** (*v*) **3** (*iii*) **4** (*i*) **5** (*iv*)

Unit 6

1 (a) Где? (b) Как? (c) Куда (d) Что? (e) Кто? **2** *Suggested answers.*

(a) Да, ру́сская во́дка и матрёшки.
(b) Извини́те, нет. (c) Да, ру́сские
папиро́сы и америка́нские сигаре́ты.
(d) Да, хоро́шие бана́ны. **3** (a) iv
(b) v (c) ii (d) iii (e) i **4** (a) ii (b) iv
(c) vii (d) i (e) iii (f) v (g) vi **5** (a)
ва́ше моё (b) ва́ша моя́ (c) ва́ши
мои́ (d) ваш мой **6** Tick everything.
Underline во́дка, пи́цца, смета́на,
пепси-ко́ла. **7** Большо́й   теа́тр,
ма́ленькое ра́дио, краси́вые цветы́,
ру́сские   папиро́сы,   интере́сная
кни́га,   молодо́й   челове́к,
ботани́ческий   сад,   хоро́шие
конфе́ты, бе́лое вино́

ПРОВЕ́РЬТЕ СЕБЯ́
1 Я хочу́ чай с лимо́ном. **2** Я иду́ в
кино́. **3** Э́то ру́сская во́дка. **4** Да,
метро́   закры́то. **5** Да, э́то мой
биле́т.

Unit 7

3 (a) ii (b) iv (c) vi (d) i (e) iii (f) v **4**
(a) Scottish (b) Portuguese (c) Irish (d)
Norwegian **5** (a) ii/4/C (b) iv/1/B (c)
i/2/A (d) iii/3/D **6** (a) iii (b) v (c) ii
(d) vii (e) i (f) iv (g) vi **7** (a) в
больни́це в Арха́нгельске (b) на
стадио́не (c) В гости́нице (d) в рес-
тора́не **8** Э́та книга, э́тот паспорт,
Э́ти сигаре́ты, э́то ра́дио **9** (a) vi
(b) x (c) vii (d) viii (e) i (f) iv (g) ii
(h) ix (i) iii (j) v

ПРОВЕ́РЬТЕ СЕБЯ́
4, 5, 2, 7, 8, 1, 6, 3

Unit 8

1 (a) 8.00 (b) 7.00 (c) 3.00 (d) 1.00
(e) 11.00 (f) 2.00 (g) 10.00 (h) 6.00
(i) 4.00 **2** (a) Час (b) Три часа́ (c)
Пять   часо́в (d) Де́вять   часо́в
три́дцать мину́т (e) Два часа́ со́рок

пять мину́т (f) Оди́ннадцать часо́в
де́сять мину́т (g) Двена́дцать часо́в
пять мину́т (h) Три часа́ два́дцать
пять   мину́т (i)   Четы́ре   часа́
пятьдеся́т мину́т **3** (a) семь встаю́
(b) во́семь за́втракаю (c) де́вять иду́
(d) обе́даю (e) во́семь (f) де́вять
смотрю́ (g)   оди́ннадцать **4** (a)
Музе́й антрополо́гии и этногра́фии
открыва́ется в оди́ннадцать часо́в.
Выходно́й день – суббо́та. Телефо́н
– две́сти восемна́дцать – четы́рна-
дцать   –   двена́дцать. (b)   Музе́й
музыка́льных   инструме́нтов
открыва́ется в двена́дцать часо́в.
Выходно́й день – вто́рник. Телефо́н
– три́ста четы́рнадцать – пятьдеся́т
три – пятьдеся́т пять. (c) Музе́й-
кварти́ра А.А. Бло́ка открыва́ется в
оди́ннадцать часо́в. Выходно́й день
– среда́. Телефо́н – сто трина́дцать –
во́семьдесят шесть – три́дцать три.
(d) Музе́й А́рктики и Анта́рктики
открыва́ется в двена́дцать вто́рник
часо́в. Выходно́й день – вто́рник.
Телефо́н – три́ста оди́ннадцать –
два́дцать пять – со́рок де́вять. **5** (a)
Чт. (b) Пн. (c) Вт. (d) Ср. (e) Сб.
(f) Вс. (g) Пт. **6** (a) 1st (ground floor)
(b) 2nd (c) 3rd (d) 5th (e) 5th (f) 6th
(g) 4th (h) 5th (i) 2nd **7** (a) обе́д (b)
за́втрак (c) у́жин **8** (a) в теа́тре
в Но́вгороде (b) в библиоте́ку (c) в
университе́те,   в   шко́ле (d)   в
институ́т (e) в поликли́нику **9** (a)
Wednesday (b) Friday (c) Tuesday (d)
Monday (e) Thursday (f) Saturday (g)
Sunday **10** (a) Mon. (b) 13.00–14.00
(c) Sat. (d) Sun. (e) 16.00 **11** Friday

ПРОВЕ́РЬТЕ СЕБЯ́
3 Когда́ открыва́ется банк? **4** Когда́
начина́ется фильм? **5** Встре́тимся
в семь часо́в в рестора́не.

Unit 9

Диало́г

George – reading, jazz, languages, travel. Lyudmila – badminton, tennis, walking. George – saxophone. Jazz concert, this evening, 5th October.

1 суббо́та пе́рвое октября́, воскресе́нье второ́е октября́, понеде́льник тре́тье октября́, вто́рник четвёртое октября́, среда́ пя́тое октября́, четве́рг шесто́е октября́, пя́тница седьмо́е октября́. (a) Thurs. (b) Wed. (c) Three sisters (d) Tues. **3** (a) Likes library, reading books, newspapers. (b) Plays badminton. Likes sport. Plays guitar. (c) Likes travel. Speaks English and French well. Doesn't like going to opera or drinking champagne. (d) Likes going to theatre and concerts. Likes music, plays balalaika. Likes pizza. **4** (a) Пе́рвое января́ (b) Седьмо́е января́ (c) Восьмо́е ма́рта (d) Девя́тое ма́я (g) трина́дцатого ию́ня, два́дцать четвёртого декабря́, три́дцать пе́рвого октября́ (h) шесто́го сентября́, тре́тье октября́, четы́рнадцатого февраля́ **5** (a) ix (b) vi (c) xi (d) v/x (e) vii (f) v (g) iv (h) iii (i) ii (j) iii/vi/vii/viii (k) xii (l) i **6** (a) 6,000 (b) 14,500 (c) 20,380 (d) 5,346 (e) 19,923 (f) 2,411 (g) 1,298 (h) 10,531 **7** (a) рабо́таю (b) говори́те (c) понима́ю (d) люблю́ (e) живёте (f) за́втракаю (g) гуля́ю **8** (a) Как вас зову́т? (b) Вы ру́сский? (c) Где вы живёте? (d) Кто вы по профе́ссии? (e) Где вы рабо́таете? (f) У вас есть хо́бби? (g) Вы лю́бите спорт? **9** (a) On Saturday 25th May, 6.00 (b) On Thursday 31st July, 9.25 (c) В понеде́льник восьмо́го февраля́, в семь часо́в три́дцать мину́т.

(d) В пя́тницу шестна́дцатого ма́рта, в пять часо́в.

Прове́рьте себя́

(b) (e) о́чень люблю́ (c) (f) люблю́ (a) не люблю́ (d) совсе́м не люблю́

Unit 10

Диало́ги

1 2 children. Parents live at dacha. **2** (a) Бе́лла (b) Серёжа (c) Tim **3** Anna prefers city, concerts, theatre, cinema, shops. Historical. Near metro. Sasha prefers countryside. Peaceful. Walks in forest.

1 (a) 63 tram or 28 bus (b) 28 bus (c) 28 bus (d) 17 trolleybus (e) 63 tram (f) 63 tram (g) 17 trolleybus (h) 28 bus **2** **Anya:** Moscow. Pharmacy. Mum and dad, sister. Cinema. Wants to speak German. **Peter:** Bristol. Teacher, school. Son. Football. Wants to travel. **Leonid:** Yekaterinburg. Train station. Wife. T.V. and sweets. Doesn't like sport. Wants to live in Moscow. **3** живёт магази́ны ку́хня её лю́бит день хо́дит **4** (a) iii (b) iv (c) ii (d) i **5 Boris:** brother, flat. **Nastya:** cat, dacha. **Liza:** car, brother, flat, dacha. **6** (a) зна́ю (b) идёте, иду́ (c) хочу́ (d) говори́т (e) рабо́таешь (f) за́втракаю (g) люблю́ (h) игра́ем (i) у́жинают

Прове́рьте себя́

1 (a) i (b) iii (c) iii (d) ii (e) iii (f) ii (g) i (h) iii **2** (a) ii (b) iii (c) iii **3** (a) большо́й (b) больни́цу (c) ва́ша (d) Магада́не (e) бадминто́н (f) гита́ре (g) пя́тое **4** (a) ii (b) iii (c) i (d) ii (e) i (f) iii (g) ii

Unit 11

1 Sport: баскетбо́л, футбо́л, бокс, пинг-по́нг, те́ннис, ре́гби, хокке́й.

Food: хлеб, бана́н, сала́т, борщ, шокола́д, котле́та. Family: ма́ма, дочь, ба́бушка, дя́дя, па́па, сын, брат, сестра́. **2** гита́ра, инжене́р, больни́ца **3** (1) теа́тр (2) студе́нт (3) метро́ (4) рестора́н (5) омле́т (6) кли́мат (7) па́спорт (8) входи́те (9) тра́ктор (10) Амстерда́м (11) октя́брь (12) вто́рник (13) телефо́н **4** кварти́ра **6** (a) восто́к (b) де́душка (c) а́вгуст (d) три́дцать (e) Росси́я

Unit 12

1 (a) 16«а» (б) white wine, бе́лое вино́ (в) 18:35, восемна́дцать часо́в три́дцать пять мину́т, 15 degrees, пятна́дцать гра́дусов **2** (a) Де́вять «б» нале́во. (б) У нас есть лимона́д, фрукто́вый сок и ко́фе с молоко́м. (в) Да́йте, пожа́луйста, фрукто́вый сок. (г) У вас есть ру́сский журна́л? **3** (a) 4 «б» (б) 10 «г» (в) 25 «г» (г) 11 «в» (д) 2.08, + 30 (e) 9.43, –5 (ж) 1.00, + 7 **4** (a) exit, no exit, boarding gate (exit to embarkation) (б) customs control, luggage reclaim, transit, passport control, flight number (в) check-in (registration), red channel, waiting room, entrance **5** до́ллары, пистоле́т, доро́жные че́ки, фу́нты сте́рлингов, ка́мера, компью́тер, францу́зские фра́нки. **6** (a) Здра́вствуй, Валенти́н? (б) Да, как дела́? (в) В пя́тницу. (г) Да, шесто́го ию́ля. (д) В восемна́дцать часо́в со́рок мину́т. (e) Да, коне́чно. (ж) Но́мер ре́йса SU две́сти со́рок два. (з) До свида́ния, Валенти́н. **7** Но́мер ре́йса ВА восемьсо́т се́мьдесят во́семь. Я бу́ду в Санкт Петербу́рге в девятна́дцать часо́в со́рок мину́т, два́дцать шесто́го января́. **8** (a) Как прия́тно тебя́ ви́деть! (б) Как

вы пожива́ете? (в) Я немно́жко уста́л/а. (г) как всегда́ (д) Мы ско́ро бу́дем до́ма. **9** (a) шестна́дцатого а́вгуста в два́дцать два часа́ три́дцать мину́т (б) пя́того ноября́ в де́сять часо́в пятна́дцать мину́т (в) два́дцать девя́того ма́я в трина́дцать часо́в пятьдеся́т мину́т (г) деся́того февраля́ в пятна́дцать часо́в два́дцать мину́т. **11** (a) 165 (б) 392 (в) 78 (г) 413 (д) 521 **12** (a) Что вы хоти́те пить? (б) Как ва́ша фами́лия? (в) Где моё ме́сто? (г) У вас есть фу́нты сте́рлингов? (д) Э́то ваш чемода́н и ва́ша су́мка? **13** (a) 5 (б) 7 (в) 1 (г) 2 (д) 3 (e) 4 (ж) 6

Анекдо́т

1 food, transport, hospitals, schools **2** You mustn't grumble in the Soviet Union, but you can grumble in America.

Unit 13

1 (a) 14 (б) on the right (в) 20-30 minutes (г) 10 minutes (д) 3 (e) на восьмо́й авто́бус (ж) пря́мо (з) Пешко́м три́дцать – со́рок мину́т. А на авто́бусе пятна́дцать. (и) Че́рез четы́ре остано́вки. **2** Smoke **3** (a) «Парк Культу́ры» the park of culture (б) «Университе́т» University (в) 4 **4** (a) Пло́щадь Револю́ции (б) Пу́шкинская (в) Арба́тская (г) Ботани́ческий сад (д) Алекса́ндровский сад. Скажи́те, пожа́луйста, как попа́сть в Кремль, в Ботани́ческий сад, на ры́нок, в Дом Кни́ги, в ГУМ? Дое́дете до ста́нции **5** (a) 6th August (б) train no. 7, carriage no. 13 (в) 10.30 (г) seat no. 2 (д) 11.00 **6** По́езд но́мер девяно́сто шесть в Но́вгород отхо́дит в де́вять часо́в три́дцать шесть мину́т. По́езд но́мер пятьсо́т оди́ннадцать в

Петербу́рг отхо́дит в двена́дцать часо́в пятьдеся́т пять мину́т. По́езд но́мер се́мьсот шестна́дцать в Ива́ново отхо́дит в два́дцать часо́в со́рок семь мину́т. По́езд но́мер во́семьдесят два в Ту́лу отхо́дит в два́дцать три часа́ пять мину́т. **7** (а) 9.40 (б) Yes. (в) На Ки́евский вокза́л, пожа́луйста. В де́сять часо́в. **8** (а) ii (б) iii (в) i **9** (а) Как попа́сть в Кремль? (б) Где остано́вка авто́буса? (в) Вы сейча́с выхо́дите? (г) Я е́ду в Ботани́ческий сад на метро́. (д) Когда́ отхо́дит по́езд?

АНЕКДО́Т 1
1 In case he loses the first and second ones **2** He has a season ticket

АНЕКДО́Т 2
1 The train conductor **2** A forest

Unit 14

1 Books about sport. **2** (а) Estonia. 15,000 roubles per kilo (б) Мо́жно посмотре́ть? (в) Ско́лько вы хоти́те? (г) Всё? (д) Напро́тив **3** (а) Lemons and mandarins (б) Edam cheese from Holland (в) Ketchup (г) Indian (д) Stolichnaya, Smirnoff, Absolut **4** Underline all except Мя́со **5** Coffee, fruit flavoured water, vodka, fruit-tea, champagne. Luncheon meat, chocolate, caramel, sauces, ketchups, sweets. **6** (а) У вас есть колбаса́? (б) ... чай? (в) ... торт? (г) ... ры́ба? (д) ... молоко́? (е) ... апельси́ны? (ж) огурцы́? **7** (а) Go round the shops. (б) Books, wooden toys, post cards and samovar. (в) No, not far. 3 stops by bus. (г) Opposite (д) она́ говори́т, что (е) The salesgirl's aunt lives in London,

and says they work there. (ж) Red, green, yellow. **8** (аспири́н – апте́ка) (ма́сло – моло́чные проду́кты/ гастроно́м /универса́м) (са́хар – гастроно́м /универса́м) (вино́ – гастроно́м /универса́м) (моро́женое – кио́ск) (цветы́ – ры́нок) (хлеб – бу́лочная) (самова́р – сувени́ры) (ша́пка – универма́г/сувени́ры) **9** (а) Matryoshka doll. «Сувени́р». Straight ahead, on the left. (б) Books. Tram 31. «Дом Кни́ги». Not far. 2 or 3 stops. (в) Cake. Grocer's on у́лица Ми́ра. Bus. **10** (а) О́птика (б) Часы́ (в) Бу́лочная (г) Антиквариа́т (д) Диети́ческие проду́кты (е) Ры́ба (ж) Музыка́льные инструме́нты (з) А́удио-Видеоте́хника (и) Автомоби́ли **11** (а) Я хочу́ купи́ть хлеб, сыр, помидо́ры и чай. (б) Где мо́жно купи́ть газе́ту? (в) Всё. (г) Повтори́те, пожа́луйста. (д) У вас есть бе́лое вино́? (е) Ско́лько сто́ит?

АНЕКДО́Т
Fish is what they haven't got in the shop opposite.

Unit 15

1 (а) A room for one with bath (б) A big room for two with shower (в) $120 (г) tomorrow (д) 7.00. 9.00. (е) yes (ж) suitcase and big bag (з) straight ahead and right **2** (а) midnight (б) downstairs on left **3** (а) Room for two with shower. (б) Room for one for 7th January. (в) Room for two for week. **4** (а) У вас есть свобо́дный но́мер? (б) Но́мер на двои́х с ва́нной, пожа́луйста. (в) Хорошо́. В кото́ром часу́ начина́ется обе́д? (г) Здесь есть лифт? У меня́ большо́й чемода́н. (д) Да, ви́жу. (е) Спаси́бо. Но́мер три́дцать четы́ре. Пра́вильно? (ж) Спаси́бо большо́е.

До свида́ния. **7** (a) Australia, 61. (б) Breakfast, tea with lemon and fruit. She feels unwell. (в) To the station, 10.00 tomorrow. **8** (a) Edna's room is hot. Window shut, because noisy outside on square. (б) Mark is cold. Another blanket required. Room 73. Tap won't turn off and TV works badly. (в) Vanessa says they have lost key. Room 16. Key at administrator's desk. Vanessa delighted. (г) Bill wants the bill. Room for 2 for week. Very pleasant stay, warm and quiet in room. Very pleased. (д) Gary is not happy. Hot water not on, telephone not working, dirty room. **9** Room 9, TV needs mending. Room 14, telephone not working properly. Room 23, tap won't turn off. Room 31, cold, window won't shut. Room 35, hot, window won't open. Room 40, noisy. Room 52, dirty. Room 55, radio not working. **10** В но́мере хо́лодно, гря́зно, шу́мно, телеви́зор не рабо́тает, кран не закрыва́ется, окно́ выхо́дит на вокза́л. Я недово́лен/недово́льна. **11** (a) New, red, American suitcase. (б) Old black bag containing visa and passport. (в) New, green coat. (г) Money: dollars, sterling and roubles. **12** Ground floor: cloakroom, lost property, restaurant. First floor: director, administrator, service desk, newspaper kiosk, snack bar. Second floor: post office, hairdresser's, bar.

Unit 16

1 (a) with lemon and sugar (б) sandwich (bread with salami sausage) **2** (a) Да́йте/покажи́те, пожа́луйста, меню́. (б) Да́йте, пожа́луйста, ко́фе и моро́женое. (в) Нет, ко́фе с молоко́м и с са́харом. (г) Я не понима́ю. Повтори́те, пожа́луй-

ста. (д) Поня́тно. Да́йте, пожа́луйста, вани́льное моро́женое. (е) Спаси́бо. Ско́лько с меня́? **3** First (ground) floor, restaurant. Breakfast, 8.00 – 10.00. За́трак начина́ется в во́семь часо́в и конча́ется в де́сять часо́в. Dinner, 13.00 – 15.00. Обе́д начина́ется в трина́дцать часо́в и конча́ется в пятна́дцать часо́в. Evening meal, 18.00 – 20.00. У́жин начина́ется в восемна́дцать часо́в и конча́ется в два́дцать часо́в. Second (first) floor grill-bar, where coffee and sandwiches can be ordered. **4** (a) Moscow salad and borshsh (beetroot soup). (б) Mushrooms in sour cream, shshee (cabbage soup), kebab (shashlik) with rice, fruit, white wine, tea with lemon but no sugar. (в) Her brother. Asks for extra wine glass and plate. **5** Да́йте, пожа́луйста, ещё ча́шку, ло́жку, нож и стул. **6** Mushrooms in sour cream, cabbage soup, shashlik, rice, red wine, bread. Another fork. Грибы́ в смета́не, щи, шашлы́к, рис и кра́сное вино́. Хлеб. Ещё ви́лка. **7** На столе́ – таре́лка, нож, ви́лка, ло́жка, рю́мка, салфе́тка, вино́, хлеб, ку́рица. **8** Да́йте, пожа́луйста, моско́вский сала́т, суп с гриба́ми, беф-стро́ганов, рис, шокола́дное моро́женое, бе́лое вино́ и ко́фе с молоко́м. Да́йте, пожа́луйста, счёт. **9** (ж) (б) (з) (а) (д) (г) (и) (е) (в) **11 Ка́ша ри́совая моло́чная:** рис – сто грамм; ма́сло – два́дцать пять грамм; са́хар – два́дцать грамм; соль – пять грамм; молоко́ – две́сти шестьдеся́т миллили́тров; вода́ – две́сти миллили́тров **12** (a) Champagne and flowers (roses). (б) Fine. (в) Mushrooms in sour cream and caviar. (г) Yes, very tasty. (д) Vodka. (е) It's late.

13 (а) Я о́чень люблю́ шампа́нское. (б) За ва́ше здоро́вье! (в) Каки́е краси́вые рю́мки! (г) Как дела́?

Анекдо́т

Someone has stolen his bike, so he does not need to avoid alcohol.

Unit 17

1 (а) iii (б) ii (в) iii **2** (а) ii (б) iii (в) v (г) i (д) iv **3** (а) Krasnodar. 861-992-54-16. Tomorrow at 10.00. Three minutes. (б) Nottingham, England. 0115-923-44-19. Today at 11.00. Eight minutes. (в) Novgorod. 816-25-13-67. Tomorrow evening at 7.00. Five minutes. **4** (а) v (б) viii (в) ix (г) i (д) iv (е) iii (ж) vi (з) ii (и) vii **5** (а) stamps, envelopes, postcards (б) 4 stamps at 500 roubles for letter to UK (в) fill in form (г) books and magazines **6** (а) три ма́рки по три́ста рубле́й (б) Что на́до де́лать? (в) Коне́чно мо́жно. (г) пра́вильно (д) Спаси́бо вам большо́е. (е) мо́жно (ж) хоти́те (з) запо́лнить (и) Э́то (к) свида́ния **7** (а) Как (б) Где (в) Куда́ (г) Кто (д) Ско́лько (е) Как (ж) Что (з) Когда́ **8** Куда́, кому́ ... Москва́, Проспе́кт Ми́ра, дом 26, кварти́ра 9, Ивано́в, А. Текст ... Я в Москве́ в гости́нице «Росси́я», у́лица Варва́рка, но́мер 331. Фами́лия и а́дрес отправи́теля ... Москва́, гости́ница «Росси́я», у́лица Варва́рка, но́мер 331, your surname and initials in Cyrillic script. **9** сын дочь/соль пе́рец/стол стул/вокза́л по́езд/я́блоки гру́ши/ма́ма па́па/теа́тр пье́са/де́вушка молодо́й челове́к **10** Росси́я 194358, Санкт Петербу́рг, Проспе́кт Э́нгельса, дом121 ко́рпус 2 кварти́ра 69, Кузнецо́ва, Т. И.

Unit 18

Информа́ция

Holiday advert. Mallorca (Spain). Aeroflot flights Moscow – Barcelona – Moscow. 3 star hotel, twin rooms, bar, café, discos, tennis, pool, golf club, shopping tour, casino, excursion around Barcelona. Staff speak Russian. One week, including breakfasts, $745.

1 (а) Go skiing in forest. (б) Cold, frosty, sunny, minus 10. (в) Sit at home and watch TV. (г) Summer, hot, can walk on beach, eat ice cream. (д) To ring Andrew. (е) 739-15-42. **2** (а) 3 (б) 4 (в) 2 (г) 5 (д) 1 **3** Tomorrow: cold, air temperature –7°, northerly wind, snow and frost. **4** На за́паде па́смурно и идёт дождь. На се́вере тума́нно. На восто́ке ми́нус 10 гра́дусов и идёт снег. На ю́ге тепло́, плюс 20 гра́дусов и со́лнце све́тит. **5** Helen is from Lancaster. Likes radio, chess, reading, films and concerts. Yura is from Krasnodar. Plays hockey, skis, walks in country, plays tennis, swims in sea, collects mushrooms. **6** Здесь мо́жно лови́ть ры́бу, купа́ться в мо́ре, загора́ть на пля́же, ката́ться на велосипе́де, ката́ться на ло́дке, игра́ть в те́ннис. **7** (а) ii (б) iii (в) i **8** (а) Sochi in hotel at beach. (б) Sunny and hot. (в) Eats ice cream and plays volleyball on beach. **9** (а) Tomorrow. (б) Eight. (в) 8 a.m. **10** (1) Enquiry office (2) tourist complex (3) hotel (4) campsite (5) architectural monument (6) museum (7) archeological monument (8) theatre, concert hall (9) stadium (10) restaurant, café, bar (11) department store (12) market (13) taxi rank (14) petrol station (15) train station (16) beach (17) garden, park. **11** Almost any excuse will do! **12** (а) 8.30, 12.30, 16.55, 19.20, 21.00,23.50 (б) 9.55, 21.40 (в) 14.20, 16.30, 20.40

(г) 11.10, 18.20 (д) 9.20, 14.00, 20.00
13 (а) Б (б) В

Unit 19

1 Vadim, 1. Tanya, 3. Anton, 2. **2** (1) нос (2) нога́ (3) голова́ (4) се́рдце (5) у́хо (6) живо́т (7) го́рло (8) глаз (9) зу́бы (10) рука́ (11) спина́ **3** (а) Brian Wilkinson. (б) Headache, hot and cold, temperature, sore throat. (в) No. (г) To rest at home and take medicine 3 times a day. **4** (а) Broken his right leg. (б) Ambulance. (в) Take an aspirin. **5** (а) Hotel Izmailovo (б) Feels bad, heart hurting. (в) Soon, in 3 minutes. **6** (а) Я принима́ю табле́тку. (б) Я иду́ к врачу́. (в) Я е́ду в больни́цу. (г) Я принима́ю лека́рство. **7** *Suggested answer*: **Леони́д** (а) ✗ (б) ✓ (в) ✓ (г) ✗ **Ири́на** (а) ✗ (б) ✗ (в) ✓ (г) ✓ **Арка́дий** (а) ✗ (б) ✓ (в) ✗ (г) ✗ **Мариа́нна** (а) ✗ (б) ✓ (в) ✗ (г) ✗ **8** (а) vii (б) iv (в) i (г) v (д) ii (е) vi (ж) iii **9** (а) го́да (б) лет (в) го́да (г) лет (д) год **10** (1) Nina Andryeyevna. 27. Back hurts. (2) Nikolay Vladimirovich. 53. Temperature. Feels sick. (3) Sergey Sergeyevich. Toothache.

АНЕКДО́Т
Doctor tells her she will live to 90 if she doesn't drink and smoke. She is already 93.

Unit 20

1 (а) On a train. (б) Wears spectacles, dressed in coat, boots and hat. Beautiful. 23 years old. (в) In restaurant 'Vostok' at 7.00. (г) Victor will wear a suit. 40 years old, smokes cigars. **2** Vanya: ✓ (в) (д) (ж) (к). Galya: ✓ (а) (б) (в) (д) (е). **3** Э́то молодо́й челове́к. Ему́ лет девятна́дцать. Да, высо́кий и худо́й. У него́ коро́ткие, тёмные во́лосы. Он в джи́нсах и в руба́шке. **4** ску́чный, лени́вый, невысо́кий, то́лстый, не лю́бит, неприя́тный, глу́пый, дли́нные, тёмные, зелёные глаза́. **5** (а) ii (б) iv (в) iii (г) i **6** (1) б (2) в (3) а **7** (а) i (б) iii (в) ii **8** (а) vii (б) iii (в) iv (г) vi (д) ii (е) v (ж) i **9** Sasha Nikolayevich Ivanov, 18, has sister and brother. Olya 10, Misha 3. Live in flat, Minsk. Father is doctor, mother is teacher. Olya likes sport, tennis. Misha not yet at school. Tall, dark hair, black eyes. Do you want photo? Likes reading and chess, most of all, going to theatre. Skiing. Please write. Where do you live? What do you like to do? Brothers or sisters? Do you live in a flat or a house?

Цифры *Numbers*

Cardinal numbers

0	ноль	11	одиннадцать
1	один	12	двенадцать
2	два	13	тринадцать
3	три	14	четырнадцать
4	четыре	15	пятнадцать
5	пять	16	шестнадцать
6	шесть	17	семнадцать
7	семь	18	восемнадцать
8	восемь	19	девятнадцать
9	девять	20	двадцать
10	десять		

21 двадцать один

30	тридцать	200	двести
40	сорок	300	триста
50	пятьдесят	400	четыреста
60	шестьдесят	500	пятьсот
70	семьдесят	600	шестьсот
80	восемьдесят	700	семьсот
90	девяносто	800	восемьсот
100	сто	900	девятьсот

1,000	тысяча
2,000	две тысячи
3,000	три тысячи
4,000	четыре тысячи
5,000	пять тысяч
6,000	шесть тысяч
7,000	семь тысяч
8,000	восемь тысяч
9,000	девять тысяч
10,000	десять тысяч
20,000	двадцать тысяч

Ordinal numbers

1st	пе́рвый	11th	оди́ннадцатый
2nd	второ́й	12th	двена́дцатый
3rd	тре́тий	13th	трина́дцатый
4th	четвёртый	14th	четы́рнадцатый
5th	пя́тый	15th	пятна́дцатый
6th	шесто́й	16th	шестна́дцатый
7th	седьмо́й	17th	семна́дцатый
8th	восьмо́й	18th	восемна́дцатый
9th	девя́тый	19th	девятна́дцатый
10th	деся́тый	20th	двадца́тый
		21st	два́дцать пе́рвый
		30th	тридца́тый

SUMMARY OF LANGUAGE PATTERNS

the/a

There are no words in Russian for *the* and *a*.

to be

The verb *to be* is not used in the present tense.

Spelling rules

1 Do not use **ы** after **г**, **к**, **х**, **ж**, **ч**, **ш**, **щ**. Instead, use **и**.
2 Do not use unstressed **о** after **ж**, **ч**, **ш**, **щ**, **ц**. Instead, use **е**.

Gender of singular nouns

Masculine nouns end in	**a consonant**	парк
	й	музе́й
	ь	Кремль
	а	па́па
Feminine nouns end in	а	кассе́та
	я	эне́ргия
	ь	дочь
Neuter nouns end in	о	метро́
	е	кафе́

Plural forms of nouns

Masculine
рестора́н/рестора́ны   *restaurant/s*
кио́ск/кио́ски   *kiosk/s*
рубль/рубли́   *rouble/s*

Feminine
гости́ница/гости́ницы   *hotel/s*
библиоте́ка/библиоте́ки   *library/libraries*
пло́щадь/пло́щади   *square/s*

Neuter
у́тро/у́тра   *morning/s*

Many neuter nouns (бюро́, кака́о, кафе́, кило́, кино́, метро́, пиани́но, ра́дио) do not change.

Adjectives

Masculine singular	Э́то краси́**вый** парк.	*It's a beautiful park.*
Feminine singular	Э́то краси́**вая** ва́за.	*It's a beautiful vase.*
Neuter singular	Э́то краси́**вое** ра́дио.	*It's a beautiful radio.*
Plural	Э́то краси́**вые** ма́рки.	*They are beautiful stamps.*

Most common endings are **–ый –ий –о́й** (*m*), **–ая –яя** (*f*), **–ое –ее** (*n*) and **–ые, –ие** (*pl*).

Possessive pronouns

Мой (*my/mine*), **твой** (*your/yours*), **наш** (*our/ours*), **ваш** (*your/yours*) change form to agree with nouns to which they refer.

Masculine	**Feminine**	**Neuter**	**Plural**
мой па́спорт	моя́ балала́йка	моё пиани́но	мои́ кассе́ты
твой па́спорт	твоя́ балала́йка	твоё пиани́но	твои́ кассе́ты
наш па́спорт	на́ша балала́йка	на́ше пиани́но	на́ши кассе́ты
ваш па́спорт	ва́ша балала́йка	ва́ше пиани́но	ва́ши кассе́ты

Его́ (*his*), **её** (*her/hers*), **их** (*their/theirs*) do not change form.

его́ па́спорт	его́ балала́йка	его́ пиани́но	его́ кассе́ты

Pronouns

Где авто́бус?	*Where is the bus?*	Вот **он**.	There **it** is. (*m*)
Где ва́за?	*Where is the vase?*	Вот **она́**.	There **it** is. (*f*)
Где ра́дио?	*Where is the radio?*	Вот **оно́**.	There **it** is. (*n*)
Где конфе́ты?	*Where are the sweets?*	Вот **они́**.	There **they** are. (*pl*)

Demonstrative pronouns

Да́йте, пожа́луйста, **э́тот** чемода́н.	*Please give me **that** suitcase.*
Э́та де́вушка – моя́ дочь.	***This** girl is my daughter.*
Покажи́те, пожа́луйста, **э́то** ра́дио.	*Please show me **that** radio.*
Э́ти биле́ты – мои́.	***These** tickets are mine.*

Personal pronouns

singular		*plural*	
я	*I*	мы	*we*
ты	*you* (informal)	вы	*you* (plural or formal)
он	*he/it*	они́	*they*
она́	*she/it*		
оно́	*it*		

As well as meaning *his*, *her* and *their*, the words **его́**, **её** and **их** mean *him*, *her* and *them* in phrases where personal pronouns are the direct object of the verb.

ты лю́бишь **меня́**	*you love me*	вы лю́бите **нас**	*you love us*
я люблю́ **тебя́**	*I love you*	они́ лю́бят **вас**	*they love you*
она́ лю́бит **его́**	*she loves him*	мы лю́бим **их**	*we love them*
он лю́бит **её**	*he loves her*		

У вас есть ...? *Do you have ...?*

у меня́	*I have*	у нас	*we have*
у тебя́	*you have*	у вас	*you have*
у него́	*he/it has*	у них	*they have*
у неё	*she has*		

Accusative case after в and на (into/to)

Masculine and neuter singular nouns do not change after **в** and **на** when motion is indicated, but feminine singular nouns change their endings from **-a** to **-y** and **-я** to **-ю**.

Masculine	*Feminine*	*Neuter*
Как попа́сть в теа́тр?	Как попа́сть на по́чту?	Как попа́сть в кафе́?
	Как попа́сть в галере́ю?	

Accusative case with direct objects

The accusative case is used when an inanimate noun is the direct object of a verb. Only the feminine singular ending changes.

- (*m*) Я люблю́ **спорт**. *I love sport.*
- (*f*) Я люблю́ **му́зыку**. *I love music.*
- (*n*) Я люблю́ **кино́**. *I love cinema.*
- (*pl*) Я люблю́ **кни́ги**. *I love books.*

Prepositional case after в and на (in)

When **в** and **на** mean *in* or *at* a certain place, they trigger the prepositional case in the following word.

Masculine	*Feminine*	*Neuter*
(институ́т) в институ́те	(шко́ла) в шко́ле	(письмо́) в письме́
(Кремль) в Кремле́		
(музе́й) в музе́е		

Verbs in present tense

Group 1 verbs

рабо́тать *to work*

я	рабо́таю	мы	рабо́таем
ты	рабо́таешь	вы	рабо́таете
он/она́/оно́	рабо́тает	они́	рабо́тают

идти́ *to go on foot on one occasion*

я иду́	мы идём
ты идёшь	вы идёте
он/она́ идёт	они́ иду́т

быть *to be* (future tense)

я бу́ду	мы бу́дем
ты бу́дешь	вы бу́дете
он/она́ бу́дет	они́ бу́дут

пить *to drink*

я пью	мы пьём
ты пьёшь	вы пьёте
он/она́ пьёт	они́ пьют

мочь *to be able*

я могу́	мы мо́жем
ты мо́жешь	вы мо́жете
он/она́ мо́жет	они́ могу́т

Group 2 verbs

говори́ть *to speak/talk*

я	говорю́	мы	говори́м
ты	говори́шь	вы	говори́те
он/она́	говори́т	они́	говоря́т

ходи́ть *to go on foot habitually*

я хожу́	мы хо́дим
ты хо́дишь	вы хо́дите
он/она́ хо́дит	они́ хо́дят

люби́ть *to love*

я люблю́	мы лю́бим
ты лю́бишь	вы лю́бите
он/она́ лю́бит	они́ лю́бят

Irregular verbs

хоте́ть *to want*

я	хочу́	мы	хоти́м
ты	хо́чешь	вы	хоти́те
он/она́	хо́чет	они́	хотя́т

жить *to live*

я	живу́	мы	живём
ты	живёшь	вы	живёте
он/она́	живёт	они́	живу́т

есть *to eat*

я	ем	мы	еди́м
ты	ешь	вы	еди́те
он/она́	ест	они́	едя́т

VOCABULARY

1 The English translations apply only to the meaning of the words as used in this book.

2 Nouns ending in a consonant or **-й** are masculine. A few nouns ending in **-а** are also masculine, but this will be clear from their meaning, e.g. **де́душка** – grandfather.
Other nouns ending in **-а** or **-я** are feminine.
Nouns ending in **-ь** may be masculine or feminine. This will be indicated by (m) or (f).
Nouns ending in **-о** or **-е** are neuter.

3 Adjectives are shown in their masculine singular form, ending **-ый**, **-ий** or **-ой**.

4 Verbs are shown in their infinitive form unless otherwise stated. If they are straightforward verbs it will be shown whether they belong to group 1 or group 2.

English — Russian

a little bit немно́жко
a lot мно́го
all right, fine норма́льно
already уже́
also то́же
always всегда́
and и
another ещё
at home до́ма
at last наконе́ц
awful ужа́сно

bad пло́хо
be быть
be able мочь 1
beautiful краси́вый
because потому́, что
better лу́чше
big большо́й
brother брат
but а, но

closed закры́т

cold хо́лодно

daughter дочь
to do де́лать 1
do you have? у вас есть?
don't mention it! не́ за что!
to drink пить 1

each, every ка́ждый
early ра́но
to eat есть
entrance вход
everything всё
excuse me извини́те
exit вы́ход
it's expensive до́рого

fairly, quite дово́льно
far, a long way далеко́
father оте́ц
favourite люби́мый
it's fine прекра́сно
fine прекра́сный
flat кварти́ра
fortunately к сча́стью
funny смешно́

to get to попа́сть
girl, young woman де́вушка
give me да́йте
go (imperative) иди́те
to go on foot идти́ 1
to go on foot (habitually) ходи́ть 2
it's good хорошо́
good хоро́ший
good day до́брый день
good evening до́брый ве́чер
good morning до́брое у́тро
good night споко́йной но́чи
goodbye до свида́ния
grandfather де́душка
grandmother ба́бушка

to have breakfast за́втракать 1
to have dinner обе́дать 1
to have supper у́жинать 1
he, it он
hello здра́вствуйте

her её
here здесь
his, him его́
house, block of flats дом
how как
how is that written? как э́то пи́шется?
how much do I owe? ско́лько с
  меня́?
how much does it cost? ско́лько
  сто́ит?
how much? how many? ско́лько
how old are you? ско́лько вам лет?
husband муж

I я
if е́сли
in English по-англи́йски
in my opinion по-мо́ему
in Russian по-ру́сски
in the afternoon днём
in the evening ве́чером
in the morning у́тром
in, into в
it's interesting интере́сно
interesting интере́сный
it он, она́, оно́
it is, this (n) э́то

just so! то́чно так!

to know знать 1

late по́здно
left ле́вый
let's go (by transport) пое́дем
let's go (on foot) пойдём
let's meet встре́тимся
to live жить 1
look (imperative) посмотри́те
to look, watch смотре́ть 2
to love люби́ть 2

man мужчи́на
man, person челове́к
may I help you? вам помо́чь!
maybe мо́жет быть
me меня́
more бо́льше

most of all бóльше всегó
mother мать
my мой

name и́мя
it's necessary нáдо
new нóвый
no нет
it's noisy шýмно
not не
not allowed, mustn't нельзя́
not far недалекó
now сейчáс

of course конéчно
often чáсто
old стáрый
only тóлько
open откры́т
opposite напрóтив
or и́ли
our наш

patronymic name óтчество
it's peaceful спокóйно
pity (what a pity!) жаль (как жаль!)
to play игрáть 1
please пожáлуйста
it's possible мóжно
probably навéрно

it's quiet ти́хо
quite, entirely совсéм

to read читáть 1
repeat (imperative) повтори́те
right прáвый
rouble рýбль
Russian рýсский, рýсская

to say, talk говори́ть 2
say, tell me скажи́те
to see ви́деть 2
it seems кáжется
she, it онá
shop магази́н
show me (imperative) покажи́те
sit down (imperative) сади́тесь
slower мéдленнее

small мáленький
so так
son сын
straight ahead пря́мо
street ýлица
surname фами́лия

thank you спаси́бо
that's nice прия́тно
that's right прáвильно
to the left налéво
to the right напрáво
their, them их
then потóм
there вот, там
there is, there are есть
these э́ти
they они́
to think дýмать 1
this (m), (f) э́тот, э́та
it's time порá
today сегóдня
tomorrow зáвтра
too, too much сли́шком
town гóрод

to understand понимáть 1
understood поня́тно
unfortunately к сожалéнию
us нас
usually обы́чно

very óчень

to want хотéть (irreg)
it's warm теплó
we мы
what have you got? что у вас есть?
what is your name? как вас зовýт?
what sort of ..? какóй..?
what time is it? котóрый
    час?/скóлько сейчáс врéмени?
what's the matter? в чём дéло?
    что с вáми?
what, that что
where где
where from откýда
where to кудá

who кто
wife жена́
with pleasure с удово́льствием
woman же́нщина
it's wonderful чуде́сно
to work рабо́тать
worse ху́же

yes да
yesterday вчера́
you (pl. formal) вы
you (object) вас
you (sing. informal) ты
you (object) тебя́
young молодо́й
your ваш, твой

Russian — English

а *but*
а́вгуст *August*
авиаписьмо́ *airmail letter*
авто́бус *bus*
автомоби́ль (*m*) *car*
администра́тор *administrator*
а́дрес *address*
а́дрес отправи́теля *address of sender*
аккордео́н *accordion*
актёр *actor*
акти́вный *active*
актри́са *actress*
алло́ *hello (on phone)*
альбо́м *album*
Аме́рика *America*
америка́нец, америка́нка *American (m, f)*
америка́нский *American (adj)*
анекдо́т *anecdote*
англи́йский *English*
А́нглия *England*
англича́нин, англича́нка *Englishman, woman*
анке́та *questionnaire*
антибио́тик *antibiotic*
апельси́н *orange*
апте́ка *pharmacy*
аспири́н *aspirin*
атле́тика *athletics*
атмосфе́ра *atmosphere*
Аэрофло́т *Aeroflot*
аэропо́рт *airport*
а́вгуст *August*
а́том *atom*

ба́бушка *grandmother*
бага́ж *luggage*
бадминто́н *badminton*
бакте́рия *bacterium*
балала́йка *balalaika*
балери́на *ballerina*
бале́т *ballet*
бана́н *banana*

банк *bank*
ба́нка *tin, jar*
ба́ня *steam bath*
бар *bar*
баскетбо́л *basketball*
бассе́йн *swimming pool*
бато́н *long loaf*
бе́лый *white*
бе́рег *bank, shore*
бери́те *take (imperative)*
(не) беспоко́йтесь *(don't) worry (imperative)*
бестсе́ллер *bestseller*
библиоте́ка *library*
бизнесме́н *businessman*
биле́т *ticket*
бланк *form*
блонди́н, блонди́нка *blond man, woman*
блу́за *blouse*
блю́до *dish*
бо́же мой! *my God!*
бокс *boxing*
боли́т, боля́т *it hurts, they hurt*
больни́ца *hospital*
бо́льше *more*
бо́льше всего́ *most of all*
большо́й *big*
борода́ *beard*
борщ *borshsh (beetroot soup)*
ботани́ческий *botanical*
боти́нки *ankle boots*
брат *brother*
бри́финг *briefing*
бро́кер *broker*
брю́ки *trousers*
брюне́т, брюне́тка *brown haired man, woman*
бу́дет *will be*
бу́лка *sweet bread roll*
бу́лочная *bakery*
бульва́р *boulevard*
бума́жник *wallet*
бутербро́д *sandwich*
буты́лка *bottle*
буфе́т *snack bar*

был *was*
быть *to be*
бюро́ нахо́док *lost property office*
бюро́ обслу́живания *service desk*

в *in, into*
ваго́н *train carriage*
ваго́н-рестора́н *restaurant car*
ва́за *vase*
ва́ленки *felt boots*
вам помо́чь? *may I help you?*
вани́льный *vanilla*
ва́нна *bath*
ва́нная *bathroom*
варе́нье *fruit preserve*
вас *you (object)*
ваш *your*
велосипе́д *bicycle*
вес *weight*
весна́ *spring*
весно́й *in spring*
ве́трено *windy*
ве́чером *in the evening*
вид *view*
ви́деть 2 (ви́жу, ви́дишь) *to see*
ви́за *visa*
ви́лка *fork*
вино́ *wine*
ви́ски *whisky*
вку́сный *tasty*
внизу́ *downstairs*
вода́ *water*
во́дка *vodka*
во́здух *air*
во́зраст *age*
вокза́л (на) *train station*
волейбо́л *volleyball*
во́лосы *hair*
вон там *over there*
воскресе́нье *Sunday*
восто́к (на) *east*
восто́чный *eastern*
вот *there*
врач *doctor*
вре́мя *time*
всегда́ *always*

всё *everything*
встаю́ *I get up*
встре́тимся *let's meet*
вто́рник *Tuesday*
второ́е блю́до *second (main) course*
вход *entrance*
входи́те *come in (imperative)*
в чём де́ло? *what's the matter?*
вчера́ *yesterday*
вы *you*
вы́дача багажа́ *luggage reclaim*
вы́звать *to send for*
высо́кий *tall*
выходи́ть *to go out*
вы́ход *exit*
вы́ход на поса́дку *boarding gate*
выходно́й день *closing day*

газ *gas*
газе́та *newspaper*
газиро́ванный *sparkling, fizzy*
галере́я *gallery*
га́лстук *tie*
гардеро́б *cloakroom*
гарни́р *side dishes*
гастроно́м *grocer's*
где *where*
Герма́ния *Germany*
гита́ра *guitar*
глаз *eye*
говори́ть 2 *to say, talk*
год *year*
голова́ *head*
голубо́й *blue*
го́рло *throat*
го́род *town*
городско́й *urban*
горя́чий *hot*
господи́н *Mr*
госпожа́ *Mrs, Miss*
гости́ная *lounge*
гости́ница *hotel*
гото́вить 2 (гото́влю, гото́вишь)
    to prepare, cook
гра́дус *degree*
гражда́нство *nationality*

грамм *gram*
гриб *mushroom*
грипп *flu*
гру́ша *pear*
гря́зный *dirty*
гуля́ть 1 *to go for a walk*

да *yes*
да́йте *give (imperative)*
далеко́ *far, a long way*
да́ча *dacha (country house)*
дверь (*f*) *door*
де́вушка *girl, young woman*
де́душка *grandfather*
дежу́рная *woman on duty*
дека́брь (*m*) *December*
деклара́ция *declaration*
(как) дела́? *how are things?*
де́лать 1 *to do*
де́ньги *money*
дере́вня *village, countryside*
деревя́нный *wooden*
де́ти *children*
де́тский сад *kindergarten*
джаз *jazz*
джи́нсы *jeans*
диа́гноз *diagnosis*
дива́н *couch*
диплома́т *diplomat*
дли́нный *long*
для куря́щих *for smokers*
днём *in the afternoon*
до́брое у́тро *good morning*
до́брый ве́чер *good evening*
до́брый день *good day*
дово́лен *happy*
дово́льно *fairly, quite*
дое́дете до *travel as far as*
дождь (*m*) *rain*
до́ктор *doctor*
докуме́нт *document*
как вы долете́ли? *how was your*
    flight
до́ллар *dollar*
дом *house, block of flats*
до́ма *at home*

Дом Кни́ги   the Book House (book shop)
до́рого   it's expensive
доро́жный   traveller's cheque
до свида́ния   goodbye
дочь (f)   daughter
ду́мать 1   to think
дура́к   fool
душ   shower
ду́шно   it's humid
дя́дя   uncle

еди́ный биле́т   season transport ticket
е́сли   if
есть   there is, there are
есть   to eat
е́хать 1 (е́ду, е́дешь)   to go by transport
ещё   another
ёлка   fir tree

жаль (как жаль!)   pity (what a pity!)
жа́рко   it's hot
ждать 1 (жду, ждёшь)   to wait
жёлтый   yellow
жена́   wife
же́нщина   woman
жёсткий   hard
жето́н   token
живо́т   stomach
жить 1 (живу́, живёшь)   to live
журна́л   magazine

за ва́ше здоро́вье!   your health!
за́втра   tomorrow
за́втрак   breakfast
за́втракать 1   to have breakfast
загора́ть 1   to sunbathe
за грани́цей   abroad
заказа́ть   to order
закрыва́ется, закрыва́ются   it closes, they close
закры́т   closed
заку́ски   starters
зал   hall
зал ожида́ния   waiting room

за окно́м   through the window
за́пад (на)   west
запо́лните   fill in (imperative)
застегни́те   fasten (imperative)
здесь   here
здра́вствуйте   hello
зелёный   green
зе́ркало   mirror
зима́   winter
зи́мний   winter (adj)
зимо́й   in winter
знать 1   to know
зову́т (как вас зову́т)   they call (what are you called?)
зоологи́ческий   zoological
зоопа́рк   zoo
зуб   tooth

и   and
игра́ть 1   to play
игру́шка   toy
иди́те   go (imperative)
идти́ 1 (иду́, идёшь)   to go on foot
извини́те   excuse me (imperative)
икра́   caviar
и́ли   or
и́мя   name
инжене́р   engineer
институ́т   institute
интере́сно   it's interesting
интере́сный   interesting
инфе́кция   infection
информа́ция   information
ирла́ндец, ирла́ндка   Irish man, woman
испа́нец, испа́нка   Spanish man, woman
Испа́ния   Spain
истори́ческий   historical
ищу́   I'm looking for
ию́ль (m)   July
ию́нь (m)   June

кабине́т   study, consulting room
ка́ждый   each, every
ка́жется   it seems
как   how

какáо *cocoa*
какóй *what sort of*
как э́то мóжет быть? *how can this be?*
как э́то пи́шется? how is that written?
кáмера *camera*
канáл *canal*
капитáн *captain*
кáрий *brown (eyes)*
картóшка *potato*
кáсса *cash desk*
кассéта *cassette*
катáться на лы́жах, конькáх, саня́х *to ski, skate, sledge*
кафé *café*
кáша *porridge*
кварти́ра *flat*
кéмпинг *camping*
кило́ *kilo*
киловáтт *kilowatt*
килогрáмм *kilogram*
километр *kilometre*
кино́ *cinema*
киноаппарáт *cine-camera*
кинотеáтр *cinema*
кио́ск *kiosk*
кли́мат *climate*
ключ *key*
кни́га *book*
кни́жечка *strip of transport tickets*
код *code*
колбасá *salami sausage*
комéта *comet*
кóмната room
компáкт-ди́ск *compact disk*
композáтор *composer*
компóт *stewed fruit*
компью́тер *computer*
кому́ *to whom*
конвéрт envelope
конéчно *of course*
консультáция *consultation*
конфéта *sweet*
кончáется *it finishes*
коридóр corridor
корóткий *short*

кóрпус *section of housing block*
космонáвт *cosmonaut*
костю́м *suit*
кот *cat*
котлéта *cutlet (flat meatball)*
котóрый час? *what time is it?*
кóфе *coffee*
кошелёк *purse*
кошмáр *nightmare*
кран *tap*
краси́вый *beautiful*
Крáсная плóщадь *Red Square*
крáсный *red*
кремль (m) *Kremlin*
крéсло *armchair*
кри́кет *cricket*
кровáть (f) bed
к себé *pull*
к сожалéнию *unfortunately*
к счáстью *fortunately*
кто *who*
кудá *where to*
купáться *to swim*
купé *compartment*
купи́ть *to buy*
кури́ть *to smoke*
кýрица *chicken*
курс *exchange rate*
кýхня *kitchen*

лáдно *OK*
лáмпа *lamp*
лéвый *left*
лекáрство *medicine*
лес *forest*
лéто *summer*
лéтом *in summer*
лимонáд *lemonade*
литр *litre*
лифт *lift*
лови́ть ры́бу *to catch fish*
лóдка *boat*
лóжка *spoon*
ложýсь спать *I go to bed*
лóшадь (f) *horse*
лунá *moon*

лу́чше *better*
лы́сый *bald*
люби́мый *favourite*
люби́ть 2 (люблю́, лю́бишь) *to love*

магази́н *shop*
май *May*
ма́ленький *small*
ма́льчик *boy*
ма́ма *Mum*
марафо́н *marathon*
ма́рка *stamp*
ма́ркетинг *marketing*
март *March*
маршру́т *route*
маршру́тное такси́ *fixed-route taxi*
ма́сло *butter*
масса́ж *massage*
матрёшка *matryoshka doll*
мать (*f*) *mother*
маши́на *car*
меда́ль (*f*) *medal*
ме́дленнее *slower*
медпу́нкт *first-aid post*
медсестра́ *nurse*
междугоро́дный *inter-city*
междунаро́дный *international*
ме́неджер *manager*
меню́ *menu*
меня́ *me*
ме́сто *place, seat*
ме́сяц *month*
метео́р *meteor*
метр *metre*
метро́ *metro*
механи́зм *mechanism*
микроско́п *microscope*
ми́ксер *mixer*
мили́ция *police*
минера́льная вода́ *mineral water*
ми́нус *minus*
мину́та *minute*
мно́го *a lot*
мо́жет быть *maybe*
мо́жно *it's possible*

мой *my*
молодо́й *young*
молоко́ *milk*
моло́чные проду́кты *dairy products*
монито́р *monitor*
мо́ре *sea*
моро́женое *ice cream*
моро́з *frost*
Москва́ *Moscow*
москви́ч, москви́чка *Muscovite man, woman*
мост *bridge*
мочь 1 (могу́, мо́жешь) *to be able*
мужчи́на *man*
музе́й *museum*
му́зыка *music*
мы *we*
мы́ло *soap*
мю́сли *muesli*
мя́гкий *soft*
мя́со *meat*

на *at, to, on*
на́бережная *embankment*
наве́рно *probably*
на́до *it's necessary*
наконе́ц *at last*
нале́во *to the left*
напи́ток *drink*
напиши́те *write (imperative)*
напра́во *to the right*
напро́тив *opposite*
нарко́тик *narcotics*
начина́ется *it starts*
наш *our*
не *not*
нева́жно *not very well*
невысо́кий *short, not tall*
недалеко́ *not far*
неде́ля *week*
недо́рого *it's inexpensive*
не́ за что! *don't mention it!*
некраси́вый *ugly*
нельзя́ *it is not allowed, mustn't*
не́мец, не́мка *German man, woman*

немно́жко *a little bit*
нет *no*
но *but*
но́вый *new*
нога́ *leg, foot*
нож *knife*
нока́ут *knock-out*
но́мер *number, hotel room*
норве́жец, норве́жка *Norwegian man, woman*
норма́льно *all right, fine*
нос *nose*
но́чью *at night*
ноя́брь *(m)* *November*

о *about*
обе́д *dinner*
обе́дать 1 *to have dinner*
обме́н валю́ты *currency exchange*
обра́тный биле́т *return ticket*
о́бувь *(f)* *footwear*
обы́чно *usually*
объе́кт *object*
о́вощи *vegetables*
огуре́ц, огу́рчик *cucumber, gherkin*
оде́жда *clothes*
оде́т *dressed*
одея́ло blanket
(биле́т в) оди́н коне́ц *one way ticket*
одну́ мину́точку *wait a minute*
окно́ *window*
октя́брь *(m)* *October*
омле́т *omelette*
он *he, it*
она́ *she, it*
они́ *they*
оно́ *it*
о́пера *opera*
орке́стр *orchestra*
о́сень *(f)* *autumn*
о́сенью *in autumn*
остано́вка *stop (bus)*
осторо́жно *carefully*
отде́л department
отдыха́ть 1 to rest, holiday

оте́ц *father*
откро́йте *open (imperative)*
открыва́ется *it opens*
откры́т *open*
откры́тка *post card*
отку́да *where from*
отправле́ние *departure*
о́тпуск *holiday*
от себя́ *push*
отхо́дит (по́езд) *departs (train)*
о́тчество *patronymic name*
официа́нт, официа́нтка *waiter, waitress*
о́чень *very*
о́чередь *(f)* *queue*
очки́ *spectacles*

пальто́ *coat*
па́па *Dad*
папиро́са *cigarette with cardboard mouthpiece*
парикма́херская *hairdresser's*
парк *park*
парфюме́рия *perfumery*
па́смурно *it's overcast*
па́спорт *passport*
па́спортный контро́ль *passport control*
пассажи́р *passenger*
пассажи́рский *passenger (adj)*
па́чка *packet*
пеницилли́н *penicillin*
пе́нсия *pension*
пепси-ко́ла *pepsi-cola*
пе́рвое блю́до *first (soup) course*
переса́дка *change (train)*
перехо́д *crossing*
пе́рец *pepper*
пешко́м *on foot*
пиани́но *piano*
пиани́ст *pianist*
пи́во *beer*
пинг-по́нг *table tennis*
письмо́ *letter*
пистоле́т *pistol*
пить 1 (пью, пьёшь) to drink

пи́цца *pizza*
пишу́ *I write*
план *plan*
плане́та *planet*
плати́ть *to pay*
плато́к *shawl*
платфо́рма *platform*
пла́тье *dress*
пло́хо *it's bad*
пло́щадь (*f*) (на) *square*
плюс *plus*
по-англи́йски *in English*
повтори́те *repeat (imperative)*
пого́да *weather*
пода́рок *present*
по́дпись (*f*) *signature*
поду́шка *pillow*
пое́дем *let's go (by transport)*
по́езд *train*
пожа́луйста *please*
пожа́р *fire*
(как вы) пожива́ете? *how are you?*
пожило́й *elderly*
позвони́ть *to telephone*
по́здно *it's late*
по-испа́нски *in Spanish*
пойдём *let's go (on foot)*
пойти́ *to go (on foot)*
покажи́те *show (imperative)*
по́лдень (*m*) *midday*
поликли́ника *health centre*
по́лночь (*f*) *midnight*
по́лный *chubby*
полоте́нце *towel*
помидо́р *tomato*
по́мню *I remember*
по-мо́ему *in my opinion*
понеде́льник *Monday*
по-неме́цки *in German*
понима́ть 1 *to understand*
поня́тно *it's understood*
попа́сть *to get to*
пора́ *it's time*
португа́лец, португа́лка
    Portuguese man, woman
по-ру́сски *in Russian*

посла́ть *to send*
посмотре́ть *to have a look*
посмотри́те *look (imperative)*
посы́лка *parcel*
(мы) потеря́ли *(we) lost*
пото́м *then*
потому́, что *because*
по́чта (на) *post office*
почто́вый я́щик *post box*
поэ́т *poet*
по-япо́нски *in Japanese*
пра́вда *truth (newspaper)*
пра́вильно *that's right*
пра́вый *right*
пра́здник *public holiday, festive*
    occasion
прекра́сно *it's fine*
прекра́сный *fine (adj)*
приезжа́йте к нам в го́сти *come*
    and visit us (imperative)
принести́ *to bring*
принима́ть 1 (лека́рство) *to take*
    (medicine)
при́нтер *printer*
прия́тно *that's nice*
прия́тного аппети́та *bon appétit,*
    enjoy your meal
пробе́йте тало́н *punch ticket*
    (imperative)
проводни́к, проводни́ца *conductor,*
    conductress
прогно́з *forecast*
продаве́ц, продавщи́ца *shop*
    assistant (m, f)
продаётся, продаю́тся *is for sale,*
    are for sale
проду́кты *provisions*
(у меня́) пропа́л *(I've) lost*
проспе́кт *avenue*
профе́ссия *profession*
прохла́дно *it's cool*
пря́мо *straight ahead*
путеше́ствовать *to travel*
пье́са *play*
пя́тница *Friday*

рабóта (на)   *work*
рабóтать 1   *to work*
рáдио   *radio*
раз   *once, time*
разговóр   *conversation*
раздевáйтесь   *take coat off (imperative)*
рáно   *early*
расписáние   *timetable*
регистрáция   *registration*
рéгби   *rugby*
рейс   *flight*
рекá   *river*
(вы) рекомендýете   *(you) recommend*
рекóрд   *record*
рéмни   *seat-belts*
ремóнт   *repair*
ресторáн   *restaurant*
рецéпт   *prescription, recipe*
рис   *rice*
рисовáть   *to draw*
рождествó   *Christmas*
рóза   *rose*
ромáн   *novel*
Россúя   *Russia*
рот   *mouth*
рубáшка   *shirt*
рýбль (*m*)   *rouble*
рукá   *arm, hand*
рýсский, рýсская   *Russian man, woman, (adj)*
рыба   *fish*
рыжий   *red-haired*
рынок   *market*
рюмка   *wine glass*

с   *with*
сад   *garden*
садúтесь   *sit down (imperative)*
саксофóн   *saxophone*
салáт   *salad*
салфéтка   *napkin*
самовáр   *samovar*
самолёт   *aeroplane*
сáхар   *sugar*
свéжий   *fresh*

свéтлый   *light*
свúтер   *sweater*
свобóдный   *free*
сéвер (на)   *north*
сегóдня   *today*
сейчáс   *now*
семья   *family*
сентябрь (*m*)   *September*
сéрдце   *heart*
серьёзный   *serious*
сéрфинг   *surfing*
сéрый   *grey*
сестрá   *sister*
сигарéта   *cigarette*
сúгнал   *signal*
симптóм   *symptom*
симфóния   *symphony*
скажúте   *say, tell me (imperative)*
скóлько   *how much, how many*
скóлько вам лет?   *how old are you?*
скóлько с меня?   *how much do I owe?*
скóлько сейчáс врéмени?   *what's the time?*
скóлько стóит, стóят?   *how much does it, do they cost?*
скóрая медицúнская пóмощь   *ambulance*
скóрый   *fast*
скýчный   *boring*
слéдующий   *next*
слúшком   *too, too much*
слóво   *word*
сломáть   *to break*
слýшать 1   *to listen*
слýшаю вас   *I'm listening*
сметáна   *smetana (sour cream)*
смешнó   *it's funny*
смотрéть 2   *to look, watch*
снег   *snow*
снýкер   *snooker*
собирáть 1   *to collect*
совсéм   *quite, entirely*
сок   *juice*
солúст   *soloist*

со́лнце све́тит   *the sun is shining*
соль (*f*)   *salt*
соси́ска   *sausage*
спа́льный ваго́н   *sleeping car (train)*
спа́льня   *bedroom*
спаси́бо   *thank you*
спать   *to sleep*
спина́   *back*
споко́йно   *it's peaceful*
споко́йной но́чи   *good night*
спорт   *sport*
спортсме́н, спортсме́нка   *sportsman, sportswoman*
спра́вочное бюро́   *information bureau*
спу́тник   *sputnik*
среда́   *Wednesday*
стадио́н (на)   *stadium*
стака́н   *glass*
ста́нция (на)   *station (bus, metro)*
старт   *start*
ста́рый   *old*
стол   *table*
столо́вая   *dining room*
стоп   *stop*
стоя́нка такси́   *taxi rank*
стро́йный   *slim*
студе́нт, студе́нтка   *student (m, f)*
стул   *chair*
суббо́та   *Saturday*
сувени́р   *souvenir*
стюарде́сса   *stewardess*
с удово́льствием   *with pleasure*
су́мка   *bag*
суп   *soup*
су́пермаркет   *supermarket*
су́шка   *dry ring-shaped biscuit*
счёт   *bill*
сын   *son*
сыр   *cheese*
сюда́   *here (motion)*

таба́к   *tobacco*
табле́тка   *tablet*
так   *so*
такси́   *taxi*

тало́н   *ticket (transport)*
там   *there*
таmöженный контро́ль   *customs control*
танцева́ть   *to dance*
таре́лка   *plate*
теа́тр   *theatre*
текст   *text*
телеви́зор   *television*
телегра́мма   *telegram*
телефо́н   *telephone*
телефо́н-автома́т   *public pay-phone*
тёмный   *dark*
температу́ра   *temperature*
те́ннис   *tennis*
тенниси́ст, тенниси́стка   *tennis player (m, f)*
тепло́   *it's warm*
теря́ть   *to lose*
тётя   *aunt*
ти́хо   *it's quiet*
то..., то...   *now this, now the other*
това́рищ   *comrade*
то́же   *also*
то́лстый   *fat*
то́лько   *only*
торт   *cake*
то́стер   *toaster*
то́чно так!   *just so!*
(меня́) тошни́т   *(I) feel sick*
тра́ктор   *tractor*
трактори́ст, трактори́стка   *tractor driver (m, f)*
трамва́й   *tram*
трампли́н   *ski jump*
транзи́т   *transit*
тра́нспорт   *transport*
тре́нер   *trainer*
три́ллер   *thriller*
тролле́йбус   *trolleybus*
туале́т   *toilet*
тума́нно   *it's foggy, misty*
тури́ст, тури́стка   *tourist (m, f)*
ту́фли   *shoes*
ты   *you (singular, informal)*

у вас есть? *do you have?*
угоща́йтесь *help yourself (imperative)*
ужа́сно *it's awful*
ужа́сный *awful*
уже́ *already*
у́жин *supper*
у́жинать 1 *to have supper*
у́лица (на) *street*
универма́г *department store*
универса́м *supermarket*
университе́т *university*
уста́л *tired*
у́тром *in the morning*
у́хо, у́ши *ear, ears*
учи́тель, учи́тельница *teacher (m, f)*

фа́брика (на) *factory*
факс *fax*
фами́лия *surname*
февра́ль (*m*) *February*
фина́л *final*
фотоаппара́т *camera*
Фра́нция *France*
францу́з, францу́женка *Frenchman, woman*
фрукт *fruit*
фунт сте́рлингов *pound sterling*
футбо́л *football*
футболи́ст *footballer*

хе́ви металл-ро́к *heavy metal rock*
хи́мик *chemist*
хлеб *bread*
ходи́ть 2 (хожу́, хо́дишь) *to go on foot (habitually)*
хокке́й *ice hockey*
хо́лодно *it's cold*
холо́дный *cold*
хоро́ший *good*
хорошо́ *it's good*
хоте́ть, (хочу́, хо́чешь, хо́чет, хоти́м, хоти́те, хотя́т) *to want*
худо́й *thin*
ху́же *worse*

цветы́ *flowers*

центр *centre*
це́рковь (*f*) *church*
цирк *circus*

чай *tea*
час *hour, o'clock*
ча́сто *often*
часы́ *watch, clock*
ча́шка *cup*
чек *receipt, chit*
челове́к *man, person*
чемода́н *suitcase*
че́рез *after*
чёрный *black*
четве́рг *Thursday*
число́ *number, date*
чита́ть 1 *to read*
что *what, that*
что вы! *what on earth!*
что с ва́ми? *what's the matter?*
что у вас есть? *what have you got?*
я чу́вствую себя́ *I feel*
чуде́сно *it's wonderful*

шампу́нь (*m*) *shampoo*
ша́пка *hat*
шашлы́к *kebab (shashlik)*
шкаф *cupboard*
шко́ла *school*
шокола́д *chocolate*
шокола́дный *chocolate (adj)*
шотла́ндец, шотла́ндка *Scot (m, f)*
шу́мно *it's noisy*

щи *shshee (cabbage soup)*

экску́рсия *excursion*
экспериме́нт *experiment*
экспре́сс *express*
электри́ческий *electric*
электри́чка *suburban train*
электро́ника *electronics*
энерги́чный *energetic*
эне́ргия *energy*
эта́ж *floor, storey*
э́та *this (f)*
э́ти *these*
э́то *it is, this (n)*

э́тот   *this (m)*

ю́бка   *skirt*
юг (на)   *south*

я   *I*
янва́рь (*m*)   *January*
я́блоко   *apple*
япо́нец, япо́нка   *Japanese man,*
    woman
Япо́ния   *Japan*
я́сли   *day nursery*
яхт   *yacht*

Teach Yourself Russian

Daphne M West

This is a complete course in written and spoken Russian. If you have never learnt Russian before, or if you want to refresh your knowledge, this is the course for you.

This revised edition of *Teach Yourself Russian* has been extensively updated to reflect the language and culture of post-Soviet Russia. It is a practical course that is both fun and easy to work through. Daphne West explains everything clearly along the way and gives you plenty of opportunities to practise what you have learnt. The course structure means that you can work at your own pace, arranging your learning to suit your needs.

Based on the Council of Europe's Threshold guidelines on language learning, the course contains:

- twenty graded units of dialogues, culture notes, grammar and exercises
- a step-by-step guide to the Russian alphabet and its pronunciation
- an extensive grammar summary
- a Russian–English vocabulary list
- an English–Russian key phrases section

By the end of the course you'll be able to cope with a whole range of situations and participate fully and confidently in Russian life and culture.

A cassette has been specially recorded by native Russian speakers to accompany the book, containing a pronunciation guide, dialogues from the book with key phrases highlighted, and exercises in listening and speaking.

Teach Yourself Business Russian

Olga Bridges with Pauline Rayner and Irina Tverdokhlebova

If you are in business and have no previous experience of Russian, or if you are a student wanting to add business Russian to your skills, this course is for you.

The authors, winners of a national award for their innovative approach, have used their extensive experience of business and language teaching to create a practical course that is fun and easy to work through. Language explanations are clear and there are plenty of opportunities to practise what you have learnt. The course structure allows you to work at your own pace, arranging your learning to suit your needs.

The course contains:

- twenty-one graded units of business conversations and tasks based on practical situations
- a pronunciation guide
- business briefings – advice, facts and figures relating to business in Russian today
- full coverage of the Russian alphabet
- a reference grammar section
- a Russian–English vocabulary

By the end of the course, you'll be able to participate fully and confidently in Russian meetings and negotiations – on the shop floor, on the telephone and in the bar after work.

Teach Yourself Czech

David Short

This is a complete course in written and spoken Czech. If you have never learned Czech before, or if you want to improve on existing skills, then *Teach Yourself Czech* is for you.

David Short has created a practical course that is both fun and easy to work through. He explains everything clearly along the way and gives you plenty of opportunities to practise what you have learnt. The course structure means that you can work at your own pace, arranging your learning to suit your needs.

Based on the Council of Europe's Threshold guidelines on language learning, the course contains:

- eighteen carefully graded units of dialogues, culture notes, grammar and exercises
- a guide to Czech pronunciation
- a Czech–English vocabulary list
- a grammar summary

By the end of the course you'll be able to cope with a whole range of situations and participate fully and confidently in Czech life.

Teach Yourself Bulgarian

Michael Holman and Mira Kovatcheva

This is a complete course in written and spoken Bulgarian. If you have never learned Bulgarian before, or if your Bulgarian needs brushing up, *Teach Yourself Bulgarian* is for you.

Michael Holman and Mira Kovatcheva have created a practical course that is both fun and easy to work through. They explain everything clearly along the way and give you plenty of opportunities to practise what you have learnt. The course structure means that you can work at your own pace, arranging your learning to suit your needs.

Based on the Council of Europe's Threshold guidelines for language learning, the course contains:

- twenty carefully graded units of dialogues, culture notes, grammar and exercises
- a guide to Bulgarian pronunciation
- a Bulgarian–English vocabulary list
- a grammar summary

By the end of the course you'll be able to cope with a whole range of situations and participate fully and confidently in Bulgarian life.

Teach Yourself Hungarian

Zsuzsa Pontifex

This is a complete course in written and spoken Hungarian. If you have never learned Hungarian before, or if your Hungarian needs brushing up, *Teach Yourself Hungarian* is for you.

Zsuzsa Pontifex has created a practical course that is both fun and easy to work through. She explains everything clearly along the way and gives you plenty of opportunities to practise what you have learnt. The course structure means that you can work at your own pace, arranging your learning to suit your needs.

The course contains:

- twenty-one graded units of dialogues, culture notes, grammar and exercises
- a guide to Hungarian pronunciation
- a Hungarian–English vocabulary list

By the end of the course you'll be able to cope with a whole range of situations and participate fully and confidently in Hungarian life.

Teach Yourself Romanian

Dennis Deletant and Yvonne Alexandrescu

This is a complete course in written and spoken Romanian. If you have never learned Romanian before, or if your Romanian needs brushing up, *Teach Yourself Romanian* is for you.

Dennis Deletant and Yvonne Alexandrescu have created a practical course that is both fun and easy to work through. They explain everything clearly along the way and give you plenty of opporunities to practise what you have learnt. The course structure means that you can work at your own pace, arranging your learning to suit your needs.

The course contains:

- twenty graded units of dialogues, culture notes, grammar and exercises
- a step-by-step guide to Romanian pronunciation
- a Romanian–English vocabulary list
- an extensive grammar summary

By the end of the course you'll be able to cope with a whole range of situations and participate fully and confidently in Romanian life.

Teach Yourself Serbo-Croat

David Norris

This is a complete course in written and spoken Serbo-Croat. If you have never learned Serbo-Croat. If you have never learned Serbo-Croat before, or if you want to improve on existing skills, then *Teach Yourself Serbo-Croat* is for you.

David Norris has created a practical course that is both fun and easy to work through. He explains everything clearly along the way and gives you plenty of opporunities to practise what you have learnt. The course structure means that you can work at your own pace, arranging your learning to suit your needs.

Based on the Council of Europe's Threshold guidelines on language learning, the course contains:

- eighteen graded units of dialogues, culture notes, grammar and exercises
- a pronunciation guide
- a Serbo-Croat–English vocabulary list
- an grammar summary

By the end of the course you'll have the language skills and knowledge you need to deal confidently with a whole range of situations.